MORAL CONTEXTS

feminist constructions

Series Editors: Hilde Lindemann Nelson and Sara Ruddick

Feminist Constructions publishes accessible books that send feminist ethics in promising new directions. Feminist ethics has excelled at critique, identifying masculinist bias in social practice and in the moral theory that is used to justify that practice. The series continues the work of critique, but its emphasis falls on construction. Moving beyond critique, the series aims to build a positive body of theory that extends feminist moral understandings.

Forthcoming books in the series by:

Amy Baehr; Maria Lugones; Joan Mason-Grant; Diana Tietjens Meyers; and Robin Schott.

MORAL CONTEXTS

Margaret Urban Walker

ROWMAN & LITTLEFIELD PUBLISHERS, INC.
Lanham • Boulder • New York • Oxford

ROWMAN & LITTLEFIELD PUBLISHERS, INC.

Published in the United States of America
by Rowman & Littlefield Publishers, Inc.
A Member of the Rowman & Littlefield Publishing Group
4720 Boston Way, Lanham, Maryland 20706
www.rowmanlittlefield.com

PO Box 317
Oxford
OX2 9RU, UK

British Library Cataloguing in Publication Information Available

Library of Congress Cataloging-in-Publication Data

Walker, Margaret Urban, 1948–
    Moral contexts / Margaret Urban Walker.
        p. cm. — (Feminist constructions)
    ISBN 0-7425-1378-5 (alk. paper) — ISBN 0-7425-1379-3 (pbk. : alk.
paper)
    1. Feminist ethics. I. Title II. Series.

BJ1395 .W34 2002
171'.7—dc21
                                                    2002009258

Printed in the United States of America

♾™ The paper used in this publication meets the minimum requirements of
American National Standard for Information Sciences—Permanence of Paper for
Printed Library Materials, ANSI/NISO Z39.48-1992.

For all my dear friends, with thanks.

CONTENTS

ACKNOWLEDGMENTS

Series editors Hilde Nelson and Sara Ruddick greeted my idea to collect these essays with encouragement and enthusiasm, for which I am grateful. I thank Eve DeVaro of Rowman & Littlefield for her unhesitant support of the project. Most of the exacting job of getting material on disk was done by Rachel Waterstradt with a contribution by Christopher Arroyo, and I thank them both for their assistance. This book was completed during a Faculty Fellowship granted by Fordham University for spring term 2002. I am grateful to Fordham for their consistent and indispensable support of my research and writing over many years. Thanks to Shelley Erikson for final proofreading and indexing assistance.

These essays appeared over a span of fifteen years in diverse venues. They are reprinted without revisions, except for making citation style uniform.

"Moral Particularity" appeared previously in *Metaphilosophy* 18 (1987): 171–85. The author gratefully acknowledges the permission of the Metaphilosophy Foundation and Blackwell Publishers to reprint this essay.

"Moral Luck and the Virtues of Impure Agency" appeared previously in *Metaphilosophy* 22 (1991): 14–27. The author gratefully acknowledges the permission of the Metaphilosophy Foundation and Blackwell Publishers to reprint this essay.

"Partial Consideration" appeared previously in *Ethics* 101 (1991): 758–74, copyright © 1991 by The University of Chicago Press. All rights reserved.

"What Does the Different Voice Say? Gilligan's Women and Moral Philosophy," was published by Kluwer Academic Publishers in the *Journal of Value Inquiry* 23 (1989): 123–34, reprinted with kind permission of Kluwer Academic Publishers.

"Moral Understandings: Alternative 'Epistemology' for a Feminist Ethics" appeared previously in *Hypatia* 4 (1989): 15–28, published by Indiana University Press.

"Feminism, Ethics, and the Question of Theory" appeared previously in *Hypatia* 7 (1992): 23–38, published by Indiana University Press.

"Seeing Power in Morality: A Proposal for Feminist Naturalism in Ethics" appeared previously in *Feminists Doing Ethics*, ed. Peggy DesAutels and Joanne Waugh (Lanham, Md.: Rowman & Littlefield, 2001).

"Some Thoughts on Feminists, Philosophy, and Feminist Philosophy" appeared previously in *Metaphilosophy* 27 (1996): 222–25. The author gratefully acknowledges the permission of the Metaphilosophy Foundation and Blackwell Publishers to reprint this essay.

"Keeping Moral Space Open: New Images of Ethics Consulting" appeared previously in *Hastings Center Report* 23 (1993): 33–40, copyright © by The Hastings Center. Reproduced by permission.

"Ineluctable Feelings and Moral Recognition" appeared previously in *Midwest Studies in Philosophy*, Volume XXII, ed. Peter A. French and Howard K. Wettstein (Notre Dame, Ind.: University of Notre Dame Press, 1998), 62–81. The author gratefully acknowledges permission of the editors of *Midwest Studies in Philosophy* to reprint this essay.

"Naturalizing, Normativity, and Using What 'We' Know in Ethics" appeared previously in *Canadian Journal of Philosophy*, Supplementary Volume 26 (2000): 75–101, published by University of Calgary Press.

"Getting Out of Line: Alternative to Life as a Career" appeared previously in *Mother Time: Women, Aging, and Ethics*, ed. Margaret Urban Walker (Lanham, Md.: Rowman & Littlefield, 1999).

"Human Conditions" appeared previously as "Feminist Ethics and Human Conditions," Inaugural Lecture of the Cardinal Mercier Chair 2001–2002, in *Tijdschrift voor Filosofie* 64 (2002): 433–50.

The author is grateful for the permission of these publishers to reprint these essays.

INTRODUCTION: THE PLACE OF MORAL THINKING

"Context" can be a loose and lazy word. "That depends on the context" can mean any number of things or nothing precisely. The "context" can mean the history of an episode, how it developed or what led up to it. It can invoke the specific nature of relationships and understandings among people involved in a situation; without knowing these one doesn't grasp how a situation appears to those in it. "Context" sometimes refers to a particular environment or set of circumstances that determine whether something is acceptable or makes sense—"But this was in a *classroom!*"—or invokes a shared understanding of the expectations that are in play in common social encounters. Depending on the context, in this sense, certain topics of discussion or styles of address are suitable, surprising, or just plainly out of bounds. "The context" can also mean something as large and complex as a culture's symbolism and its interpretation of particular human behaviors or modes of expression. Sometimes, though, "I'd need to understand the context" simply means: I don't know any details, in other words, I don't really know what happened at all.

"Context" is in fact an indispensable, even if free-floating, placeholder for information crucial to understanding what we or others are doing. There are always presupposed conditions or background assumptions that make all the difference in how we understand the things people say and do, and whether we can understand them well, or at all. All of us are schooled in particular settings and steeped in specific assumptions that sink into the background as we learn to negotiate our social, intellectual, working, and personal lives. Frames of reference that once challenged us become as invisible to us as the glasses on our noses sometimes do. This feature is shared by academic "disciplines" and other specialized trainings. Part of the object of these trainings is to make us effortlessly use specialized languages, selective points of view, and uncommon formats for framing and addressing certain kinds of problems. When this becomes effortless, we no longer remember that we are using them, or how particular and peculiar they are. Nor do we often reflect on the extensive training that we had to undergo in order to take these assumptions for granted, once we have been fully initiated into those ways of thinking and behaving. From learning the language and the various rules of one's cultural world and local communities, to becoming fluent in the understandings of particular institutions or certain disciplines, we are steadily acquiring and refining the ability to read meanings in varied contexts, having ceased to pay much attention to the contexts themselves.

The essays in this book explore the significance of context in moral thinking, paying special attention to that disciplined and systematized thinking about morality that is called "moral philosophy" or "ethics." Moral philosophy is a theoretical practice of examining reflectively and testing critically the nature of our moral values, judgments, and responsibilities. It purports to discover or construct (depending on whether the theorist sees morality as given in the nature of things, or as a human construct subject to change and refinement) what is true or best in the way of morality for human beings. This theoretical practice of ethics is now largely professionalized and contained in academic settings as part of disciplines like philosophy, religious studies, political theory, or social sciences. There are two dimensions of context that shape our understanding of morality in ethics. There are, first, the contexts that frame and guide ongoing moral thinking and action as we get on in our lives, making judgments and taking responsibility in matters of value and concern (or, of course, failing to do so when we should). And there are also contexts— academic, institutional, professional—that configure and constrain the *theories* some of us, in philosophical and other academic ethics, make about how human beings should live: about what values really deserve to command our allegiance, what relationships should determine our obligations, what principles or guidelines should steer or ground our judgments, what persons or other beings we should take responsibility for.

The essays collected here were written over an extended period. They embody my repeated attempts to identify contexts that are not given due importance in dominant styles of philosophical ethics even though these contexts fundamentally shape human lives. They also aim to expose contexts that are in fact decisively shaping work in ethical theory, but which are taken for granted and so not examined critically. Those contexts that shape the daily choices and perceptions of human beings but are not always given their due in ethics include our individual personal journeys and histories, our limited awareness and our awareness of human limitations, and our social positions and institutional roles. They include relationships that define us in our own and others' eyes and cultural settings and forms of social organization that elevate particular ideals, images, and roles to special status and visibility. Finally, they include the specific moral idioms we learn to speak in certain times, places, and communities. Ethical theories sometimes idealize unrealistically the perspectives that human beings can take on their lives, or simplify the burdens of understanding others and ourselves. Theories often allude to "us" or to "the moral agent" in ways that homogenize or universalize what are really very different situations within the same society or community, or circumstances that vary starkly among societies and communities.

Contexts of academic theory in ethics include disciplinary paradigms and specialized languages—formats for writing a paper or a treatise on moral matters—that become entrenched in university classes, in professional preparation and training, and in work considered acceptable for presentation and publication in professional venues. The actual spaces and activities that house these paradigms—the classroom, the conference, the learned society, the graduate program, the publisher's list or journal refereed by networks of people with professional credentials—are contexts, too. And they are decisive in shaping how "moral theory" looks, and what it looks at or ignores. Yet these contextually defining features of academic and professional discourse rarely become a topic for critical reflection within that discourse, which tends to see itself instead as the embodiment of the most highly skilled and insightful thinking about profound issues of value, judgment, and responsibility. These issues are indeed profoundly important, but sustained and disciplined thinking about them can fail to achieve mere adequacy when context of either kind—of daily life or moral theory—is ignored or denied.

When context is ignored or effaced in theorizing, what we get is irrelevant or bad theory: theory that does not connect with life; theory that distorts, rather than reveals and clarifies its subject matter; theory that becomes a pastime and even a competitive game for theory-makers independently of whether the theory enhances our understanding of its subject matter. In the case of ethical theory, the subject matter is the moral responsibilities of human beings. But ethical theories can be worse than bad theory. They can be insidiously misleading, covering over features of our human and social conditions that require us to be *morally* examined and challenged. They can become "ideological," enforcing patterns of thinking that make existing conditions and distributions of authority and power in human societies seem natural, inevitable, or normal when they are elaborately constructed and defended by human beings, open to assessment and deliberate alteration by human beings, and productive of many kinds of humanly enforced norms. Some of these norms will not survive honest and informed critical reflection.

In these essays I have, for more than a decade, explored varieties of moral contexts. My interest was at first motivated by a sense of the remoteness of moral philosophy from the lives human beings lead. Under the impact of feminist thinking, however, I began to see this remoteness, abstraction, and detachment differently. Unrealistic idealizations, wholesale and reductive abstractions, and generalizations that papered over great differences among human lives and at the same time covered over some truly inevitable and universally shared features of it, did not do so randomly, nor did they represent universal "human" longings and aspirations. Generalizations and idealizations tended in fact to mirror conditions and positions more likely to be familiar to, or entertained as possibilities by, some people rather than others. The likelihood that certain generalizations and idealizations would make sense or appear plausible seemed to track not only cultural and historical periods, but specific social positions within those periods.

Feminists in the 1980s and 1990s developed numerous sustained critiques of suspicious convergences between ideals of agency, character, judgment, and action in moral theory and the life opportunities and social expectations of men relatively privileged by their race, gender, class, and professional locations. Once exposed, these connections seemed obvious. Why, for example, did the image of a self whose ultimate achievement was a self-chosen, willfully unified, and consistently plotted "career" or "life-plan" loom so large in late twentieth-century moral philosophy done by educationally privileged white men within a culture of individual enterprise that reserved this life-pattern for such men by consigning women, nonwhites, and men of the lower classes to supporting roles? Why have universalist modern moral theories focused largely on relations among nondependent peers who might be strangers in male-dominated public worlds of work and politics, rather than exploring the complex of dependencies that make up the varied forms of attachment and connection in everyone's everyday life? Feminism's explorations of gender bias in moral theory turned out to be vulnerable in many cases to its own neglect of context—as relatively privileged white women in academic professions were found in turn to project their own uncontextualized images (and their socially specific—not universal—gendered situations) into feminist moral and other theory. But the larger lesson remained: there are layers and dimensions and aspects of context that beg to be identified, and their impact on our theorizing examined. To fail to do this, as moral agents and thinkers, is to fail to take responsibility for the distinctive features, biases, and limits of our situations which are no less operative when we are constructing theories of ethics than when we are going on with the rest of life. These essays try to underscore the significance of layers and aspects of context, in some cases to account for the suppression or masking of these contexts, and in all cases to remark on the implications of contexts insufficiently noted and examined.

Part I includes the earliest of these papers. They look at substantive assumptions as well as formative imagery in philosophical ethics that seem to deny or misrepresent some fundamental features of what we might still call "the human condition." The backdrop of our moral judgments is one already sharply contoured by prior commitments and kinds of concerns that vary widely both among individuals and within individual lives over their course. The significance of our sharing a kind of generic moral personhood need not and should not eclipse the human and moral importance of our leading the particular lives we do, in which not all forms of moral excellence or value can or should have the same place in different lives, or in the same one over its entire course. People and values that shape our lives and responsibilities concretely come to do so in ways that are not necessarily completely designed and controlled by us—the particular parents we happen to have, the conditions of ease or challenge to which we are heir, the facts of our social environments. Nor are all the meanings and consequences of our actions under our control. We find ourselves responsible for what has *in fact* come about due to our actions and omissions, and not only for those things we have mindfully decided to do. Our thinking about responsibility must encompass the reality that our impact on the world and each other *characteristically* exceeds our control and foresight. Our human agency is this potent but blinkered kind of agency, and this needs to be an initial premise in our thought about the practices in which we hold each other to account. Finally, while it is impossible to make adequate moral judgments without understanding who we are and what we are doing and have done, attaining this understanding is a complicated business. Opaque features of human actions and intentions interact with helpless confusion, intended and unintentional evasiveness, inexpressiveness, or lack of attention to make our knowledge of self and others an achievement requiring skill and effort. Pictures of moral understanding or deliberation that pass over these daunting challenges lightly, or that eliminate these challenges by declaring unnecessary the more taxing forms of understanding, are not pictures human agents need or can put to use. The essays in Part I explore our particularity, vulnerability to chance, and challenging opacity to ourselves and each other.

The critical methods of feminist theory have provided a key to unlocking the role of social contexts in defining distributions of responsibility and understandings of agency in moral theory and in life. It is obvious that academic philosophical ethics has been until just very recently almost entirely a product of some men's intellectual authority, but in most societies moral authority itself (and its close kin, religious, social, and political authority) have been reserved to or monopolized by men, and even denied to women. Gender, however, is not the only dimension of hierarchically organized social power that confers and restricts the authority to define the shared terms of common moral life; hereditary, racial, economic, and other privileges do so as well, and gender itself always works with and through these other arrangements, not independently of them. (In Euro-American societies the gender of white women of respectable class status—and later educational and professional attainment—has often conferred a form of moral authority concerning the "household" spheres of intimacy and nurturance, while women of stigmatized racial groups and the lower classes are often viewed as lacking the moral virtues for responsible motherhood and disciplined housewifery. At the same time, race, economic, and educational privilege can confer on some women a presumption of moral rectitude or sensitivity denied of many men.)

While feminist critique thus opens up a wider field than that of gender bias in ethics, feminist insight into the shaping of morality and moral theory by gender has been one powerful force for exposing many exclusions and distortions in the moral philosophy authored by privileged men. The idealization, especially, of formalism and impersonality in moral thought, and the privileged place of independence and full reciprocity in human relations, reflect the position of those whose social roles are *not* organized significantly around care-taking and responding to inevitable human vulnerabilities of infancy, illness, incapacity, or frailty. Largely exempt from caring labor, they can envision their true society as one of independent peers from whom they seek respectful affirmation and mutually acceptable noninterference. This has led to a regimented "arm's-length" moral epistemology that values uniformity and repeatability of judgments—a kind of moral legality. It has also, disturbingly, evaded the urgent task of thinking through deeply and candidly the meanings of dignity and equality in light of the *full* range of *common* conditions of ability and incapacity, immaturity and decline, asymmetry and reciprocity that are part and parcel of human lives. Feminist analysis has been willing to look squarely at the impact of social power on moral understandings in life and in theory. Rather than "reducing" morality to power, this maneuver has instead exposed the unjustifiable transposition of social differences into moral ones, and subjected unearned powers to moral criticism. At the same time, this form of critique has opened up a space for thinking candidly about uses of social power and the cultivation of moral powers of which we can approve without deception or subterfuge in our social relations and in our moral theories. The essays in Part II make this case for a feminist approach to ethics.

The brief concluding piece in Part II was originally part of a 1995 symposium of the Pacific Division of the American Philosophical Association on feminist philosophy. It studies the curious and not necessarily innocent confusions that result from failures to recognize (or accept) that feminist philosophy is a *philosophical methodology*, an analytical program designed to reveal and test presuppositions of philosophical discourses, and to construct alternative philosophical theories of knowledge, morality, personal identity, and other aspects of reality that philosophers traditionally address. No one is a feminist philosopher just by being a woman, or a woman philosopher, or even a woman philosopher and a feminist. Men and women are feminist philosophers when they wield a critical perspective and an analytical methodology of a particular kind, one that sees gender and other power-laden social differences as creating social, symbolic, and discursive contexts with significant impacts on philosophical theories.

Part III continues a theme of the previous section, asking moral philosophers to think about the actual environments from which they are theorizing, and the actual effects of what they have to say on some social practices and institutions. Over several decades, for example, academically trained ethicists have been recruited in ever larger numbers to study and critically assess practice, and to participate in setting policy, in one of our societies' most pervasive and invasive institutional networks, health care. If philosophers should be careful to scrutinize the entitlements to authority in academic ethical theorizing, how much more urgent to do so in the context of a practice—ethics "consulting" in clinical settings—in which people's well-being, dignity, and lives are at stake.

Moral philosophy as a cultural voice can also be unhelpful and, worse, misleading when a priori reflections on human relations and responses are allowed to float free of some sad and ugly realities of how human beings can live together, effacing these realities rather than confronting them in our lives. If philosophers need to look and see, and not simply try to deduce or imagine, how human beings are capable of thinking about and responding to each other, still the reflective and normative enterprise of moral philosophy does not collapse into some kind of observational science. To "naturalize" ethical thought in the right way is to avoid the pitfalls both of a scientistic reductionism about ethics and of an insistence on a pure nonempirical core of moral knowledge that excuses moral philosophers from an obligation to inform themselves about diverse human lives through what scientific, artistic, and humanistic inquiries can teach us.

There is a synergy between academic discourses of ethics and more broadly disseminated cultural figurations as well. A rather abstract philosophical conception—for example, of "autonomy" as a premier moral value in modern Euro-American thought—can become intertwined with, and expressed through, specific cultural associations and concrete exemplars when it circulates outside academic philosophical quarters. "Situated" theory, especially in ethics, might keep track of this synergy when philosophical ideas are interpreted concretely in popular, professional, and policy discussions. In the example of discourses on aging, the interpretations and applications of autonomy as an ideal are not benign.

A concluding essay in Part IV draws together several strands of this project of putting moral thinking in context. There really are human conditions of vulnerability and interdependency, of limited awareness and control, of fallible and imperfect insight into human hearts and minds, of having to live in a very particular world at a very particular time with only modest powers of imagination about what other worlds there have been or might yet be. These are the conditions no human beings evade, nor should moral reflection try to escape or deny them. But there are also conditions in which our moral thinking is rooted, which give rise to it and make sense of it, that are the products of human will and are themselves something for which human beings are responsible. These humanly created human conditions make possible essential moral powers; in moral and social forms of life we learn modes of self-understanding, self-control, and accountability to others. We learn how to participate in a shared life which produces some valuable expressions of human insight, creativity, and responsiveness. Yet these conditions also are often ones that permit or require cruelty, suffering, waste, and deception, the subjection of some by others, the denial of our common human abilities and our shared human plight.

Moral thinking and moral philosophy are undeniably *reflective*—analytical, critical, probing real and imagined comparisons, pondering multiple relationships between theory and practice, keeping track of the respective roles and the constant interactions of reality and idealization in the looping, halting process of figuring out whether how any of us live is how to live. But moral philosophy needs, as I hope these essays show, to take responsibility for which particular experiences it reflects upon, how they shape its conclusions at a given time, and how its conclusions in turn might affect our common life. Moral philosophy should view itself as a densely situated and fallible, empirically obligated, open-ended and improvable practice of reflecting on our human conditions of both types, making use of all the information of every type that it can get.

I

CONTEXTS ABSENT OR IGNORED

1

MORAL PARTICULARITY

An assumption common to diverse sorts of widely held moral theories is the assumption that all relevant considerations in what any one person is truly obliged, permitted, or forbidden, (etc.) to do in a situation is the very same for any other similarly placed. I call this prevalent assumption, sometimes embodied explicitly in universalizability requirements, *moral universalism,* and theories which assume it *universalist.* I defend in this paper a view about the nature of morality and moral judgement which directly repudiates universalism. According to the *moral particularity thesis* (MPT) there are identity constitutive structures and features of an agent's life which can give some particular content to the agent's moral position. By a "moral position" I mean the array of prohibitions, obligations, prerogatives, and opportunities for merit, mediocrity, or deficiency of a moral sort that may be judged with adequate reason to apply to a person in a given situation at a specific time. If MPT is true not everyone may be claimed to stand necessarily under the same moral constraints even in very similar situations, nor under the same ones with equal stringency. This is not a claim about diminished responsibility, mitigating circumstances, or exceptional cases, but a claim about the nature of one's moral position over the general run of affairs, exceptional or quotidian. The view MPT represents is not only a view about what sorts of considerations can bear on the making of a moral judgement, but a view about *how* these considerations can bear. MPT allows certain individuating and defining features of an agent's life (referred to herein as "particulars" or "particularizing features") to matter for that agent's moral position in some cases; more controversially, it allows these to matter where they do in some cases in a way that is not universally generalizable.

3

As an illustration of what is at issue, consider the following example (to which I will return throughout). A man, Jeff, knows that continuing to care for his increasingly irrational, incontinent, and unpredictable aged mother is creating a severe strain on the entire household. The family could, with considerable sacrifice, afford institutional care for his mother, but Jeff cannot forget that more than once he told her he intended to keep her at home. Jeff's mother is well past the point where she might participate genuinely in decisions regarding her welfare. What ought Jeff to do with respect to his mother's future care?

This kind of case seems susceptible of various morally *acceptable* solutions in line with general values or common principles. On MPT there is a natural way of extending the moral ordering beyond a selection of merely acceptable alternatives determined by general principles or values. It may matter what kind of relationship Jeff has had with his mother. Or, it may be that his mother is (or had been) a certain kind of person, to whom certain values—whether loyalty, sacrifice, independence, or dignity—matter(ed) most, in herself, her son, and others. Or, Jeff's marriage to his wife Kathy may be premised on an acceptance of mutual sacrifice, or on putting their children first, or on certain religious understandings, or something else. According to MPT these and other particulars, not present in another case otherwise extremely similar, may contain the materials for specific moral (and not merely practical) guidance.[1] Singly or in some combination factors like these might even be compelling: they might underwrite a refined judgement that Jeff ought morally to do A, or ought not morally to do B. Yet it might be that in another, extremely similar case, say that of Jeanne, particulars of Jeanne's life might render A-type and B-type alternatives equally morally acceptable at a refined level, or render B morally superior to A *for her.* MPT allows that the acknowledgment of particulars as moral grounds can lead to situations where X ought morally to do A and Y ought morally to do B (or ought not morally to do A) even though X and Y find themselves in extremely similar circumstances.[2]

A universalist will reply that since the particulars are among the relevant circumstances, either X's and Y's situations are *not* similar in just those morally relevant respects (i.e. the particulars) or that those respects are not morally relevant. Either way, the universalist can claim that what one is morally permitted or constrained to do in any case is what anyone else in a truly relevantly similar case is likewise permitted or constrained to do. A particularist view of the type described must be able not only to defend the moral relevance of certain particulars in cases like these, but to offer an account of how such factors may determine an agent's moral position in a non-universalizable way.[3]

In Section I, I argue that a satisfactory rationale for countenancing particulars morally at all must be of a certain kind. In Section II, I argue that this same rationale explains the irreducibly particular character of certain moral judgements. The central claim is that certain identifying features are the materials for, and irreducibly particular judgements are the exercise of a special although familiar kind of moral competence. I call this competence *strong moral self-definition*. It is the ability of morally developed persons to install and observe precedents for themselves which are both distinctive of them and binding upon them morally. I claim possession of this capacity is evident in the behavior of morally admirable persons, and that it is a capability to which every moral agent should aspire. In Section III I defend the reality and desirability of this special moral competence. If universalism cannot acknowledge it, universalism falsifies or effaces a significant dimension of our moral experience.

I

The intent of a particularist view is to treat specific features which give meaning and direction to an agent's life as potentially contributing to defining an agent's moral position, rather than as extra-moral motivations, non-moral concerns, or commitments presumptively antagonistic to doing what one ought.[4] In recent literature defenses of the moral legitimacy of one or another kind of particularizing feature as motive or end are not uncommon.[5] But to defend the moral relevance of just deep relationships *or* social roles *or* personal ideals *or* constitutive projects *or* group loyalties raises the question of why one sort of particularizing feature should be sponsored and not others. The obvious multiplicity of bases for attachment and concern, commitment and relationship begs recognition. We are born into the emphases and values defining historical periods, cultures, ethnic groups, classes, social milieus, families. We are thrust into or incur or adopt roles, debts, commitments and affiliations, and experience loyalties, feelings of identification, patterns of affection and aversion. We set goals, look to ideals and models, and give ourselves to values, causes, institutions, modes of life and religious devotions, in varying degrees. We take up tasks, works, projects, and jobs.

We like, love, despise, admire, worship, revere, or respect various things, beings, and persons. However, what one wants is a unified rationale for the moral recognition of these possibly deserving particulars. I argue that elements of all these kinds (and perhaps of other kinds) are candidates for moral relevance, if any of them are, because (1) any instance of a particularizing feature can be defended as morally relevant only as one of a *kind,* and (2) these kinds can be plausibly defended as morally relevant only in a certain way.

A justification of the moral relevance of any such specific features is going to have to be *generic* in order to be persuasive at all. It is wholly inadequate simply to say, "But Jeff loves his children more than anything," or "Christine couldn't live with herself if she felt she betrayed the cause." It is inadequate, unless the enterings of such possible bases for moral decisions implicitly refer to the role various *kinds* of commitments and attachments play in human development, meaningful experience, or self-direction of the sort that enhances moral performance, or even renders it possible. If one could not appeal to the necessary, important, or at least positive role that *types* of commitments and attachments play in moral formation and cultivation, one would have to wonder why anybody *should* care in a context of moral decision about Jeff's fatherly love or Christine's political dedication, even though Jeff and Christine in fact *do.* That individuals are gripped by their projects and partialities is evident. What is needed is a reason to countenance such kinds of motivational currents as legitimate or even necessary conduits to a morally good life.

There is a general rationale for doing this. The kinds of features mentioned above are identity-constituting in an obvious way: to have to forsake, betray, deny, or damage them can cause one to feel that a part of oneself has been lost or deeply altered. But unlike physical traits, mannerisms, and many habits or accidents of circumstance which may also be components of identity in the broad sense, the aforementioned particulars are the materials for a certain kind of conception and formation of oneself: the constitution and recognition of oneself as a bearer, servant, guardian or champion of certain *values* which provide bases for choice. If this formation of oneself makes a direct and irreplaceable contribution to one's capacity for moral discrimination and performance—one's moral competence—it is entitled to be called *moral self-definition* in those applications in which it so contributes. How such applications are possible and in what they consist is the subject of Section II; their reality and importance is defended in Section III.

The moral relevance of any particular in any specific case, then, requires generic defense along certain lines. In this way a particularist view honors an important intuition which may initially seem universalist: that morality is about the activities and treatment, interests and well-being of "human beings as such." This intuition is deep and important. It suggests that moral reflection is a medium of exploration and adjustment for human beings, within their own lives and between their own and others', which always allows us to transcend the merely local and individual or even the historical and cultural in our situations. I consider this intuition central to the concept of morality and to set it off dramatically from the empirical, functional notions of "mores" or "value systems." But this deep, valuable sense of morality as transcendent and ideal does not require moral universalism, and is not abandoned by particularism.

The notion that morality concerns "human beings as such" might be taken to imply (a) that for an obligation or constraint to be moral, it must attach to everyone just as human (i.e. the only moral obligations are absolutely general and strictly universal, owed to all by all); or (b) that for an obligation or constraint to be moral, it must concern features or interests any human being just as such (without special position, privilege, capacity or relationship) could have (e.g. pleasure and freedom from pain); or (c) that for an obligation or constraint to be moral it must derive from universally shared kinds of features or interests of human beings as such. Clearly, MPT is at odds with (a) and (b): it will say that there are truly moral constraints which are less than universal or even general, and which are rooted in specific features or interests which it does not make much sense to say "any human being just as such" could have, unless that means they are in the range of human possibility. However, moral particularity need not and cannot in a plausible version collide with (c). That there is particularity in our moral positions rests on the fact that human beings (within all but the catastrophic reaches of experience) are the kinds of beings who deeply care about, find meaning and identity, in certain sorts of structures and features of their lives, even if in quite different *versions, combinations,* and *weightings* of these elements. A fully developed particularist moral view would require a generic typology of such structures and features, and would prompt detailed studies of how specific cases may be understood, motivationally and axiologically, in terms of them. The topic of this paper, however, is the logical burden of particularism—to show how certain moral judgements relate moral positions to their particular grounds or bases in a non-universalizable way.

II

Particulars should be accorded *moral* relevance at all only if and to the extent that they play an important role in supporting and enhancing our *moral competence.* Moral competence is our ability to act in ways consistent with the constraints values and principles impose on us morally. It is, minimally, the capacity to acknowledge consistently that certain values or principles do so constrain us, a capacity which manifests itself paradigmatically in morally acceptable performance in which there is typically at least some awareness that it is morally acceptable performance.[6] There is a significant kind of moral competence which goes beyond the minimum, moral self-definition in its *strong* form. It is the argument of this section that the exercise of strong moral self-definition consists in making and acting upon irreducibly particular moral judgements. By requiring implicit universality, universalism denies the possibility of strong moral self-definition.

Consider first how a minimal kind of moral self-definition is manifest in plain moral competence. In recognizing that certain values or principles place moral constraints upon the choices and acts of persons generally, including oneself, and to act in accordance with that recognition is, to that extent, to identify with one's status as a *moral* being, as opposed, say, to seeing oneself as a creature of impulse, a wanton, a pure maximizer of self-interest, a non-moral zealot of some kind, or whatnot. Moral judgements made in this spirit are morally self-defining in a weak sense. They are not incompatible with universalizability; indeed universalizability may be viewed as a standard check on the authenticity of judgements of this sort, i.e. whether they do represent what they purport to represent, a kind of non-individuated subscription to the general moral force of considerations of certain kinds. Judgements of this sort include those understood as direct instantiations of exceptionless principles; those made on generic grounds (e.g. "A life would be lost") in standard order (e.g. human life over convenience); and those based on particulars (e.g. well-entrenched and definitely specified social roles) whose constraining content (where relevant from a moral point of view) is understood strictly or as a matter of course (e.g. "A priest must...," "A military officer may not...."") Most moral judgements we make are of this sort; they manifest plain moral competence, are viewed correctly as instances of universalizable connections between grounds invoked and position affirmed, and represent non-individuated submission of oneself to "the right (or decent, or morally acceptable) thing."

How then may a valid moral judgement be irreducibly particular?[7] The non-universalizability of such judgements cannot be due simply to the fact that some grounds of the given judgement are particular. This does not suffice to show that the judgement is any less an instance of and an implicit assent to a universal principle linking just the kind of grounds appealed to, however particular, with just the moral position the judgement affirms.[8]

The universality universalism requires is compatible with minute specificity of content; it is the universality of the connection between grounds acknowledged and position affirmed.

Irreducibly particular judgements are possible because the relevance, rank and weight of particulars is not a given, a uniformity over all agents. Rather, particulars are aspects of ourselves up for moral scrutiny and possibly for revaluation at any turn in our moral lives, and so are part of the matter for moral consideration ongoing. Their relevance is not presupposed to decisions in which they figure as grounds, because their relevance derives from the commitments made, fixed, sustained, or renewed in those very decisions.

Irreducibly particular judgements consist in an agent's assigning to particularized grounds a discretionary value (compatible with generally acceptable orderings of generic values) in the act of affirming a certain moral position on their basis.[9] Such moral judgements do not instance a standard viewpoint, but either establish or renew a precedent which derives what force it has from the agent's identification with it: it is presumed to commit the agent in future acts and valuations to allowing the countenanced particulars special scope, weight, or centrality where they apply. What is systematic and nonarbitrary in the relation between grounds and position in this kind of case derives not from a uniformity over all moral agents, but from an existing or prospective uniformity over performances of *this* moral agent. Call this uniformity the agent's *moral persona,* actual or intended. It is moral judgements which extend or are purported to constitute a distinctive moral persona which are irreducibly particular ("I ought to A in C, but I make no judgement whether anyone else ought to A in C").[10]

Consider four possible deliberative resolutions of Jeff's quandary:

(D1) My mother has been the most significant person in my life. Not to continue to care for her at home would mean to me a kind of abandonment, even betrayal, at the time she is in most desperate need. It is painful for me to ask Kathy to accept the fact that my debt to and love for my mother runs as deep with me as my relationship with my wife. Still, I must give my mother what I feel is due her.

(D2) Kathy and I see this as a question about what is owed between parents and children: between me and my mother, between our children and us. I think I've done as much for mother as she herself would think loving and fair. There is much I can and want to give the children, whom she loved too. The competent care and reasonable comfort she needs now can be given her outside our home, and I really ought to arrange for that.

(D3) I'm grateful to mother for all she has been to and given to me, but my relationship with my wife means more. It is the center of meaning in my life, and next to that ideas about duty or loyalty to my mother seem abstract. I'll do everything necessary for proper care for her, but mustn't further jeopardize our marriage by continuing to keep her at home.

(D4) Up to now I've seen myself first and foremost as her dutiful son. It's time to admit that that was as much a form of dependency as loyalty. Other people need me now to be a husband and father first, things I haven't always done as I should. Sometimes I think I've insisted on keeping her home this long because I needed her here, not because she needed me. I should arrange for outside care.

Along each of these (schematically depicted) deliberative routes three things happen on the way to a terminating judgement which render that judgement particular. First, the agent identifies particulars (e.g. profound indebtedness to a parent, surpassing love for a spouse) alongside or in terms of more general values, exploring their relevance not simply to this kind of situation, but to himself in this kind of situation. Second, the agent discerns a course of action which expresses the significance of certain particulars and represents a certain strength and type of commitment to them. Third, the connection between particulars weighted and the position that in the agent's view ratifies their force is endorsed with an understanding that the endorsement bears on the agent's future. I elaborate these features in turn.

(1) In irreducibly particular judgements particulars presumed to apply on the basis of past concerns and commitments may be revoked or revised, as well as renewed. The pertinence of particulars is itself subject to scrutiny in any case. To affirm a moral position on the basis of weighting certain particulars is either, then, to sustain an extant moral course or to chart (or at least set) a new one. In the examples given, Jeff is seen either as honoring a long-standing pattern of emphasis (D1 and D3), bringing one to explicitness (D2), or inaugurating one (D4). Jeff should not want to say whether another's situation with closely similar particulars applying must be resolved on the same weighting and ordering of particular bases that his own terminating judgement embodies. He's established these relevances in the first place through progressive moral self-definition. Every choice which impinges on the self-defined areas of relevance requires of him an exercise of the very capacity that established those relevances, and which can sustain or revoke them. In uni-

versalizing his judgement, he would be exercising strong moral self-definition but failing to acknowledge that others can or may do likewise.

(2) In irreducibly particular judgements the agent's accepting a certain moral position on particular grounds *is* the determination of how forceful and central those grounds are for the agent. Given that certain particulars have potential application to deciding a case, it falls to the agent to determine (a) whether and (b) with what degree of force they will be applied. On each score there is latitude for discretion, and the exercise of that discretionary authority is what moral self-definition is.

(a) That particulars *could* be brought to bear morally in the resolution of a situation may not suffice to settle whether they should be or need be. As in many non-particularized cases, where there is room for dispute about whether an opportunity for action or case for decision should be defined in moral terms at all, or in which respects it should be, so one may confront the same ambiguity where particulars have some grip. That Jeff, for example, construes (or cannot fail to see) some aspects of his situation as *morally* weighty already reflects his degree and kind of moral self-definition. The perception that debt and betrayal are crucial issues pervades D1 but is wholly absent from D3; D4 is unique in suggesting that the agent's honesty and integrity are at the fore. Not everyone has reason to see, or would be able to see, these aspects in those ways; only those who were already used to viewing certain patterns or relationships in a moral dimension might. The sensibility apparent in constructing the situation in a certain way is itself endorsed in the particular judgements which respond to that sensibility.

(b) That particulars *will* be brought to bear morally in resolving a situation still requires a determination of appropriate force. In particular judgements an agent may affirm "mays" and "shoulds" as well as "musts" and "must nots," and findings of the better or worse too. Just as some general values are higher in the standard ordering than others, some particulars are more central to the moral definition of a given life than others are. In D1 and D3 Jeff's terminating judgements attribute virtually coercive force to the particular invoked, whereas D2 and D4 attribute strong, but respectively less compelling force. The patterns of attribution in an agent's particular judgements define an ordering of that agent's individuated moral commitments.

Strict universalism forbids grounds of judgements and consequent affirmings of moral positions which are not compelling for all alike. That is to forbid the exercise of a strong and special moral competence, or to deny that there is such a thing. Under universalist assumptions agents are not entitled, or are not believed to be able to find and form themselves morally in this way.

(3) Irreducibly particular judgements are *undertakings,* because the strong moral self-definition these judgements embody is progressive and prospective. Every valid particular judgement and the action which fulfills it strengthen the moral persona from which it proceeds, and creates a stronger claim on the agent to apply certain particulars henceforward or a claim on the agent to apply certain particulars more widely in the future. While instances of particular judgement manifest strong moral self-definition, no instance in itself suffices to establish this special moral competence, any more than the production of an isolated well-formed English sentence demonstrates linguistic competence in English. In either case, there must be more where that came from for it to be what it appears. The agent needs the appropriate sort of moral record. Because an agent may be at the start of that record, or some way along it, particular judgements may function either rather more like declarations or rather more like findings.[11] They will function rather more like findings if the agent has a well-established moral persona, for in that case they may represent a reckoning of how the situation at hand is to be assimilated to the extant record. If the situation is one which prompts the agent to strike out anew the judgements inaugurating the novel direction will function to declare the way chosen. But either way, these judgements are committing; what one finds or establishes are the bases for binding oneself, and what one declares in favor of is the binding of oneself in a certain way and to a certain degree. As discussed in (1) and (2) respectively above, these are the things one does *in* making particular judgements, but binding oneself thusly is what one does *by* making them. That is their point: they constitute moral self-definition because by them one enacts and imposes on oneself particular constraints, and purports to stay or embark on a moral course *not* for all. Since these judgements constitute, progressively and prospectively, an individuated moral identity, universalizing them amounts to legislating one particular moral identity for everyone. Kant, the prototypical universalizer, had just this in mind: rational wills are as such morally interchangeable. Moral interchangeability is incompatible with the reality of strong moral self-definition; a particularist view denies it in defense of the reality of strong moral self-definition.

III

A particularist view denies strict universalism in order to accommodate theoretically irreducibly particular judgements.[12] It is judgements of this sort which introduce or sustain an individuated moral persona, and so, judgements of this sort are signal exercises of strong moral self-definition: not simply the identification of oneself as a moral being, but identifying oneself with the bearing, serving, guarding, or championing of *certain* morally significant values.[13] Dramatic instances of this are the stuff of moral heroism, but more common, less conspicuous instances are found in remarkably good people, who are always remarkably good in some particular way(s) (generosity, courage, kindness, justice, etc.) and in some particular arena(s) (important roles, personal loyalty, public service, etc.). This capacity for strong moral self-definition, for setting oneself a moral course of distinctive but no less genuine requirements (and correlatively, of distinctive possibilities of failure or achievement), is reflected as well in many morally unexceptional lives. Many people show unmistakeable vigor and wholeheartedness, or notable finesse and perceptiveness in precincts of keeping faith or doing good which matter to them specially. The phenomenon of particular people stewarding particular values is undeniable. It is admired, and is truly admirable: few would choose to live in a world with less, rather than more of it, other things (like the prevalence of common decency) equal. I claim it is natural and right to see this phenomenon as a high degree of *moral* achievement that is the product of a special kind of *moral* competence. I have assumed that this competence (moral self-definition), its exercise (irreducibly particular judgements), and its fruition (moral distinction of some type) are actual, and I have defended the general lines of a particularistic view which would show how they are possible. I turn in concluding to a brief defense of their actuality and even briefer comment on their desirability.

Universalism must deny that we can compel or constrain ourselves *morally* with the intent and effect of individuation. If there exist dedications and achievements of roughly that admirable and evident sort referred to, these dedications and achievements aren't moral ones, within universalist assumptions. The two principal sorts of objections one anticipates are that truly particular constraints defended here are not really *moral* ones, or not *real* ones at all. They may be said on the first score to be instead personal, or aesthetic or practical; on the second, to lack a kind of objectivity which could make them serious or real. On either score, it may be claimed that the phenomenology of situations of the sort described, the sense or feelings of being constrained, should be accounted for psychologically without needing to be reckoned with ethically. These are large issues, obviously. I attempt here limited replies.

It is hard not to beg the question about the nature and reach of "the moral" from any side.[14] Still, if people do accept certain cares and commitments as imposing serious bounds on their choices and behavior and requiring from them weighty determinations of acceptability in light of which they may succeed or fail in deep ways it is hard to see how the constraints imposed are, if real, "aesthetic". It is hard to dismiss the specific kind of depth and consequence felt in situations calling forth these resolutions by labelling them "merely practical" either. This implies that decisions beyond universalist limits are just questions of appropriate means or workable choices or prudent planning, and that those who cannot see this are overwrought. A situation like Jeff's however will not easily be made to appear as simply a rather sticky means-end problem or matter for cost-benefit analysis once cruelty, neglect, fraud, theft, etc. are barred. Choices like this are felt, often keenly, as grave and fateful, and do reverberate through the agent's perception of the substance or meaning of his or her life. Even where the eliciting situations are not dramatic we are often aware that to carry through in a self-defined fashion is to be "true" or "faithful" to something which determines "the kind of person" we are. Now, is this "merely personal"? According to a particularist viewpoint it is precisely personal, i.e. having to do with the definition and formation of a person, but it is not for this reason nonmoral. What is being defined and formed is a capacity for responsible, well-ordered and effective deliberation on matters of fundamental value and meaning. This kind of self-development, unlike body-building, memory improvement, heightened social grace, or better grammar certainly *looks* moral. The concept of a 'person' is after all a moral concept or a concept the application of which is intimately linked with the application of moral concepts.

The supposed constraints here discussed may still appear fatally 'personal' in another way—too subjective to be taken seriously as real constraints at all. This is not an area where anything which seems right to me is going to be right for me, however. Mistakes of several sorts are possible, mistakes which consist either in faulty discernment or in running aground on, or running up against the facts. One may, for example, misappreciate the existence or meaning of particularized precedents one believes to be a part of one's record. Patterns of action, attention and response are often ambiguous or multivalent, and this can cause us to misrepresent ourselves to ourselves and to others. People can mistake self-interested largesse for generosity, possessiveness for dedication, penitence for loyalty. Loyalty may look like respect, and honor like dignity. Fidelity may issue from fairness, rather than affection, and respect from gratitude rather than admiration. And not only the natures but the objects of our commitments can be obscure, as when we find we cherished a person and not an ideal. In cases of out and out self-deception one may claim things matter (or don't) which demonstrably don't (or do). Gross and obvious or fine and subtle, such mistakes are familiar in kind and may defeat the relevance claimed for particulars to concrete cases. Cases may be falsely construed as well, as matters of charity, or of justice, or of honesty, etc., when they are not. All these sorts of mistakes have analogues in the moral ignorance or poor judgement that can vitiate moral decisions in non-particularized cases.

In addition, the commissive nature of truly particular moral resolutions provides for a category of mistake with special poignancy. One may licitly and wholeheartedly attempt by a particular resolution to set or continue a distinctive moral course and find oneself *unable* to honor the resolution and/or the future commitment it sets in play. One may drift, or balk, or break down instead. Jeff, for example, may make a perfectly conscientious moral choice about his mother on certifiable particularized grounds, and then be rent or defeated or emptied in the sequel as he discovers he cannot make good on the presumptions and implications of his choice. In these cases it is not just that one cannot do what one ought in the usual sense, but that one cannot be what one in a profound and internally motivated way wants and needs to be (and perhaps assumed one was). The authority of agents to effect individuated moral resolutions is earned by demonstrating competence in strong moral self-definition. One may only pretend to such authority; or one may lose what standing one had. These aren't matters in which wishing or saying can make it so.

The irreducibly particular judgements discussed herein are apparently moral and possess objectivity of familiar kinds. Furthermore, the concept of individuated moral persona seems to capture something real. We expect and usually find a certain amount of convergence and continuity in what a given person cares about, values, and willingly takes responsibility for, despite the non-negligible incidence of ambivalence, akrasia, and compromised performance in our lives. The notion of moral persona is the idea that there are often patterns of morally acceptable or laudatory valuation or concern which are consistently expressed in people's lives, and which can be extrapolated toward a coherent and mutually sustaining set of value commitments.[15] A particularist view urges us to take this actual structure, and its potential for refinement seriously, as the basis for a special and specially valuable kind of moral competence.

Indeed, there is reason to hold that the cultivation of a well-defined moral persona is a higher-order value for any moral agent, that strong moral self-definition is not only something we can do, but something we ought to do. The degree to which a moral persona is defined in a given agent is directly proportional to the *scope of the relevance* of particularity in the agent's moral life. That is, lives in which the valuational emphases are blurred, random, or relentlessly ambiguous provide little ground for *any* appeal to particularity; they can legitimately follow *only* the common ways of moral judgement along the lines of general values standardly ordered. Lives which are instead sharply etched and strongly integrated by evident uniformities of valuation contain the basis for frequent appeals to particulars and for such appeals over a wider scope. To create and maintain a distinctive moral persona is to provide oneself as one goes with additional resources for moral deliberation, and ones which are progressively more refined and powerful. One will be able by virtue of these resources to achieve more determinate moral resolutions of greater numbers of morally problematic situations. So increasing clarity of moral persona renders moral deliberation more effective and complete. This would seem to be something moral agents ought to do over and above doing what they ought or must or should in the first-order sense. On the conception of irreducibly particular judgement defended here, however, we need not see the acquisition of greater moral-deliberative acumen as "over and above"; we can see ourselves as doing just that in those acts of first-order moral resolution which embody strong moral self-definition. Recognition of this special moral competence is central to a person-centered moral viewpoint which centers on persons pretty much as we know them—creatures whose lives derive meaning, value, intelligibility and direction from specific attunements and extended commitments, not the same for all.[16]

NOTES

1. The view of morality as setting *only* boundary conditions is explicitly defended on behalf of "rationalist" moral systems by Alan Donagan, "Consistency in Rationalist Moral Systems," *Journal of Philosophy* 81 (1984): 291–309, and by Barbara Herman, "Integrity and Impartiality," *Monist* 66 (1983): 233–50, on behalf of Kant. Donagan calls decisions within moral limits but not dictated by them "practical" (307–9). If universalist ethics can only ever set boundaries this may be a disturbing limitation of universalism. Part of what is disturbing is that ways of settling indisputably practical questions which may be quite acceptable or at worst foolish (e.g., flipping coins, rolling dice) seem shameful, scandalous, or despicable in cases like Jeff's. I rejoin this matter briefly in section III.

2. Particularism is not metaethical relativism and does not deny the objectivity of moral judgements. Both particularism and relativism deny universalism, by implying the possibility of different moral positions for different persons in the same sort of case. But relativism implies this because it denies a claim to unique rightness

of any moral theory. Particularism supports possible divergence of moral positions by a conception of the structure and issue of moral deliberation (see section II) which is compatible with objectivism about ultimate values or standards.

3. Jonathan Dancy, "Ethical Particularism and Morally Relevant Properties," *Mind* 92 (1983): 530–47, defends a view called "ethical particularism," which like my view denies that moral judgements must instance universal principles. Dancy's view, however, is an epistemological particularism which jettisons the idea of "morally relevant respects" whereas my view is a logical particularism which incorporates the idea of generic relevance (see section II).

4. Harry Frankfurt, "The Importance of What We Care About," *Synthese* 53 (1982): 257–72, represents the latter position unequivocally. The domain of "ethics" which deals with "how to behave" and orders "our relations with *other people*" is prized off sharply by him from the field of "what to care about" and "what to do with ourselves." This view represents a prevalent tendency in modern ethical thought and poses in stark form a challenge to any claim that what people care about has anything to do with morality at all.

5. Examples are: Alasdair MacIntyre, *After Virtue* (Notre Dame, Ind.: University of Notre Dame Press, 1981), on social roles in historical settings (from whom I adopt the term "moral particularity"); Larry Blum, *Friendship, Altruism and Morality* (London: Routledge and Kegan Paul, 1980), and John Cottingham, "Ethics and Impartiality," *Philosophical Studies* 43 (1983): 83–89, on love, friendship, and personal ties; Bernard Williams, *Utilitarianism For and Against*, with J. J. C. Smart (Cambridge: Cambridge University Press, 1973), *Problems of the Self* (Cambridge: Cambridge University Press, 1973), and *Moral Luck* (Cambridge: Cambridge University Press, 1981), on constitutive projects and personal relationships; Andrew Oldenquist, *Normative Behavior* (Washington, D.C.: University Press of America, 1983), on loyalties and affiliations.

6. Philosophers who defend the moral importance of one or other particularizing features are often in fact concerned with keeping moral theory consonant with a plausible psychology. I understand this as a concern with moral competence. See, for example, Cottingham, "Ethics and Impartiality," 92–94; Blum, *Friendship, Altruism and Morality*, 36; Williams, "Persons, Character, and Morality" and "Internal and External Reasons," in *Moral Luck*. See also Michael Stocker, "The Schizophrenia of Modern Ethical Theories," *Journal of Philosophy* 73 (1976): 453–66.

7. The following discussion concentrates on certain first-person moral judgements. There are also particular second- and third-person moral judgements which require parallel or complementary accounts I do not attempt here. The position developed herein reflects a general view of moral reflection and discourse in which clarification and elicitation of commitments and mutual disclosure as well as self-definition are central features. Stanley Cavell, *The Claim of Reason* (New York: Oxford University Press, 1979), suggests this general view persuasively (see part III).

8. For instance, Richard Hare, *Freedom and Reason* (London: Oxford University Press, 1963), says that universalizability requires one in making a moral judgement

to make a precisely similar moral judgement about any case like the original "in the relevant respects . . . those which formed the grounds of the original judgement" (139–40). But the universal moral principle implicitly invoked may be of "unlimited specificity" including a specification of personal characteristics and motivational states (Hare, *Moral Thinking* [Oxford: Clarendon, 1981], 41 and 108).

9. I here suppose that the application of particulars is restricted to the area of what is morally acceptable on generic grounds. A stronger case may be possible, i.e., that particulars may sometimes morally justify actions contrary to those licensed on generic grounds, especially where the former actions are supererogatory. I do not broach the stronger claim here. On the permissibility of supererogation in place of fulfilling obligation, see Frances Myrna Kamm, "Supererogation and Obligation," *Journal of Philosophy* 82 (1985): 118–38.

10. Michael Pritchard, "Self-Regard and the Supererogatory," in *Respect for Persons*, ed. O. H. Green (New Orleans: Tulane University Press, 1982), defends this kind of refusal to universalize in connection with supererogation. An appealing feature of a particularist view is that it makes supererogation integral, rather than marginal or mysterious. But I think irreducibly particular moral judgements should be understood to encompass more of moral life than is naturally thought of as "supererogatory." Some reasons for this will be apparent in section III.

11. Peter Winch, defending the non-universalizable character of some first-person moral judgements in cases of moral conflict, has claimed "they seem to span the gulf between propositions and expressions of decisions," and that in deciding the agent is finding out something about himself. I hold this sort of thing is not confined to conflict cases, and that the agent is not only finding something, but may be intentionally making something. See Winch, "The Universalizability of Moral Judgements," *Monist* 49 (1965): 196–214, esp. 209–12.

12. This makes any truly particularist view "fully agent-centered" in the sense of Samuel Scheffler, *The Rejection of Consequentialism* (Oxford: Clarendon, 1982), 4–5. Such views will provide for both agent-centered prerogatives (permissions in some cases to do otherwise than produce the best outcome, impersonally considered) and agent-centered restrictions (prohibitions in some cases against producing the best outcome, impersonally considered). The rationale for MPT underwrites both types of agent-specific moral constraints. Hence, if the present case can be made, Scheffler's "asymmetry thesis," that it is possible to identify a principled rationale for agent-centered prerogatives but not for agent-centered restrictions (82), is false. My rationale for particularism is based, like Scheffler's preferred one for agent-centered prerogatives, on the "natural independence" of the personal point of view (56–61) but is neither a "maximization strategy" (60) nor a "liberation strategy" (62). One might call it an "incorporation strategy."

13. Compare Edmund Pincoffs, "Quandary Ethics," in *Revisions*, ed. Stanley Hauerwas and Alasdair MacIntyre (Notre Dame, Ind.: University of Notre Dame Press, 1983), who also stresses the way "the conception that I have of myself as a moral being" (103) is revealed in the demands I make upon myself (104); but Pin-

coffs subscribes to universalizability as a test of rightness (111) allowing one's moral persona to determine *how* one will fulfill the universal requirements, not *what* requirements fall upon one.

14. Martha Nussbaum, "Aeschylus and Practical Conflict," *Ethics* 95 (1985): 233–67, provides a nice discussion in connection with moral conflict of the artificiality of a strict moral/non-moral distinction, and of the diversity of distinctions which generate "a messier continuum of claims judged to have various degrees of force and inevitability" (240).

15. This is, to be sure, both idealized and simplified. I do not here entertain the interesting questions about abrupt or dramatic changes in moral persona (conversion, character reversals, epiphanies) or about persistently dissonant or alternating themes, but the pursuit of these questions is dictated by the view presented.

16. Much earlier versions of some of these ideas were presented to members of the National Endowment for the Humanities Institute on Human Action at the University of Nebraska–Lincoln in July 1984. I thank the endowment for this opportunity and the Director, Robert Audi, for additional comments on later drafts. Special thanks to Arthur F. Walker. I have previously published under the name Margaret Urban Coyne.

2

MORAL LUCK AND THE VIRTUES OF
IMPURE AGENCY

> One's history as an agent is a web in which anything that is the
> product of the will is surrounded and held up and partly
> formed by things that are not, in such a way that reflection can
> go only in one of two directions: either in the direction of say-
> ing that responsible agency is a fairly superficial concept, which
> has a limited use in harmonizing what happens, or else that it
> is not a superficial concept, but that it cannot ultimately be
> purified—if one attaches importance to the sense of what one
> is in terms of what one has done and what in the world one is
> responsible for, one must accept much that makes its claim on
> that sense solely in virtue of its being actual.
>
> Bernard Williams, *Moral Luck*[1]

Moral luck consists in the apparent and allegedly problematic or even
paradoxical fact that factors decisive for the moral standing of an agent
are factors subject to luck. While several variants have been noted, the ones
commanding most attention are luck in the ways our actions and projects turn
out (sometimes called *resultant* luck), and luck in those circumstances we happen to encounter which provide opportunities for excellence or disgrace
(*circumstantial* or situational luck).[2] Favored examples of the former include the
negligent driver who is unlucky enough to strike and kill a pedestrian, as opposed to the equally negligent driver who is lucky enough not to. In the latter category, we may consider the bad fortune of someone who has the opportunity to become a Nazi collaborator and the character that prompts her
to do so; for one fit for heroic resistance, this same opportunity amounts to
being luckily in just the spot for admirable moral achievement. In such cases
someone winds up a killer or collaborator, someone else merely negligent or

a moral heroine, and the substantial, even vast differences in the moral standings of such agents is due as much to luck as to anything these agents do.

Three positions on moral luck are recognizable in the contemporary literature: that moral luck is real, but constitutes a paradox in the context of other ordinary and central assumptions about morality; that moral luck is illusory, a misleading impression based on insufficiently fine analysis of belief and practice; and that moral luck is real and not paradoxical, even if wishfully distorted or simply inadequate views of the human condition make it appear so. In what follows I argue for the reality and deep importance of (resultant and circumstantial) moral luck in human life, and against the view that assumptions which render moral luck paradoxical are truly ordinary or central to conceiving or conducting moral life. My view is thus a variant of the third sort of position. In Section I, I overview the terrain of the discussion to date, identifying what is thought to constitute the problem. In Sections II and III, I defend the ways in which moral luck is in fact and indeed ought to be central to our conceptions of agency, responsibility, and our common good.

I

The "problem" of moral luck resides in a sense that persuasive general beliefs about the conditions for moral responsibility are at odds with our actual common practices of moral assessment in cases involving an element of luck. Common belief is said to endorse the principle—a "control condition"—that factors due to luck are "no proper object of moral assessment and no proper determinant of it, either"[3] or, more simply, that people cannot be morally assessed for what is due to factors beyond their control.[4] Yet common practice shows that uncontrolled happenstance indeed figures in the assessment of particular sorts of cases. For example, the negligent driver who cannot control the unlucky, untimely emergence of the child whom he strikes and kills is perceived as committing a greater offense than a merely but equally negligent, non-killing driver, and is held to be worthy of greater blame. What is to be said about the differential moral assessment of cases where the difference is an element due to luck? What is to be done about the apparent persistent slip between persuasive principle and common practice?

Bernard Williams and Thomas Nagel, who introduced the problem into contemporary literature and baptised it so disconcertingly, held that moral luck, the determination of moral assessment in some cases by happy or unhappy contingency, is altogether *real* but constitutes a full blown *para-*

dox in "our conception" of morality or "the ordinary idea of moral assessment" when viewed in light of intuitive notions linking moral responsibility to the agent's control.[5] A paradox requires a remedy which restores consistency but neither Williams nor Nagel proposed one. Instead they suggested darkly that the reconstruction of principle required by practice might alter our understanding of ourselves or of the role of morality in our lives beyond recognition.

Others have argued, contrary to Williams and Nagel, that moral luck surely *cannot* be real; they find it deeply unfair, if not incoherent. The "control condition," the intuitive principle limiting moral assessment to just such factors as an agent controls, is held to be virtually self-evident. Further, its corollary that "one cannot be more culpable or estimable for anything than one is for that fraction of it which is under one's control," shows that differential assessments where the sole difference in cases is a factor due to luck cannot be correct.[6] Hence, for example, the lucky and unlucky negligent drivers *are* both blameworthy, but can only be *equally* so; that one case resulted in a killing is a matter due to luck. Assuming that practice just can't be so wildly at variance with self-evident truth, these critics adopt the strategy of explaining away the appearance of moral luck in order to restore consistency.

Henning Jensen and Norvin Richards in such recent attempts to show moral luck illusory, allow that we do *seem* often enough to allow matters of luck to figure in our moral assessments, but aim to show through closer scrutiny and additional distinctions that the control condition is not in fact violated.[7] Unfortunately, the assumptions at work in their accounts are at least as counter-intuitive as they take moral luck to be. Richards's account rests on the dubious assumption that we *in fact* consider only a person's character, and never acts or their results, worthy of praise or blame. Jensen's account requires us to accept the troubling assumption that actually causing the harm one risks merits no more blame than merely risking that harm without causing it.[8]

A third avenue is to take moral luck seriously enough to call into question theoretical principles that won't cohere with it. Martha Nussbaum's extensive and vivid study of moral luck as a defining theme of classical Greek thought demonstrates how long its recognition has been with us and how the *wish* to deny or contain moral vulnerability is a philosophical quest as old as the western tradition.[9] Judith Andre reminds us that our long tradition of ethical thought makes for "hybrid" concepts, partaking of different (though not necessarily contradictory) strains; moral responsibility, for example, has more or less Kantian as well as rather Aristotelian applications and connections, the latter of which allow for the impact of luck in the sphere of moral value.[10] If the recognition of moral luck is so deeply rooted, our theoretical pictures of moral value and responsibility should accommodate it. If they do not, the acceptability of those pictures needs defending.

From Nagel and Williams through Richards and Jensen, however, the control condition stands curiously undefended.[11] Yet the principle is not self-evident (and certainly not a tautology). It expresses a substantive view about the conditions under which we should see ourselves and others as responsible for actions and their outcomes. By consequence, it marks out the area in which various responses (owning up; assuming or accepting blame or liability; experiencing sorrow, anguish, shame or guilt; offering reparative gestures) are appropriate for the actor, and various others (imputing responsibility or holding blameworthy; experiencing indignation, outrage, disgust or disappointment; expecting or demanding reparation, apology, or other fitting acknowledgement; developing or losing trust) are appropriate for others. The moral assessments at issue, then, in the contest between moral luck and the control condition are not only bare imputations of responsibility but evaluations of a full repertoire of perceptions, judgements, expectations, responses, attitudes and demands with respect to ourselves and to others in the matter of our conduct, its meaning, and its impact.

It is in light of this that I propose to defend the reality of moral luck and to reject the view that it generates an insoluble problem. Elsewhere I have argued that moral luck threatens paradox only in the context of a view of moral agents as noumenal, or virtually so.[12] But we are human agents and as such are hopelessly "impure" in Williams's sense—agents of, rather than outside, the world of space, time and causality, agents whose histories and actions belong to it. The beautifully simple regimentation of responsibility embodied in the control condition represents an alteration of our common life far more drastic than may at first be supposed. To accept it, I will argue, would rid us of far more than an alleged kink in our philosophical thinking.

In the following section I explore, albeit very briefly, some deep and extensive connections between our causal inextricability, which combines limited control with significant efficacy, and the moral significance of our response to it. I claim that the reality of moral luck alone makes sense of an important arena of assessment in which agents are found satisfactory or deficient, even admirable or base, to the extent that they understand their causal position and the appropriate responses to it. Judgements in this area center around the matter of an agent's *integrity*. In section III, I consider why certain responses *are* so widely considered appropriate: they are too valuable to us in our vulnerability and interdependence to dispense with. To show this I explore the disparity between an understanding of human agency which accommodates moral luck and one which refuses to accommodate it. Considering two pictures of agency polarized along the dimension central to the moral luck problem, the relation of control to accountability, I propose that the stakes in affirming one or the other of these pictures are high ones, and that we have good reason to go with our luck.

II

How do we commonly regard and what do we expect of agents in actual situations of having "unluckily" caused serious harms or having "unluckily" confronted moral tests which their characters did not prevent them from failing miserably? Here only vivid and closely described cases could generate precise and specific results. It will matter whether a negligent killing driver drove knowingly with faulty brakes, drove 105 m.p.h. in a residential area, drove home in exhaustion to get to a dying parent's bedside, or refused friends' assistance and drove himself home very drunk. It will matter whether a woman with hungry children keeps a lost, money-filled wallet which contains identification, whether a child is caught up in a Nazi youth group at school or an adult informs on his Jewish neighbor for political advantage, whether someone lied out of humiliation or greed. These differences will matter for our judgements on the degree and type of wrong, and on the appropriateness of blame, its amount, and its nature. Yet in most, if not all, such cases of uncontrolled upshots or unchosen circumstances, there is one thing I think we will find at least faulty if not completely unacceptable: that the agent should *shrug it off.*

Suppose the agent says, in effect, "It's really too bad about what happened and the damage that's been done, but my involvement was just a happenstance that it was my bad luck to suffer. I admit my negligence (dishonesty, cowardice, opportunism, etc.) and accept such blame as is due these common faults. But it would be totally unfair of you to judge, let alone blame me for unlucky results and situations I didn't totally control, and stupid or masochistic of me to let you." It is hard to imagine any variation on this sort of agent response not striking us as untoward. Given the nature of the case, it could be disappointing or irritating, shameful or indecent, shocking or outrageous. Even where we as third parties are disposed to be compassionate, fair-minded, and humane, we would be taken aback, and perhaps indignant. If our indignation were met by the agent with a cool reminder that we were conceptually befuddled about assessment and control, our estrangement would, I suggest, be aggravated rather than relieved. We would think there was something wrong with that agent that went deeper than the initial offense. What the agent's stance puts in question is how responsible or responsive he or she is. We might say that he is cavalier, or that she is kidding herself, or more simply and strongly, that this person lacks integrity. We might just experience the equivalents of these by feeling disgust, resentment, indignation, loss of trust.

Such responses are common phenomena of our moral lives together when we do not simply imagine ourselves as the ideal moral judiciary, or as officers of the moral police armed with sharp instruments of blame. When we do not restrict ourselves to thinking about this problem in the "juridical" mode—that of sitting in judgement and levying blame—we are more apt to remember the variety of assessments and considerations that will concern us, including ones about trust, confidence, and reliability, and the responses that will express our grasp of these. The reality of moral luck renders these more varied phenomena intelligible, if we take moral luck for what it appears to be: a fact of our moral situation and our human kind of agency. The *fact* is our perfectly predictable entanglement in a causally complex world, with imperfectly predictable results. Part of the normal and required self-understanding of human agents is a *grasp* of that fact, of the loose and chancy fit between undertakings and impacts, and between where we'd choose to find ourselves, and where we actually do. This fact requires us to understand and respond to our actual situation of being at moral risk, i.e. of being subject to assessment both for results of what we have (uncontroversially) done and for our actions under circumstances morally fraught, where these results and circumstances are determined in important part by luck. The truth of moral luck which the rational, responsive moral agent is expected to grasp is that *responsibilities outrun control*, although not in one single or simple way.

This truth in turn renders intelligible a distinctive field of assessments of ourselves and others, in terms of how we regard and respond to just this interplay between what we control and what befalls us; to, as Williams might say, the "impurity" of our agency. Here we expect ourselves and others to muster certain resources of character to meet the synergy of choice and fortune which is especially burdensome in the case of bad moral luck. Here agents are found to have or lack such qualities as integrity, grace or lucidity. These qualities might well be called "virtues of impure agency." As is said of dispositions which are virtues, they issue in acceptable or even meritorious behavior which contributes "in extensive and fundamental ways" to our living well in concert with others a distinctively human life.[13] They are corrective of temptations and deficiencies of sorts to which human beings are commonly susceptible with typically or overall undesirable results.[14] They are constituted in important part by a reliable capacity to see things clearly, to take the proper moral measure of situations, so that a fitting response may be fashioned.[15] While acceptance of responsibility, whether in excess of control or not, will often prompt reparative attempts which enlist various of the familiar virtues—courage, justice, benevolence—bad moral luck taxes agents in distinctive ways to which the qualities mentioned distinctively respond.

Integrity is a quality of character hard enough to describe in any case, but impossible to capture fully without reference to the vicissitudes of moral luck. The "intactness" or "wholeness" which are its core meanings imply freedom from corruption, spoilage, shattering, or decay. What integrity so protects, however, is not one's goals or goods or social standing, but one's *moral self*, that center of moral commitments in oneself from which morally fitting and valuable responses flow in a sure and steady way. From the viewpoint of others, the agent's firm moral center guarantees *dependability* in the matter of morally responsible conduct not just in the long run or in the sphere of the everyday, but more especially in trying times where unwanted circumstance proposes more severe tests. What integrity is a bulwark against is not just lapses or simple wrongdoing, which are always possible, but a deeper or more catastrophic loss or lack of moral center.

The conditions which most threaten us with this kind of loss or most unequivocally reveal this lack are just those constituting moral luck: the decisive moral tests one did not invite, and which may reveal one's moral competence or commitments as a pretense; the faulty or horrifying results that one invited but did not control, and which one is expected to find resources to address or redress without taking refuge in denial, demoralization, or paralysis. People we know to have integrity are those who have been challenged in just such ways; their integrity consists in the fact that they are able to stand and respond in terms that embody ongoing moral commitments or such new ones as may be required. They keep or make whole and well what might otherwise suffer deformity, collapse, or desertion: a coherent and responsible moral posture. Temptations to avoidance and denial are successfully countered.[16]

It is also true that integrity can be caricatured in an unseemly and narcissistic "heroism" or self-glorifying but ineffective martyrdom (literal or symbolic). There are morally unlucky cases, for example where a life is lost or a deep human bond severed, where there remains little place for meaningful reparation to others, and where the self-reparative work of integrity seems small even if necessary response to an inexpungeable loss. Acceptance, non-aggrandized daily "living with" unsupported by fantasies of overcoming or restitution, may in its quiet way be as profoundly admirable as integrity in those situations which permit no reconstructive address. I would call this, simply, *grace*; it also has its place in far less grievous situations, where it is one's good moral luck to have received forgiveness or mercy and where one should not succumb to self-absorbed or exhibitionistic contrition.

Further, integrity and grace depend critically on *lucidity*, a reasonable grasp of the nature and seriousness of one's morally unlucky plight and a cogent and sensitive estimate of repairs and self-correction in point. Temptations to self-deception, self-indulgence, and wishful thinking here require overcoming. As in the other cases, the capacities in question can be virtues only if they are relatively fixed dispositions; but their fixity may indeed be relative, varying concretely by degree or even, perhaps, with respect to contexts.

Perhaps 'lucidity' is just a name for the reliable perceptual capacity that grounds integrity, as 'grace' may refer to integrity's understanding of the limits of its own effectiveness. But whether these virtues are distinct or aspects of one thing, they are possible and necessary only for agents whose natural situation involves vulnerability to luck, and so part of whose distinctive achievement will rest on how well and truly they reckon with that. Virtue, James Wallace has said, "must tend to foster good human life in extensive and fundamental ways. It must be the perfection of a tendency or capacity that connects or interlocks with a variety of human goods in such a way that its removal from our lives would endanger the whole structure."[17] If integrity is the capacity required to deal morally with the impurity of luck-ridden human agency, its general absence should be disfiguring of human life in ways broad and deep. For the same reason, a way of conceiving agency that attempts to banish the impurity which gives integrity its point should produce under examination an alien and disturbing picture of moral life. And so it does. I turn to this now.

III

The "moral luck problem" is one about conceptions of agency and responsibility of the sort that morality requires. Moral luck is part of a picture of *impure agency*: agency situated within the causal order in such ways as to be variably conditioned by and conditioning parts of that order, without our being able to draw for *all* purposes a *unitary* boundary to its exercise at either end, nor always for *particular* purposes a *sharp* one. Such agents' accountabilities don't align precisely with their conscious or deliberate choices or undertakings, and are not necessarily limited by them. Rather, the match between choice and action on the one hand, and accountability and desert on the other, is inexact and conditional, and is mediated by complex social understandings which these agents are expected to appreciate and to share.[18] To be sure, matters of control and faulty intention will be *elements* in these understandings; but so will matters of foreseenness, foreseeability, magnitude of adverse impacts, significance or conspicuousness of causal contribution, as well as (loose or precise) appreciation of probabilities of different sorts. Part of the complexity of these understandings consists in the fact that there appears to be no single equation of responsibility in which each or all of the elements play fixed roles. Still, an underlying assumption of these understandings is that responsibilities are apt to outrun deliberate commitments, intentional choices, and even their foreseen or foreseeable entailments. On this picture, we are players within the complex causal set-up, where the price of our often decisive participation is exposure to risk.

The view against which moral luck offends is that of *pure agency*: agency neither diluted by nor implicated in the vagaries of causality at all, or at least not by causality external to the agent's will, itself understood as a causal power. This view is epitomized by Kant's conception of the moral agent as noumenally free, so outside space, time, and causality entirely. But it also comprehends non-transcendental pictures of agency which share with Kant's just the feature of immunity to luck. Such views do not need to withdraw agency entirely from the realm of causality in order to secure this.[19] It is sufficient that the possibility of assessment be allowed to stretch only so far as does that causality which may be identified with the agent itself, e.g. the causality of character or of intention. Nagel has recently given striking expression to the ideal aspiration of pure agency:

> What we hope for is not only to do what we want given the circum-
> stances, but also to be as we want to be, to as deep a level as possible, and
> to find ourselves faced with the choices we want to be faced with, in a
> world that we can want to live in.[20]

It is, at last, the drive "to be able to encompass ourselves completely, and thus become the absolute source of what we do."[21]

It is characteristic of those who view moral luck as philosophically problematic or paradoxical to claim it is so in light of "our" or "the ordinary" concept of agency, assessment, or moral responsibility. Yet no one denies that facts of the matter *seem* to resist. I have argued that they are indeed facts, that in some precincts especially our practice shows a grasp of our causal inextricability and some burdens we take it reasonably to impose. At the same time, I do not mean to ignore the existence of some lively, "principled" intuitions to the effect that such practices embody an unfortunate mistake. Rather than prolong indecisive proprietary disputes about intuitions, I turn instead to the question of what is at stake in the contest between the actual practices I have emphasized and some possible ones purified along lines provided by the control condition. We should ask: what is it *like* to live under the strict correlation of moral assessment and responsibility with control? What is it like to be, and to be among, pure agents?

First, pure agents will have far less to account for, and will bear, in total, far less responsibility than many of us think we and others currently do. No unforeseen results will place them at risk of assessment, let alone of blame; even foreseen but uncontrolled upshots of their intentional performances will not properly place them in question. Presumably, no fewer damages, hurts, harms, deprivations, violations, cripplings, and killings will occur. Indeed, pure agents have fewer moral reasons to take care for these eventualities, even if they still have various social and practical ones. But these sufferings and misfortunes will go more often unattributed; they will be *other people's* hard luck.

Pure agents will not only be responsible for less, but will bear a special kind of relationship to their responsibilities: they will unilaterally control and constitute them. Each pure agent is free, on her own, to determine what and how much she may be brought to account for by determining the intentional acts and commitments she will undertake, and recognizing the limits to her control beyond these. What will no longer be true, if it ever was properly thought to be so, is that the realities, potentials, needs, vulnerabilities, and sufferings of other things and people might be part of what constitutes her responsibilities. Relationships, situations, and encounters in which emerge uncontrolled and uninvited needs, demands, and opportunities to enable or harm will not be thought to ground morally legitimate claims upon us or in our behalf, in ways we might have thought or hoped. Even if we have invited these relationships, situations or encounters, we will not have controlled all of the demanding possibilities they give rise to. I may have decided to have a child, but will probably not have decided to have a sickly and difficult one; I may have entered into a friendship, but surely will not have controlled the death of the friend's wife, and the desperate neediness with which he turns to me. That legitimate moral claims can overreach deliberate commitments, that need or suffering can even sometimes *impose* responsibilities it would be indecent to ignore do not seem to be realities in the world of pure agents.

Being accountable and actually bearing responsibilities is burdensome. Being accountable means exposure to possibilities of criticism, rebuke, and punishment; to valid demands of reparation, restoration, or compensation; to proper expectations of regret, remorse, self-reproof, and self-correction. It would be nice to have to do and accept so much less of this, and pure agents enjoy such relief. Having conceptually divested themselves of much of their moral property, they have secured unusually favorable rates of moral taxation. In respect of any particular performance or default, they are rendered far less vulnerable to many burdens of these sorts that might have applied if features due to circumstantial and resultant luck had not been rendered morally unaccountable. Concomitantly, however, all other pure agents are thereby rendered a great deal more vulnerable. Their augmented burdens involve needs, pains, and frustrations deriving from various injuries and misfortunes which result from the actions of other, morally unburdened pure agents; the latter have achieved impunity in such respects, but the former can no longer rightfully propose or expect compensation or repair, nor even enjoy the mild satisfactions (or relief) of others' appropriate regret or fitting remorse.

Pure agents, in sum, are freer on the whole from responsibility; are freer to define for themselves what and how much responsibility they will bear; and hence are freer from the varieties of burden to which responsibility renders one subject. Pure agency is a model of *independence*. Unlike the Stoical independence of withdrawal from worldly, bodily, or common life, however, we see here independence of a more robust and worldly sort, reserving the full field of action while paring responsibilities to fit consent, commitment, and contract—the markers of voluntary control.[22] In pure agency we recognize the template of versions of the clearly bounded and rationally self-controlling agent of neo-Kantian and contractualist moral philosophies, and the socially discreet, rationally self-disposing self of liberal political theory.[23]

One cannot deny that pure agents are enviably free, in certain ways, of unhappy fate and of each other. Their enviable independence, however, cannot help being at the same time a worrisome and unpleasant *undependability*. Their unilateral control of responsibility and their exemption from reparative demands in all areas beyond strict control make clear that such agents may not reasonably be looked to for much. In particular, pure agents may not be depended upon, much less morally required, to assume a share of the ongoing and massive human work of caring, healing, restoring, and cleaning-up on which each separate life and the collective one depend. That the very young and old, the weak, the sick, and the otherwise helpless—i.e. all of us at some times—depend on the sense of moral responsibility of others unlucky enough to be stuck with the circumstance of their need will not be the pure agents' problem. It is alarming to anticipate life in a world where people routinely and with justification walk away from the harmful, cruel, or even disastrous results which their actions were critical even if not sufficient, in bringing about. In a technologically advanced society in which some people's actions can have disproportionate impact on huge numbers of unknown others, the prospect is worse than alarming. All these prospects are real ones in a world from which moral luck has been banished and agency purified.

Impure agents are saddled with weighty responsibilities and the open-ended possibility of acquiring more due to circumstances beyond their control. Yet agents who recognize their vulnerability to fortune are primed for dependability of humanly invaluable sorts. These are agents on whom we can depend, or at least to whom the presumption of dependability applies, and so whose undependability in many cases can be duly registered as failure. To the extent that these agents are people of integrity, they won't fail us even under the blows of bad fortune or odd turns of fate which might otherwise prompt denial or opportunism; to the extent that we ourselves are such agents and possesses integrity, we can depend, morally, on ourselves even in a bad spot.

Anyone may fail morally in the particular dimension of facing bad moral luck. There are also cases so trying as to be virtually beyond human endurance, circumstances or results so shattering that maintaining integrity would be supererogation. They are the stuff of tragedy. But the association of moral luck with tragedy should not obscure the fact that the tragic case is a rare one, while more pedestrian instances of moral luck are ubiquitous, and its common challenges are everyday matters. In a world where we need so much from each other so often, acceptance of our impurity is not the worst we can do.[24]

NOTES

1. Bernard Williams, "Moral Luck," in *Moral Luck* (Cambridge: Cambridge University Press, 1983), 29–30.

2. Thomas Nagel, "Moral Luck," in *Mortal Questions* (Cambridge: Cambridge University Press, 1979), 28, describes four types of moral luck: constitutive (luck in the kind of person one is); circumstantial (luck in the problems and situations one faces); luck in how the will is determined by antecedent circumstances; and luck in the way one's actions and projects turn out. The first and third types are often seen, correctly, as representing the metaphysical problem of freedom and determinism, while the second and fourth have drawn most interest as representing the problem of moral luck proper. Nagel's and Williams's discussions (the latter's "Gauguin problem" being of the fourth type) are the locus of the contemporary debate.

3. Williams, "Moral Luck," 20.

4. Nagel, "Moral Luck," 25.

5. Respectively, Williams, "Moral Luck," 22, 39; Nagel, "Moral Luck," 27.

6. Nagel, "Moral Luck," 28.

7. Henning Jensen, "Morality and Luck," *Philosophy* 59 (1984): 323–30; Norvin Richards, "Luck and Desert," *Mind* 95 (1986): 198–209. In a similar move, Michael Zimmerman, in "Luck and Moral Responsibility," *Ethics* (1987): 374–86, claims that the killing driver's being to blame for a death just means that he is "to blame for more events" but not "more to blame." But being "to blame for a death" is here reduced to the death's being "an indicator" that one deserves a negative evaluation, the *same* negative evaluation one deserves for negligent driving alone (383). This move appears to be a terminological maneuver; what is described isn't "being to blame for a death" but is just being to blame *for negligence* in light of, or in view of, or because of a death.

8. Richards, "Luck and Desert," 206–7, admits that his position looks more like a wholesale "utilitarian" revision of common understanding than an interpretation of it. Jensen, "Morality and Luck," 327–28, elaborates a complex and interesting account of blaming in order to show how equally blameworthy persons might be in practice differentially blamed. But Jensen, while explaining why harmless negligent acts often escape active blame entirely and why malicious acts with or without harmful results typically receive blame, never does explain the specific case at issue, our propensity to actively blame (even punish) people for negligent acts with harmful but not completely controlled results. It is not clear to me that he can get the answer he needs. See Jonathan Adler, "Luckless Desert Is Different Desert," *Mind* 96 (1987): 247–49, for a strong reply to Richards.

9. Martha Nussbaum, *The Fragility of Goodness* (Cambridge: Cambridge University Press, 1986).

10. Judith Andre, "Nagel, Williams, and Moral Luck," *Analysis* 43 (1983): 202–7.

11. In fairness to Williams, I should note that he does emphasize the role of immunity to luck (secured by limiting accountability to control) in rendering acceptable the idea that morality is ubiquitous in scope and supreme in authority. Williams thus locates the control condition in an ensemble of features of a certain vision of morality he argues cannot be right.

12. Margaret Urban Coyne [Walker], "Moral Luck?" *Journal of Value Inquiry* 19 (1985): 319–25.

13. James Wallace, *Virtues and Vices* (Ithaca, N.Y.: Cornell University Press, 1978), 153.

14. Phillipa Foot, *Virtues and Vices* (Berkeley: University of California Press, 1978), 8.

15. See John MacDowell, "Virtue and Reason," *Monist* 62 (1979): 331–50; John Mackie, *Ethics* (New York: Penguin, 1977); and Iris Murdoch, *The Sovereignty of Good* (New York: Schocken, 1971). See also William May, "The Virtues in a Professional Setting," *Soundings* 67 (1984): 245–66, on the importance of viewpoint, and not only action, in facing the "perennials" of human existence: birth, death, incapacitation, generational conflict, and, I would add, moral luck.

16. This does not, of course, constitute a theory of integrity, but I believe it expresses the core of a plausible one. The central idea is that integrity is the capacity for reliably

maintaining a coherent moral posture, and that this capacity is only proven under challenge. Whether the posture in play must meet some minimal standards of correctness or adequacy, and whether it must be in some way "authentic," i.e., truly or reflectively the agent's own, are questions a more complete discussion might address.

17. Wallace, *Virtues and Vices*, 153.

18. Joel Feinberg, "Action and Responsibility," in *Philosophy in America*, ed. Max Black (Ithaca, N.Y.: Cornell University Press, 1965), provides a useful discussion of the several senses of responsibility that may be distinguished in connection with human actions, and the fact that just a bit of causal contribution suffices for some kinds of responsibility, while no causal contribution is even necessary for others. Robert Audi, "Moral Responsibility, Freedom, and Compulsion," *American Philosophical Quarterly* 11 (1974): 1–14, nicely analyzes a variety of conditions, including normative ones, which constitute, diminish or cancel moral responsibility. For a probing conceptual examination of some intricacies in the legal understanding of connections among causal involvement, responsibility and liability, see Judith Jarvis Thomson, "Causation and Liability," in *Rights, Restitution, and Risk* (Cambridge: Harvard University Press, 1986).

19. Richards, "Luck and Desert"; Jensen, "Morality and Luck"; and Zimmerman, "Luck and Moral Responsibility" are examples.

20. Thomas Nagel, *The View from Nowhere* (New York: Oxford University Press, 1986), 136.

21. Nagel, *The View from Nowhere*, 118. For Nagel these are expressions of what moral agency requires, even though the conditions set are impossible of attainment, and so the appetite for autonomy is insatiable.

22. I thank Martha Nussbaum and Neil Delaney for suggesting to me that the Stoic approach to the neutralization of luck in human life deserves more thought. The contemporary discussion rather naturally tends to fix overmuch on Kant. A more just treatment would need to explore fundamental differences in meaning and motivation between the ideals of *autarkeia* and *autonomy*, as well as the important similarities.

23. The foregoing discussion of pure agency is not offered as a refutation of such moral or political views, but as a response to those who propose the control condition as limiting moral responsibilities. I do intend, however, to raise the question of the adequacy of an entirely constructivist or consensual view of responsibility to the role of contingency in our lives. An admirably concise and effective critique of attempts to ground all special moral responsibilities to particular persons or categories of persons on consent or agreement is found in Robert Goodin, *Protecting the Vulnerable* (Chicago: University of Chicago Press, 1985).

24. Two opportunities to present earlier versions of this paper were helpful to me: I thank the Vanderbilt University Philosophy Department Colloquium audience, especially Alasdair MacIntyre and John Post, for their comments; and those present at the University of Santa Clara conference on Agency, Causality, and Virtue (1987). Thanks to John Arthur, Robert Audi, Christopher Gowans, and Arthur Walker for helpful suggestions and criticisms. I am grateful to Fordham University for the Faculty Fellowship leave during which I wrote earlier drafts of this paper.

3

PARTIAL CONSIDERATION

It is no wonder that impartiality, in some form, is so widely viewed as a constitutive norm of correct moral thinking.[1] A requirement of impartiality warns us off fixations and distortions of feeling, challenges the exclusions of inattention or bias, and picks away at the parochialism of our own small worlds of interest and narrow horizons of experience. These predictable pitfalls which impartiality confronts threaten equally the most substantively diverse kinds of moral thinking; inattention, distortion or bias may beset us as we reckon with rights or with welfare, with virtuous conduct or with responsibility in relationships. So one can hardly deny the central claim of impartiality as a regulative ideal of moral thinking, enjoining the kind of consideration of each affected party that will genuinely enable us to count her or him for at least one. In the face of possible deformities of incomplete attention or positive bias, impartiality sets us the (ideal) goal of full and undistorted appreciation of the situation of each in the service of fair application of moral norms to all.[2] Put in this way impartiality may seem incontestable. Who would deny that each affected party is morally owed a sincere attempt at adequate consideration? Yet I aim to show that standard ways philosophers envision the nature of impartial thinking mislead us as to how beings such as we might possibly achieve this goal.

A moral ideal needs an implementation, a way of bringing it into contact with actual possibilities and practices of moral reflection and judgement. The ideal of adequate consideration of each might seem to put pressure on moral agents to achieve refined and detailed understanding of the positions and interests of potential moral patients, with all the attention to specifics of circumstance, history, desire and expectation that would involve. This would seem to invite philosophical scrutiny of those communicative, deliberative, imaginative and empathetic skills which are required to elicit and organize the wealth of information required by a full and undistorted view. Reflecting impartially in order to make more adequate moral judgements seems like a very epistemically complex and labor-intensive process of acquiring, refining, and amplifying information.

Yet philosophical discussions of impartial thinking seem lax, where not actually reductive, with respect to this epistemically demanding ideal. Often the real possibilities and problems of achieving insight and gleaning information, especially about people, are simply ignored. Where models, devices or techniques for impartial thinking are stipulated, they often involve eliminative maneuvers, directing us to detach or disconnect ourselves, or to surpress, exclude, or limit the impact of many kinds of information.

Nowhere is this more evident than in certain images invoked repeatedly by philosophers in connection with impartial consideration: God's eye, the ideal observer, the third-person spectator, the disinterested judge.[3] Such pictures are a familiar part of the prevailing *rhetoric* of impartiality—the way the concept is "deployed" in standard tropes, repeated images or common patterns of description by philosophers. My claim is that the rhetoric of impartiality embodied in these forcefully suggestive pictures in standard use creates recipes for very *partial*—that is, incomplete or distorted—moral consideration indeed. It is not that impartial consideration is logically incompatible with minute attention to all manner of specific information bearing on moral choice. The problem is that trying to direct historically situated, imperfectly observant, and inveterately interested agents—us—to that information in terms of these images is misleading or distorting where it is not simply unhelpful or irrelevant. I will try to show how these images in practice steer agents like us away from ways and means of moral understanding which could give us access to what we need morally to know and to suggest in conclusion, very briefly, the direction an alternative moral epistemology could take us. But as this involves an exercise in "moral pragmatics," a comment on method is in order.

I

Much contemporary moral philosophy is devoted to defining key moral concepts, articulating and refining possible moral principles or theories, and examining the logical connections, presuppositions, and entailments of these. When I speak of the *pragmatics* of moral thinking, I refer to a different set of concerns than these. From the standpoint of moral pragmatics we ask questions about how moral concepts, principles, and theories are fitted with certain social patterns, kinds of activities, and forms of communication to which they are appropriate and in terms of which they make sense. We also ask how people's selection and exclusion in discussions of morality of certain ways of thinking and speaking expresses something about those people: their preoccupation with certain problems, modes of relationship, or social responsibilities, or their greater familiarity with some situations, institutions, roles, social arrangements or opportunities.[4] Most generally, the pragmatics of moral thinking asks what things people actually do with moral vocabularies and patterns of emphasis in the use of them, and what is done to people's moral thinking and moral lives thereby. It is about why and how it matters to say one thing at one point rather than another, and why it matters that some things are not (or rarely) mentioned at all. The point of moral pragmatics is not to disparage or ignore the standard concerns of moral philosophers, but to supplement them, by reminding ourselves that moral thinking is a real-time, socially situated, interpersonally effective phenomenon.

Looking at moral discussions and discussions of morality from the viewpoint of use and impact, it is not inappropriate to speak of a particular *rhetoric* at work.[5] By this is meant the stock of key words, images, metaphors, favored examples, and methods of presentation that people share when they occupy the same universe of moral discourse and thus enjoy within that universe a certain degree of unimpeded mutual comprehension. "Rhetoric" is, after all, a package of devices for effective and persuasive communication. Many contemporary philosophers think of philosophy as a business of fashioning and testing arguments. Argument, in the logic textbook sense, is one way of organizing information, and the use of arguments is one type of persuasive presentation. Focus on rhetoric does not slight argument, but recognizes argument as one aspect of philosophical rhetoric, and the claim of reliance on argument as the mark of a particular rhetorical stance.

In what follows, I do not examine arguments for impartiality. I look instead at some parts of the other, supporting machinery of the rhetoric of impartiality. Some of the machinery shapes our sense that arguments are (or are not) appropriate and significant at certain sites in moral-theoretic discussion. But this function is only one aspect of a broader one: drawing attention to some problems and possibilities of moral understanding while obscuring others. It is this chiaroscuro of philosophical rhetoric that primarily interests me here. I explore, in examining a cluster of its repeating and central images, where and how this portion of the rhetoric of impartiality casts light and throws darkness.

II

Let us suppose we want to give due consideration to the interests of affected parties in arriving at a moral judgement, establishing a moral principle, or determining the mode and relevance of applying a moral view or principle to a particular case at hand. There is a great fund of facts of several kinds we may have to establish and synthesize in achieving a view unblemished by arbitrary exclusion, positive bias, simple carelessness, or remediable ignorance. We may need to determine whose interests are actually (or potentially) affected; which interests at stake are morally relevant and significant, in kind or by degree; just how the interests affected are most adequately characterized, including the meaning and importance of such interests to the affected parties; and, perhaps, the relative importance of these various interests of various parties when brought together on some common scale, or through some technique of ordering.[6] We also need to bear in mind the reliability of all of the (not necessarily mutually independent) sorts of information just mentioned, which may well influence the weight or role we might reasonably assign to it.

R. M. Hare, a proponent of rigorous impartiality (in the service of maximizing at the critical level of moral thinking), is unusually sensitive, as these discussions in moral philosophy go, to the vicissitudes and burdens of acquiring, assessing, and using moral information of some kinds just mentioned.[7] Hare notes that determining moral relevance will often involve "guesswork" and "experiment" in which principles mentioning the possibly relevant features are tried out (189), and that the trying out itself will require us to know "what it is like to be those people in that situation," that is, knowing what something is like for someone and not merely that something is happening to him (92). Hare's expectations of us are modest here, for the right reasons: "The difficulties are all practical ones of acquiring the necessary knowledge and correctly performing some very complex thought-processes" (111). "Nobody supposes that in practice human beings will be able to find out all the facts about other people's preferences and their strengths which would be necessary for a secure answer to all moral questions" (122). Most critically, "We cannot know everything about another actual person's concrete situation (including how it strikes him, which may make all the difference)."[8] Hare's remarks display a clear awareness of how information-hungry impartial consideration should be, and hungry for types of information with their own vexing and peculiar obscurities. Unless we are already very sure we're in a position to say what's what, with respect to intention, act, meaning, importance, and impact for everybody upon whom our decisions bear, we must view the goal of full and accurate appreciation as quite challenging, perhaps even in ordinary cases. Hare's way of giving form to the very real difficulty he spots for interpersonal (and self-) understanding, however, is strikingly typical of the way this problem is marked and imaged in a great deal of philosophical literature. "In difficult cases," Hare remarks, "it would take an archangel to do it."[9]

Hare's archangel joins a cast of like characters who are supposed to mark the spot from which things are impartially viewed: the ideal observers, the third persons, the disinterested judges, God's eye (left behind, like the smile of the Cheshire Cat, when God disappeared), and Sidgwick's crypto-version of the divine oculus, "the point of view of the universe."[10] These are images of transcendence or encapsulation, and their prevalence suggests that an account of morally adequate attention lies not in close perusal of the many talents and techniques that ordinary folk, or persons with specially refined or schooled skills of interpersonal (and self-) observation, make use of to discover "what it is like to be those people in that situation," including how it "strikes" them. We do not often in articles on moral philosophy see the moral agent at deliberation imaged as a close friend, loving parent, concerned teacher, or perceptive advisor, much less as a gifted counselor, seasoned psychoanalyst, shrewd sociological observer, or trained anthropological field worker.[11] Yet all such individuals possess special capacities and opportunities for gleaning recondite information of just the right sorts in some situations where human interests and perceptions are paramount. Many familiar ways and means of knowing what is going on or is likely to go on with people do not appear in most moral philosophy.[12] More importantly they not only do not appear, but the "place" where they might appear—the part of the discussion that takes up issues of how to know or see what must be understood for adequate moral consideration—is preempted by images of nonhuman or superhuman viewers, or human viewers specially blinkered by role or distance. Let's now consider some of these images in turn, asking what sorts of cognitive skills, patterns of interest or attention, modes of perception and lines of access these philosophically preferred symbols of moral intelligence possess.

III

The view from "God's eye" (or its secular, but not demythologized, surrogate the "point of view of the universe") expresses in one way an obvious ideal of morally adequate vision, but in other ways is an image of deep obscurity. The obvious suggestion is that everything is seen from this viewpoint, and hence everything that is possibly relevant to a moral response is seen. Because human agents labor always under conditions of limited information and understanding, and since the familiar limitations include that of not always reliably knowing exactly in which respects one's understanding is incomplete, the invitation to look through God's eye is an exhortation to expand our grasp of morally relevant information.

Yet the image of God's eye responds to the real problem of limited information in a particularly uninstructive way. The divine viewpoint is a pointlessly extravagant expression of the ideal of fully adequate information, for moral agents do not need to know the state of every leaf and sparrow, and there is the real problem of how much raw information it is possible and optimal for a human agent to attempt to ponder in pursuit of a morally adequate view. But when we try to work this image to define *relevance* (leaving aside the very important question of manageability), we run up against the imponderable: God sees everything, but how should we imagine the salience and priority for God of what God sees from God's point of view, and what has this to do with (our) morality? Here perhaps it is felt that a divine perspective is superior to the "universe's point of view." It is tempting to imagine that the universe's point of view would very likely be, "So what?" whereas God, understood in familiar Judaeo-Christian traditions as a person, is commonly thought to possess such attributes as benevolence in addition to omniscience. But even if we do assume that God sees everything, and sees it under the aspect of benevolent concern, we must still be puzzled about what *God* would think best for us, for we surely cannot assume that God must (or is likely to) see this as we do.

The point is not that there cannot be theories about this but that philosophical fondness for this image is not accompanied by any interest in moral theology, so the image remains blank for purposes of specifying the full and undistorted view. On the other hand, if the appeal of the image derives from the thought that we're not inscrutable before God even if we are often enough to each other, that God "sees into the heart of each," then we do not need a theology for our moral purposes. But we very much need a different kind of moral epistemology, one which gives instruction in how, with our limited provisions, to better approximate God's feat. The exhortation to fullness of appreciation cannot help us without indicating what specific forms that could take for us. And it does not touch the question raised before and which I rejoin below in connection with ideal observers: what is the status of a superhuman creature's view for our tasks of moral understanding?

This image, then, gives little help. Worse still, though, it does damage. The image powerfully projects the idea that a morally ideal grasp of things is essentially a view (sight, observation) from a place apart, perhaps timeless as well. I'll say more on observers, ideal and otherwise, below. The suggestion of placelessness and timelessness, however, is no innocent idealization. In morality we think to live and act and be able to give an account of ourselves, not just to have a "view." Human beings have to "live with" and "stand by" moral determinations and their issue. Some of the most common expressions one hears when people discuss weighty and difficult moral decisions is whether they can live with certain solutions, whether they or others will be haunted or damaged, whether ensuing burdens (psychological, reparative, or both) will be bearable, whether they will be able to make others understand. In actual morality there are real stakes and real costs, of value, self-esteem, relationship, future options, coherence in one's own eyes (as well rewards of several kinds).[13]

It is not insignificant that we don't typically think of God's privileged view connecting with God's ensuing actions and their results. (That is, God's view is invoked in connection with our choices, not usually pondered as the ground of God's.) It seems a joke to say of God's pursuit of a certain course, "Well, she or he will have to live with that." It is no joke for us that we can and often must think this about ourselves, for it conditions some of what we will take to be morally relevant reasons and so determines the relevance of some forms of information (especially about results and costs and others' perceptions and our own ability to make sense of ourselves). Neither God nor the universe has to "live with" the sequels to and moral repercussions of their actions, in the sense in which human beings do. Neither do they have to "stand by" moral implications of the commitments and valuations their moral resolutions express, or at least it is not clear they have any costs to sustain if they do not, for who is in a position to call them to account? That there may be such repercussions and entailments for oneself and others, that we and others call ourselves to account, is morally relevant information of which we need to make ourselves aware in making moral decisions. The idea lacks sense for the divine or cosmic case.

Bringing the divine perspective into firmer contact with the human situation leads to the imaging of some (presumably) more useful, because mongrel, types of morally exemplary viewers. Hare's archangel, with "superhuman powers of thought, superhuman knowledge and no human weaknesses" might be recognized immediately as a colorfully celestial version of that more common theoretical construct, the ideal moral observer, described in Roderick Firth's classic contemporary statement as omniscient, omnipercipient, disinterested, dispassionate and consistent, but "in other respects . . . normal."[14] Like God's viewpoint, that of the ideal observer stands in for an unrealizable limit of perfect understanding. Yet it is purportedly derived by extrapolation from actual human capacities and by erasure of identifiable human defects. As Firth said, "We must try to determine the characteristics of an ideal observer by examining the procedures which we actually regard, implicitly or explicitly, as the rational ones for deciding ethical questions."[15] While this sounds right, the characteristics selected for emphasis are transhuman or nonhuman in the extreme. Questions about the appropriateness and intelligibility of the ideal, analogous to those raised about God's view, arise.

Do we really understand the epistemic position of the ideal observer in Firth's version, for example? The observer not only knows everything that is the case but can also imagine everything that might be. Yet the observer lacks susceptibility to essentially particular interests, and the capacity for emotions with essentially particular objects (where 'particular' indicates those that can't be defined without use of a proper name). How is it then that we are to imagine what the observer grasps about the nature and significance of so many particular interests and emotions which matter to us, and how it is that the observer grasps them? What is it for the ideal observer to apprehend and appreciate "what Mark means to Sheila," or what *this* child (not "a child" or even "a child of mine") means to me? If the archangel has no human weaknesses, how does the archangel assess the cost of humiliations, shames and losses? One of the commonest and most severe impediments of human moral understanding is the limitation of sympathy or even of recognition that arises from simple lack of experience of what others endure. So why is an observer so dis-equipped ideal? As Richard Brandt remarked in his reply to Firth, "If a person were really incapable of particular emotions and particular interests, would he be ethically sensitive? . . . If the absence of particular interests and emotions resulted from the absence of relationships which might generate them, e.g. because like God he had no mother or children or friends, we might wonder if the conditions necessary for the development of ethical sensitivity could be realized."[16] Emotions, attachments, and evaluative reactions have a grammar grounded in human experiences and possibilities; certain forms of literacy are required in reading and understanding attachment and commitment, loss and continuation. How could and why would the ideal observer appreciate what matters to us and how it matters? Conversely, how could and why should we consider this alien's perceptions normative, or indeed, ideal?

The observer was to be constructed by extrapolation from the known human case, but what results is not really extrapolation but a wholesale negation of certain irremediable features of our human placement, motives, and paradigms of concern. The observer seems not to have all of our equipment, and we surely lack hers. The problem is: How really are we supposed to get there from here, and then back, where our moral perceptions and our conduct must make sense to ourselves and others of our kind? The ideal observer is hardly less impenetrable than God. Firth conceded that beyond the somewhat imponderable properties mentioned, the specific properties of an ideal observer are "apparently not capable of precise definition."[17] But it is not clear that even those mentioned are capable of the kind of characterization that would guide our own moral thinking. Similarly, Hare refers to the "superhuman powers of thought" which enable the archangel to tap into all the relevant information, but while Hare tells us to "approximate" to the thought-processes of the archangel (122), it remains unclear how we can know we are doing that, or how well.

Once again, while the ideal observer imagery explains little, it powerfully suggests some very questionable things. The ideal observer observes; and the archangel wrestles with unimaginable masses of data processed through inconceivably sophisticated thought processes. Like God, they are, in their exemplifying role, spectators who embody an ideal justificatory process which we imagine them traversing *in foro interno*. They are, in Seyla Benhabib's image, "like geometricians in different rooms who, reasoning alone for themselves, all arrive at the same solutions to a problem."[18] This they may do, because the stipulation of total information and perfect epistemic prowess bypasses questions of techniques and means of acquiring relevant information, especially those interpersonal methods of pooling and sharing and interpreting information for greater completeness and mutual correction. It is true that there is no stipulation that ideal observers will not or need not elicit, converse, inquire, debate, exchange interpretations, collaborate on imagining scenarios, or mediate a consensus on the way to full and accurate consideration. But nothing is said of these inquisitive, conversational, or hermeneutic maneuvers, which are blanketed over with stipulations of omniscience, and the like. That the observers are so well supplied with morally relevant information appears as if it were something instantaneous, hence magical, in our human terms. That is why they end up, after all, as demigods, able to leap chasms of interpersonal confusion or ignorance at a single bound.

There are some common images of impartial consideration which are not mysteriously out of human reach. These are the *disinterested judge* and the *third-person observer*. They have in common that they are truly human images, ones which ask us only to imagine our actual human experiences of moral situations structured in certain ways, not to remodel them along bafflingly superhuman lines. So these really are images of available human moral postures. More clearly than in the cases already discussed, these images emphasize certain restrictions and exclusions as essential. As before, it is important to look at what they do and don't imply or emphasize.

Consider the third person. To urge us to examine moral situations from the point of view of a third party is, of course, to counsel us toward greater objectivity where our own interests or attachments are at stake; what grips me in the first person may have a looser hold on me in the third. Further, even if the value or importance of concerns remains constant under first-to-third person transformations, one's vision of alternatives, prospects, and possibilities may from the spectator's position be "cooler," less disturbed by the passions or intensity of direct engagement. Here precisely the characteristically human business of moral costs and stakes and the future may receive more lucid appraisal if one can succeed in viewing these, however briefly, as someone else's. The third person perspective, then, seems to offer distinct benefits over the first. But the third person is an alternative not only to the first but to the second person as well, whose home is in communication, direct address. The third person, then, is constitutively not communicating, not addressing the involved parties, but observing them. One might act "on" the engaged parties and remain a third person, but one cannot engage with them and remain so.

The second person is a position largely neglected in moral philosophy. This shows up especially clearly in the way philosophers do talk about "taking the other's position." What this means typically is to construct for (by?) yourself the other's point of view. This can take rigorous game-theoretic forms or the more usual ones of temporarily trying out somebody's "shoes". (These dress rehearsals are almost always described as "imaginatively" performed; it is virtually never suggested that I might concretely sample somebody's burdens or woes.) What's really involved is thinking *for* others.[19] What is usually unexplored in such discussions is thinking *with* others. These round robins of role-taking are tournaments of monologic reasoning. One might not guess from the frequency of the theme of each of us "thinking for" all the others that a great deal of our best evidence about how it is with others requires talking with and listening to them. That asking, telling, repeating, mutually clarifying, mulling over, and checking back are the most dependable, accessible, and efficient devices for finding out how it is with others (a home truth for successful teachers, managers, marriage counselors, spiritual advisors, and other perceptive souls) could not be guessed from reading most moral philosophy. But this theme of thinking for, or imaginatively identifying, will loom large for any moral philosophy which recognizes the inescapability of assessing some human interests and yet does not insist on *communication* as a central constituent, where available, of adequate moral consideration. Since it is available in the vast majority of cases, where our moral courses implicate family, friends, intimates, neighbors, co-workers—that is, perfectly accessible others—the strong philosophical predilection for the game of imagination is alarming.[20]

The disinterested judge, on the other hand, is both observer and participant. A judge in a courtroom (or wine tasting or dog trial) may engage the contestants (or their representatives) in the search for more information or greater clarity. Still, the second-person opportunities of judges in proper exercise of their roles as such are strongly regimented. For one thing, the judge must always remain a third person in the sense that the judge's own interests must never be allowed to be at issue, at stake, or in any way influential. Further, the judge's expertise consists in having mastered the predetermined standards of relevance for the context under judgement; these may be interpretable within limits by the judge but are not, in the event of the judgement, open to discussion, reevaluation or revision in the process. Finally, the judge's decision simply closes that case (at least for that judge), and beyond that closure sequels and outcomes may be significant for the judge as a judge only with respect to future cases, or significant to the judge as (we like to say) a human being in ways quite outside the judging role. How does this model fare with respect to morally adequate consideration?

Its merits are clearer than any of the others. Unlike the God's eye view, the judge's presupposes some already established, relevance-defining categories of assessment, without which moral deliberation could not begin. It allows the moral agent to be both observer (practicing certain forms of detachment) and participant (with opportunities for communication). The judge does not merely achieve a view but imposes a decision in ways that have real impacts and results as well. The judicial image does, however, emphasize the regimentation of testimony and adherence to precedent to an extent misleading for the moral situation. The model of legal interrogation or institutional competition is a model of one kind of eliciting process, and one which would be inappropriate or useless for a variety of other interpersonal encounters (physician and patient, friends, parent and child). The idea of relevance predetermined suggests either that everyone understands the categories of assessment similarly and agrees to them or that it suffices if the agent/judge simply applies what she assumes to be the common or correct understandings. But in non-institutional moral contexts, the power to "appeal" on the spot for a review of the relevance or meaning of even basic moral assumptions and categories is a critical opening for deepened mutual understanding and significant corrections of insensitivity, blindness or rigidity. Finally, the moral "judge," like God and the archangel and the ideal observer, does not clearly have to live with and in the wake of his or her decrees in the sense in which moral agents do. It is part of judicial authority to be freed from personal responsibilities to contestants or litigants, whereas part of the cost of certain moral choices may be further moral obligations or a reconstellation of the relationships affected and their attendant moral claims.[21] The moral judge, then, models some features of all moral contexts in part, but fails to represent the whole of any noninstitutionalized moral encounter, or represents these in terms which may distort or preclude some of our most effective ways of getting to relevant truths.[22]

Various themes weave in and out of these leading and guiding images of the impartial viewpoint: disengagement or detachment; absence of interaction and dialogue as a part of deliberation; unilateral decision-rendering; the picture of a moral problem as a case to be closed or an instance to be disposed of by a decision or verdict. Themes of cost-exemption, interpersonal evasiveness, discontinuity, and personal inexpressiveness saturate central images of moral impartiality. Let us now assess what those elements of the rhetoric of impartiality examined do and do not contribute to understanding (and achieving) adequate moral insight.

IV

A moral ideal of impartiality of the kind discussed here aims us at full and undistorted consideration of each. We must neither fail to consider any information which is morally relevant nor give force to any which is not. This ideal of impartiality thus addresses both the problem of incomplete attention and that of positive bias. When we examine central and powerful images which illustrate or exemplify impartial viewing, however, we find them blank, distorting, or misleadingly limited as depictions of the fully informed agent. We also find them largely preoccupied with themes of detachment: one is to observe rather than engage, cogitate rather than converse, dispose of moral cases rather than situate them coherently in a continuing history of responsibilities, evaluations and relationships.

The conspicuous emphasis on detachment, screening, and eliminating perhaps reflects a special preoccupation with one problem of bias, the problem of misleading irrelevancies or preoccupations. But the exclusion of diverting or dangerous irrelevancies, important in its own right, need contribute nothing to full-informedness. It is not as if our perceiving and registering morally significant features of our circumstances were a straightforward matter once certain distorting factors have been controlled, the way, for example, accurate color perception is, for the most part, with normal perceivers. Acuity of moral perception, especially as regards the interests and perspectives of people, must result from the exercise of many complex, learned, and indefinitely improvable skills of attention, communication and interpretation. Seeing whether an act is disloyal, an intention magnanimous, an attitude disrespectful, or an outcome demeaning is often less like seeing whether something is green than seeing whether a shadow on an x-ray is a kind of tumor, or whether a painting is in the style of Perugino. Even if one is acutely aware of how not to look, accurate "seeing" is not thereby a matter of course. Marking common impediments, distractions, and aberrations in moral appreciation doesn't itself illuminate the positive capacities, techniques, and processes that can make available what we morally need to know. One's moral grasp may easily be at once unbiased and drastically incomplete.

Worse, moral inattentiveness or imperceptiveness limits our flexibility in recognizing subtle or covert forms of bias. If disengaged, solitary reflection is sometimes a powerful source of clarity in moral appreciation, it is sometimes an extremely effective blind. Reflective withdrawal may close out input, appeals, and invitations to reconsider which are not already standard in the reflector's repertoire. So it is in much of everyday moral life. Stock images of omniscience or unexplained informedness, of majestic isolation or role-prescribed encapsulation, of solitary imaginings and of disposing of moral cases by authoritative decree may sometimes serve to extend or assist moral understanding. They may assist us in organizing what we know and help us not to be overwhelmed by the possibilities of culpable blindness or disguised prejudice. But repetitive and virtually exclusive use of these exemplars suggests neither the actual limiting conditions of our moral grasp on situations nor the real forms of encounter, skill, communication, and mutual adjustment that allow us to get beyond these, albeit in irremediably piecemeal fashion. Failure to direct our attention in these ways implies that the real-time modes of moral understanding we must master are too obvious or too unimportant to be the subject of moral philosophy, and that these idealized images and some few highly schematic moral categories, decision methods, or principles give us the important part of the story about what moral understanding is like.[23] I have argued that these images obscure at least as much as they reveal and that what is obscured is at least as important, if not more so, than what is emphasized.

V

I have claimed that some very familiar images of impartial viewing embody a questionable view of the forms of intelligence and practices of thinking that reliably yield adequate moral judgements. But I do not suggest that this questionable conception is simply a mistake. It is a response to a real tension between the ideal goal of full and undistorted consideration of all affected parties, and the severe practical limitations of attention, skill, and access which keep this ideal goal at an immeasurable distance from human moral agents. The problem, conceptually and existentially, is how to do justice to the noble norm of impartial concern within our modestly provisioned, all too human moral-epistemic situation. Very schematically, there are two very different implementations of the ideal of impartiality that may attract us.

One is to emphasize uniformity of attention, by cleanly regimenting moral thinking along the lines of some very general, paradigmatic categories of status, right, role, duty, etc., applied in the same ways to all. We may feel it matters less to achieve a fine-grained appreciation of people's circumstances and perceptions than to insure that all have been considered under the same dimensions of assessment or that all have been measured, if only imprecisely, on a common scale. This strategy is in fact or by implication that adopted in a great deal of moral philosophy, where the primary goal is to discover and defend the right highly general schemata or parameters of moral assessment. If the issue of more acute or nuanced moral appreciation is joined at all on this common approach, it may be deemed philosophically (as opposed to "psychologically" or "practically") uninteresting, or it may be seen as involving questions of detail that must (and can) await perfection of the larger scheme. Practically speaking, however, this approach carries the message: what's important are the categorial uniformities, not the nuances of the particular case and the practical know-how that reveals them. The kind of regimentation thus effected, however, does not achieve a "view from nowhere" which successfully eludes all possibly deforming particular interests. It achieves instead a particular, highly selective view which expresses its peculiar interest in certain specific, and very generic, features of persons, relationships and situations, and which embodies a particular kind of concern—with even-handed application of policies—which is not unfairly called "administrative" or "procedural."[24]

There is an alternative, although philosophically less traveled, strategy. Suppose we continue to recognize the demand of adequate consideration of all but put primary emphasis on adequacy, that is, fullness and precision of appreciation within the (often narrow) limits our situations establish. It is after all true that the vast majority of our moral situations involve accessible others in fairly small numbers. It is further true that our habits of moral perception, native moral vocabularies, stock of reflex principles, and entrenched evaluative priorities will practically guarantee a substantial degree of categorical uniformity in our approach to moral assessments. Theoretical rigorism is no match for the inertia of concepts and character. What we might foster is a lively and wary consciousness of that inertia, that tendency to the fixed and formulaic and blandly categorial, for it is in fact one of our best defenses against the vivid and morally demanding reality of specific others with whom we must come to terms.[25] One methodical corrective is vigorous emphasis on facing up to the particular reality of each person and case and on refinement of perception, acuity of communication, flexibility of perspectives, and use of a range of moral categories closer, in variety and nuance, to our full nonmoral resources of interpersonal description and expression. This approach amounts to a wholesale shift in moral epistemology, to a different set of questions about how to know how it is with each other, and what it is we are trying to know.[26] It suggests that concern for substantive adequacy go before and after concern for uniform attention.

Nor is this approach suited only to the small scale and close by, the "personal" rather than the social or political. A reorientation to refined perceptions, communication, and shared interpretations suggests critical scrutiny of "representative" political and social institutions, of intellectual elites who control public discourses on "people's" needs and interests, and of institutional mechanisms which render groups of individuals silent and invisible, to mention just a few points of application.[27] It is not that uniformity of consideration should be slighted, especially on the institutional level. But we need to worry more about the provenance and adequacy of public representations of the perspectives and interests to which we are to give comparable consideration or even (in political and institutional contexts) equal weight.

VI

The moral of this meditation on the philosophical figuration of impartiality is this: moral understanding will never be anything but partial, that is, incomplete, aporetic, limited. This is in the nature of us and the nature of things. But it is not foretold which way moral understanding must be partial. This is a matter of what kind of incompleteness we will tolerate and even justify, in life and philosophy. Different choices here give different results.[28]

NOTES

1. A sampling of contemporary views includes: the demand for "equal and impartial positive consideration for their respective goods and interests" in Alan Gewirth, "Ethical Universalism and Particularism," *Journal of Philosophy* 85 (1988): 283–302, esp. 283; for "principles which impartially maximize the satisfaction [of given preferences]" in R. M. Hare, *Moral Thinking* (Oxford: Clarendon, 1981): 226; for regarding each person's total set of basic interests as "making the same initial claim to fulfillment" in Paul Taylor, "On Taking the Moral Point of View," in *Midwest Studies in Philosophy, Studies in Ethical Theory*, vol. 3, ed. Peter A. French et al. (Morris: University of Minnesota, 1978): 35–61, esp. 49; for a view containing "nothing . . . tailored to fit your particular situation" in Adrian Piper, "Moral Theory and Moral Alienation," *Journal of Philosophy* 84 (1987): 102–18, esp. 105; for rising "above his own feelings, to take stock of the situation from the third-person point of view" in Sarah Conly, "The Objectivity of Morals and the Subjectivity of Agents," *American Philosophical Quarterly* 22 (1985): 275–86, esp. 275; for the view of "an independent, unbiased, impartial, objective, dispassionate, disinterested judge" in Kurt Baier, *The Moral Point of View* (New York: Random House, 1965), 107; or even for the "impersonal standpoint of all eternity" from which "total world histories" might be evaluated without privileging any particular temporal locations of morally preferable states of affairs, as discussed by Michael Slote, *Commonsense Morality and Consequentialism* (London: Routledge and Kegan Paul, 1985), 125.

2. It does not follow from this "adequate consideration" conception of impartiality that moral norms require us to give equal weight to the interests of all. Many philosophers defend a narrower, substantive requirement of impartiality that does demand each count, in the process and issue of moral judgement, for exactly one, i.e., that the comparable interests of each count the same. This might be called the "equal treatment" conception of impartiality. The plausibility of this conception (at the heart of classical utilitarianism, for example) continues to be disputed by moral philosophers. (See, e.g., John Cottingham, "Ethics and Impartiality," *Philosophical Studies* 43 [1983]: 83–89; John Kekes, "Morality and Impartiality," *American Philosophical Quarterly* 18 [1981]: 295–303; Lawrence Blum, *Friendship, Altruism and Morality* [Boston: Routledge and Kegan Paul, 1980]; or Bernard Williams, "Persons, Character and Morality," *Moral Luck* [Cambridge: Cambridge University Press, 1981].) I reject this narrower conception of impartiality, but that is not my concern in this article. Even so, some of what I have to say may bear on the application of the equal treatment conception as well.

3. I do not consider here another powerfully influential family of images involving imagined or hypothetical bargainers or contracts. For a critical discussion of some features of these and other devices for modelling impartial thinking in Rawls, Darwall, Kohlberg, and Nagel, see Marilyn Friedman, "The Impracticality of Impartiality," *Journal of Philosophy* 86 (1989): 645–56. I profited greatly from studying this paper in writing the present one.

4. A number of distinct intuitive, political, or historical approaches qualify as "pragmatics" in my sense. Stanley Cavell explores moral discussion as a medium for expression and mutual clarification of the participants' "cares and commitments" and possibilities of relationship in *The Claim of Reason* (Oxford: Oxford University Press, 1979), part 3. Feminist moral critique provides extensive discussion of the way gender determines who gets to define "morality" and strongly constrains what they define it to be. See, e.g., Cheshire Calhoun, "Justice, Care, Gender Bias," *Journal of Philosophy* 85 (1988): 451–63; Annette Baier, "The Need For More Than Justice," in *Science, Morality and Feminist Theory*, ed. M. Hanen and K. Nielsen (Calgary: University of Calgary Press, 1987); and "Trust and Antitrust," *Ethics* 96 (1986): 231–60; and many essays in E. Kittay and D. Meyers, eds., *Women and Moral Theory* (Totowa, N.J.: Rowman & Littlefield, 1987). Other analyses of moral conceptions in relation to social practices, political power, and intellectual authority include Sabina Lovibond, *Realism and Imagination in Ethics* (Minneapolis: University of Minnesota Press, 1983); Alasdair MacIntyre, *After Virtue* (Notre Dame, Ind.: University of Notre Dame Press, 1981); and Anthony Skillen, *Ruling Illusions* (Atlantic Highlands, N.J.: Humanities Press, 1978). The more pointedly "rhetorical" (rather than social-critical) approach I take here has been, I believe, less widely developed.

5. In their valuable systematic and historical study of casuistry, Albert Jonsen and Stephen Toulmin remind us that practical reasoning in the Greek and medieval traditions was often explicitly considered to be in the domain of rhetoric, where "the task is to make a case that is capable of carrying conviction" by marshalling a preponderance of convincing arguments on one side (*The Abuse of Casuistry* [Berkeley: University of California Press, 1988], part 1, 72).

6. I do not mean to restrict the discussion to moral views that are in some very direct way "interest-based." I doubt, though, that any deliberation which is recognizably a moral one could avoid invoking concepts, whether in describing agents, acts, intentions, or situations, which do not, directly or indirectly, depend on what someone intends, what happens to someone or what it means. An intuitionist deontologist may need to figure out whether some action counts as "betrayal"; one committed to the way of virtue may need to assess the difference between being generous and being patronizing, and so on. In this sense I think some reckoning of interests and meaning cannot be avoided in moral reasoning.

7. Hare, *Moral Thinking*. Page references will be in parentheses in the text.

8. R. M. Hare, *Freedom and Reason* (London: Oxford University Press, 1963), 48.

9. Hare, *Moral Thinking*, 111. The celestial deliberator reappears throughout the book, 24, 44, 46, 89, 111, 122, and 211.

10. For Sidgwick's famous phrase, see *The Methods of Ethics* (1907) (Indianapolis, Ind.: Hackett, 1981), 382. Aside from many references, central and incidental, in the literature of moral philosophy, it is to the point for the present discussion that everyone reading this article instantly recognizes this family of pictures. It is part of the standard rhetorical repertoire of moral philosophy, and we have heard these phrases tens of times from our first moral philosophy classes onward. If I put before you the

image of the moral agent as "the corner bartender" you would be alert to novelty, would not already know how the application of the picture was to go.

11. One notable exception is Blum's *Friendship, Altruism and Morality*. Blum's continuing concern with specific skills of attention and perception is evident as well in "Moral Perception and Particularity," in *Ethics* 101 (1991).

12. There is a school of thought in moral philosophy that urges us to mine great literature for its penetrating moral insights. The chief proponent of this view in its strong form is surely Martha Nussbaum. In addition to *The Fragility of Goodness* (Cambridge: Cambridge University Press, 1986), see also "Flawed Crystals: James's *The Golden Bowl* and Literature as Moral Philosophy," *New Literary History* 15 (1983): 25–50, and "Narrative Emotions: Beckett's Genealogy of Love," *Ethics* 98 (1988): 225–54. I agree that nuanced characterization and the ability to portray vividly multiparty situations both from outside and inside the involved parties might well prime or exercise capacities of moral understanding. Aside from some problems about the actual or intended verisimilitude of fictional creations or our responses to them, I want to stress instead the largely untapped wealth and diversity of resources for the understanding of actual persons which is known to us in everyday life and special professions, rather than in fictional elaborations.

13. An extended discussion of moral or value costs in relation to moral conflicts is given by Michael Stocker in *Plural and Conflicting Values* (Oxford: Oxford University Press, 1990).

14. Hare, *Moral Thinking*, 44; Roderick Firth, "Ethical Absolutism and the Ideal Observer," *Philosophy and Phenomenological Research* 12 (1952): 317–45, esp. 344.

15. Firth, "Ethical Absolutism," 332.

16. Richard Brandt, "The Definition of an 'Ideal Observer' Theory in Ethics," *Philosophy and Phenomenological Research* 15 (1954): 407–13, esp. 411.

17. Firth, "Ethical Absolutism," 344–45.

18. Seyla Benhabib, "The Generalized and the Concrete Other," in *Women and Moral Theory*, ed. Kittay and Meyers (Totowa, N.J.: Rowman & Littlefield, 167).

19. Hare gives a central place throughout his work to "thinking for." Lawrence Kohlberg associates it with the most mature approach to moral reasoning, e.g., in *The Psychology of Moral Development* (San Francisco: Harper & Row, 1984), 310, 367, and 454. Susan Miller Okin, in "Reason and Feeling in Thinking About Justice," *Ethics* 99 (1989): 229–49, construes thought in the Rawlsian original position as requiring each to "think from the point of view of everybody, of every 'concrete other' whom one might turn out to be" (245). But see also Michael Sandel's discussion about how the apparent plurality of the original position is an idle wheel, in *Liberalism and the Limits of Justice* (Cambridge: Cambridge University Press, 1982), chapter 3.

20. See Benhabib, "The Generalized and the Concrete Other," for an acute critique of the monological-hypothetical stance.

21. It might also be argued, more controversially, that there are discretionary elements in moral judgement that allow for the progressive development and expres-

sion by moral agents of a distinctive moral identity, whereas the image of judge implies the judge's commitment to speak strictly for "the law" or "the standards," and not in any sense for himself or herself. This issue is too complex for meaningful discussion here. I have defended the view about individuated moral identity in "Moral Particularity," *Metaphilosophy* 18 (1987): 171–84.

22. The actual functions of judges, especially in a judicial system at various levels, are enormously more complex than indicated, and the difference between the real and the commonly imagined determinants of judicial activity complicates matters more. For my purposes here it is the commonplace assumptions that matter more than the complex reality (although it is the latter that matters for constructively exploiting the positive insights of the judicial analogue). For a suitably nuanced interpretation of what judges actually do in review of hard cases, see Ronald Dworkin, "Hard Cases," in *Taking Rights Seriously* (Cambridge: Harvard University Press, 1978).

23. Several articles in this symposium [*Ethics* 101 (1991)] do explore the need for a better understanding of how values, norms, feelings, and perceptions interact to produce our moral views and responses (see Blum, "Moral Perception and Particularity"; Herman, "Agency, Attachment, and Difference"; and Piper, "Impartiality, Compassion, and Modal Imagination").

24. Thomas Nagel speaks of "administrative" justifications in connection with utilitarian thinking in "War and Massacre," in his *Mortal Questions* (Cambridge: Cambridge University Press, 1979), 68; Bernard Williams likens the understanding of practical reasoning in modern moral philosophy to characteristically modern views of "public" rationality in *Ethics and the Limits of Philosophy* (Cambridge: Harvard University Press, 1985).

25. Marilyn Friedman in "The Practice of Partiality," *Ethics* 101 (1991): 818–35, well identifies the dangers of unexamined moral postures both within and toward the sphere of special or personal relationships.

26. For a somewhat fuller account this approach, see Margaret Urban Walker, "Moral Understandings: Alternative 'Epistemology' for a Feminist Ethics," *Hypatia* 4 (1989): 15–28.

27. Two revealing discussions of these problems are provided by Iris Young, "Polity and Group Difference: A Critique of the Ideal of Universal Citizenship," *Ethics* 99 (1989): 250–74; and Nancy Fraser, "Talking About Needs," *Ethics* 99 (1989): 291–313.

28. Thanks to Christopher Gowans for helping with a central conceptual issue, to Charles Kelbley for insight into the image and reality of the disinterested judge, and to Arthur Walker for advice on earlier drafts.

II

FEMINISM AS THEORY AND CONTEXT

4

WHAT DOES THE DIFFERENT VOICE SAY? GILLIGAN'S WOMEN AND MORAL PHILOSOPHY

Many want to see psychologist Carol Gilligan as advancing the view that there are 'male' and 'female' moral voices, a view which she disclaims early on in *In a Different Voice* and in later writings.[1] Gilligan does advance the hypothesis that the different voice—or "care perspective"—is "characteristically a female phenomenon in the advantaged populations that have been studied" and holds that this hypothesis receives support from studies other than her own (R, 330). But she continues to maintain that what makes this voice different is that it offers "a moral perspective different from that currently embedded in psychological theories and measures" (R, 327), one which embodies distinctive conceptions of self, relationship, and responsibility (R, 326).

Much discussion of Gilligan's work has centered on whether she has adequate evidence for the claim of significant gender-related differences in moral thinking. I pursue another set of questions here, because the interest of the different voice for moral philosophy lies primarily in what it expresses, perhaps some significant part of moral truth.[2] My questions are: whether the differences in moral thinking she outlines amount to a unified perspective on morality; what that perspective is; and whether this (*possibly* more characteristically "feminine") viewpoint represents an important or interesting addition or correction to prevailing philosophical views.[3]

In Section I, I distinguish two themes apparently characteristic of the different voice, and in Section II show how plausible versions of each may appear separately in already well-known types of moral views. In Section III I consider two ways in which versions of the themes might be internally related to produce a view which is both unified and distinctive. One of these interpretations is found superior as a rendering of Gilligan's subjects' views; it is also a plausible moral outlook which significantly challenges standard

57

philosophical conceptions about morality. In conclusion (IV) I remark that while the existence and significance of a different moral voice remains in question, women's voices surely matter for moral philosophy in any case.

I

Gilligan holds that the different voice is "characterized not by gender but theme" (2). The characterizing theme is referred to by her variously as "care," "responsibility," or "response" (in contrast to the alternative theme of "justice" or "fairness" or "reciprocity"). But in reviewing her presentation of and commentary on those particular quoted voices which are held to exemplify the care perspective, one hears not one theme but two, and these two themes appear not only distinct, but mutually independent.

One focal description of the care and justice perspectives which comes early on in *In a Different Voice* makes the two themes readily apparent:

> In this [care] conception, the moral problem arises from conflicting responsibilities rather than from competing rights and requires for its resolution a mode of thinking that is contextual and narrative rather than formal and abstract. This conception of morality as concerned with the activity of care centers moral development around the understanding of responsibility and relationships, just as the conception of morality as fairness ties moral development to the understanding of rights and rules (19).

This passage touches on both the *substance* of moral concern in the alternative visions, and on the *method* of definition and construction appropriate to the solution of moral problems. Both strains recur throughout the book's discussion, sometimes intertwined, sometimes discretely. I will call the substantive one a *care and response orientation,* the methodological one a *contextual-deliberative picture* of moral thinking.[4]

Often Gilligan seems to identify the different voice in terms of a kind of *value* orientation, i.e. what it sees as calling for moral concern. For example:

> The moral imperative that emerges repeatedly in interviews with women is an injunction to care, a responsibility to discern and alleviate the 'real and recognizable trouble' of this world. For men, the moral imperative appears rather as an injunction to respect the rights of others and thus to protect from interference the rights to life and self-fulfillment (100).

The care orientation resides in "sensitivity to the needs of others and the assumption of responsibility for taking care," (16); it is concerned with "equity" in light of persons' very different needs (164). An "overriding concern with relationships and responsibilities" (16–17) makes connection and attachment (19, 45, 48), compassion (71) and intimacy (17) central moral concerns. As little girls are reported to terminate their games rather than threaten the continuance of their relationships (10), so adult women recognize "the continuing importance of attachment in the human life cycle" (23); it "creates and sustains the human community" (156).

Sometimes Gilligan's characterizations are ambiguous between caring as instrumental to the goods of need-fulfillment or non-violence, and caring as itself the object or attainment of moral endeavor. But these are not exclusive alternatives, and often enough Gilligan seems to be saying, and is heard by others as saying, that women care specially *for* relationships or attachments as themselves fundamental goods of our lives. Jean Grimshaw, for example, in a searching consideration of the idea of a "female ethic" concedes: "There is evidence, both from common experience and from the work of Carol Gilligan and others, that women often perceive the maintenance of relationships as very important in their lives, and see it as a moral priority."[5] In a care and response orientation, then, caring relationships and the responsive attitude which sustains them are particularly morally valued, whether as means, ends, or both.

Gilligan, however, understands these women to be describing and exemplifying a different structure of moral understanding as well as a certain set of concerns. Here the difference between care and justice is marked by method, approach, and the standards for defining and solving moral problems. Here thinking that is "contextual and narrative" contrasts with thinking that "abstracts the moral problem from the interpersonal situation" (32) so that a "formal logic" of fairness can take hold (73). The justice perspective drives toward classification of cases at a high level of generality so that antecedently ordered rules and formulas can do their work in deciding the particular case. The different voice, however, strains against schematically depicted situations toward further concrete information about the particular case (100–101). It is mistrustful about the relevance of prior, abstract moral orderings (101). And it does not necessarily expect moral dilemmas to yield to resolution without remainder on which "all rational men can agree" and no conflicting claims retain authority.[6] This contextual deliberative view rejects a top-down, nomological picture of moral decision as a deductive operation, it views typifications of actions and situations as only, at best, heuristic, and it leaves room for moral remainders. For it a moral problem is not "a math problem with humans" (28) and there is no moral decision procedure, no guarantee of neat closure. Instead, a "narrative of relationships that extends over time" (28) may supply materials for a context-sensitive adjudication of claims.

Here are the two themes, consonant but seemingly addressed to different questions: one to *what* we must think about morally, one to *how* we must do so. This seems not simply an ethic of care nor simply a context-sensitive, particularistic ethic, but instead a *contextualist ethic of care*. Is this *one* thing, or *two* things contingently juxtaposed?

II

It is not difficult to see how a care and response orientation and a contextual deliberative view might be separate commitments. A contextualist, after all, could have many other value orientations than the care and response one. She might believe that what matters morally is self-realization, or eudaimonia, or something else. She might think many things matter—courage, wisdom, integrity, dignity, gratitude—and each in several ways. She might think care matters too, but not see it as a specially dominant or highest-ranked value. But her way of structuring moral deliberation and achieving resolution will not be a logical deduction or computation defined in advance by a strict formal program, but a minute and concrete exploration of the particulars. She might like "Sharon" in Gilligan's book "try to be as awake as possible, to try to know the range of what you feel, to try to consider all that's involved" (99) and then, to borrow a phrase, let the decision rest with perception.[7] But her perception might be informed by more than considerations of care and response, and perhaps by other kinds of considerations entirely. Aristotelians, ethical individualists, Bradleyian self-realizationists, and Christian agapeists can be (although may not be in every version) contextualists in the relevant sense.

In turning to the reverse case, of an ethic of care that is not particularistic, but is principled and rigorously logical in carrying theory into practice, consider classical utilitarianism (and many contemporary variants) which could lay claim to being the ultimate in care perspectives.[8] The utilitarian sees the world in terms of a single value, happiness, where that is specified in terms of fulfillment, contentment, satisfaction, pleasure, or preference, i.e., the well-being of others in their own terms.[9] But utilitarians are not content to let the concern for well-being play itself out in the commonplace and parochial ways, and so insist on unqualified and impartial commitment to caring—caring for all, counting each for one and no more. When joined to the positive injunction to produce the greatest aggregate amounts of well-being possible, the strenuousness of this caring seems hard to outdo. Further, full-blooded act utilitarians are known for their mitigated commitment to justice: in the face-off between care and justice that is one recurring motif of Western ethical thought,[10] utilitarians know what side they are on.[11]

Utilitarianism thus can see itself as raising on the ground of human interdependence and fellow-feeling a system for responding to human want without compromise and for extending the care of each over the whole human community, and perhaps over the wider community of all feeling, needing beings.[12] Utilitarians also sometimes claim for their view the virtue of sensitivity to context, inasmuch as rights and wrongs are reckoned afresh case by case. But they are reckoned rigorously, by a procedure laid out in advance, one which allows no competitors and which promises decisive resolution where applicable at all. The narrative of relationships could only matter in providing data for prediction of outcomes and payoffs. Utilitarian moral decision making *is* a math problem with humans.

Is the different voice then whole in some way other than being the sum of these two separable parts? Does it matter? Before proceeding to the first question, I touch here briefly on the second.

I think the unity of the different voice does matter. For Gilligan, it must have mattered originally in a special way in her critique of Kohlbergian developmental theory. In laying down the gauntlet on page one of her book, Gilligan claimed that the two ways of speaking about morality, self, and other which she discerned were an ongoing contrapuntal structure of moral life rather than "steps in a developmental progression," i.e., that the ordering of these ways as higher or lower stages à la Kohlberg was a mistake. But this challenge itself takes the view that these perspectives on morality are equally *like* Kohlbergian stages—internally differentiated but "logically unified, functionally *holistic* structures" of moral thought—at the *same* level.[13] For the different voice to have been a fragment of a view or worse an unordered set of moral *apercus* would have made a lame case, in Kohlbergian terms.

The interests of moral philosophy are not those of Kohlbergian theory, and moral philosophy is properly eager for any pieces of moral insight with claim to intuitive entrenchment. Still, what seems *exciting* about the different voice for moral philosophy is that it might reveal or suggest a unified and comprehensive view of moral life—one might say a "moral vision"—which is genuinely alternative in important ways to those which are prevalent

philosophically. It would not be negligible, although it would not be so exciting, I think, if the news were that women tended to align, say, with Mill
on value but with Aristotle on method.

III

The consideration of utilitarianism as a care-ethic provides a useful comparison case in seeking a picture of the different voice whole. Utilitarians
are fully committed to caring about welfare, about the "well-being of others in their own terms," about assessing the particular, present situation, and
do not traffic in advance ordering of different values (for there is only one)
but in reckoning actual consequences. These are all marks of the care perspective Gilligan describes (e.g., 78, 101). But clearly, Gilligan has not meant
that women have a bent for utilitarian thinking. This would leave out the
emphasis of the different voice on care focused in terms of relationship, intimacy, attachment, and "natural bonds" (17, 19, 32, 48, 132). Magnification
of the "impartial viewpoint" has put both utilitarianism and Kantian ethical views under suspicion of unwisely demoting or neglecting just the special caring bonds on which the different voice dwells.[14] Seeing care in terms
of relationship is a clue to understanding how care and contextualism may
be more than accidentally conjoined.

I see two different ways of bringing the care-orientation and the
contextual-deliberative view into more intimate union. Both turn on an
identification of care primarily with the loving attention characteristic of
specific personal bonds. This identification joins them in common cause
against the utilitarian ideal of uniform, generalized benevolence—
"administrative care" one might call it, as it undertakes the task of reckoning in common terms the satisfactions of persons close by and familiar
alongside those who may be any, distant, and unknown. The emphasis on
personal bonds also provides each of these ways with a clear basis for finding universalism and legalism either inappropriate or derivative as views
about the structure of moral reasoning and resolution. But these two ways
part company decisively over a fundamental issue. On one, the creation and
maintenance of caring relations is *itself* the human good; on the other, caring relations are a necessary condition for the practice within which varied human goods might emerge and flourish. The first way is neater, but it
is also more reductive about the direction and point of moral life than is
the second way. The divergence corresponds to the ambiguity noted earlier in Gilligan's own descriptions of women's valuation of caring.

The first way is represented lucidly and without compromise by Nel Noddings. In *Caring: A Feminine Approach to Ethics and Moral Education*[15] Noddings anchors morality in the human affective response of natural sympathy and its characteristic issue of natural caring, transformed reflectively into a moral ideal of oneself as one-caring. The caring this ideal demands consists in direct relations in which loving attention and minute recognition flow toward the one cared for, who completes the caring by responding in ways which show its nurturant and supportive power (C, 79–84). Such relations can arise only in actual encounters. Since this is so and since the acts constituting care are determined by close perceptions of individuals, the only appropriate methods of moral thought and resolution are those which embody as much concrete detail as possible and which represent as specific a response as can be mustered. Subsuming people's "cases" under generalization and treating them by rule would be not simply inadequate, but a denial of the very nature of the moral demand and a foreclosure of the achievement of the only moral value. Noddings makes this clear: "Rule-bound responses in the name of caring lead us to suspect that the claimant wants most to be credited with caring" (C, 24). A care-ethic of this kind is necessarily contextualist because of the value it demands be realized morally (a completed instance of a specific caring relation) and the nature of human beings who participate in its realization (psychologically non-interchangeable individuals whose ways of wanting, needing, perceiving, and receiving may be very different). Legalistic reasoning and impartial computations are wholly inapplicable on this view, and the respect or generalized benevolence which are their attitudinal correlates—their "carings"—are found counterfeit, period. On Noddings's view caring is just one thing, and it is, morally speaking, the *only* thing. The presence, ordering, and extent of moral obligations for her varies with encounters and the possibility of completion, but the object of obligation is invariable; care is both ground and object of the demands morality places upon us.

Noddings's view is one candidate for a consistent systematization of what the different voice is saying. It suggests that women, including Gilligan's subjects, tend to care, ultimately, *about* caring; that is what they seek to initiate or complete in their lives, or at least what they feel (in Noddings's view correctly) obligated to realize. It also suggests that if care as a specific relation is itself what is valued, then caring will be kept close to home, since direct encounters, and primarily those embedded in a prior history of relationship, are the only obligating occasions. Generalized concern—whether benevolence or that yet more astringent attitude, respect—and its concomitant sense of obligation are on this view illusory (C, 18, 29, 90). It is in just these respects that I find Noddings's view less than satisfactory either as a rendering of what resides in Gilligan's subjects' voices, or as a moral vision on its own feet.[16]

Are Gilligan's women properly described as caring about care itself? It seems not; different of the different voices invoke, as decisive or central grounds for moral choice, such values as equality (64), honesty (65), authenticity (52), growth (159), safety from danger and hurt (129), self-preservation (111). Further, a striking feature of a number of cited responses is a tendency to extend the scope of concern very widely indeed. One woman feels strongly "responsible to the world" and obligated to better it if only on a small scale (21). Another finds mundane practical decisions open onto agonizing vistas of others' poverty, unknown children in need, and a world full of trouble and headed for "doom"; and it is clear that she does not dismiss the claim this seems to make on her (99). "Claire" articulates the sweeping view positively: other people are *part of* you," so that link by link is formed a "giant collection of people that you are connected to" (160). A number of Gilligan's women seem not at all hesitant to generalize concern and to ponder, troubled, the overwhelming implications. What they seem *not* to do is to generalize the *other persons,* to view them abstractly as generalizable kinds of cases (11). The distinction is important and is needed to make sense of a certain kind of strain in these voices. A different way of modeling the moral sensibility at work here captures this.[17]

On this second way, an ethic of care might be seen as affirming the *generative* role of caring relations in morality. Caring relations initiate new human beings into the kind of interpersonal acknowledgment that full moral concern requires: of the separate reality of other persons, of the complex and precarious process of communicating and understanding. Ongoing opportunities to care and be cared for continue the education of those dispositions and capacities which allow us to know how it is with another and to make ourselves known as well. Caring relationship provides a *paradigm* of the understanding that determines full and appropriate response to persons: it must be direct, personal, and specific; it requires minute attention, identification in thought and feeling, precise communication. It will be, among other things, "contextual and narrative," that is, defined by reference to rich circumstantial detail, to the history of the episode, and ideally to the history of the person. This understanding carried through to appropriate action, on this view, is caring. But to carry through to *appropriate* action requires more. It requires a *conception of human good,* a picture of what's worth aiming at; there is no reason to think that this cannot be a rich and varied conception in which many important goods (intrinsic, in-

ternal, contributory) are complexly related. Care itself, this attentive relation of acknowledgment and understanding, will no doubt reappear *within*
this conception of value. It is one of those things worth spending the hard-
won understanding of care on reproducing. Care plays a very special role
in moral life, on this view, but not that of sole or even dominant end. Care
appears instead as a condition for the fullest and most direct pursuit of such
goods as there may be.[18]

Full, minute, and sensitive attention is a paradigm of how the materials for the exercise of moral concern are had. It is a *paradigm* because it represents the *best* case: it is in this way I know "fully and directly" to what and
to whom I am responding. Yet many cases are not, cannot be, of the best
type. Connection may be attenuated, access blocked. If I am not in a position to care in the paradigmatic way I may be reduced to applying incomplete versions of care, or even resorting to surrogates: general benevolence,
respect, fair consideration may be the best I can do. It is, I think, important
to let this way remain open. The different voice need not be seen as denying any role to generalized concern, but as marking its incompleteness. This
truly rotates the usual order of philosophical precedence 180°, saying that
the particular is always first, and the application of rules or generalized standards to someone as a kind of "case" is not just a derivative, but in fact a de-
generate instance. The conviction that moral *adequacy falls off in the direction
of generality* seems to be one of the plaintive notes in this style of moral discourse. The note struck is plaintive because it is understood that this kind
of inadequacy is recurrent and inevitable. What is condemnable from this
perspective, then, is *not* doing one's inadequate best where that is all one can
do, but denying or ignoring how far the principled, universalistic view may
be from adequate moral response in many situations, and how much responsibility one has evaded in adopting it. This is our situation when truly
personal understanding eludes us. Gilligan's recent work, interestingly, is
more concerned with different understandings of the nature of persons, and
with questions of adequate knowledge and disclosure than with particular
structures of moral judgement.[19]

The combination of indefinite openness to responsibility and of the
particularistic paradigm of understanding persons accounts for a certain
kind of strain I discern in these voices. The fact of human connectedness
that makes for endless vistas of responsibility (both with respect to *any* person and with respect to *all*) runs up against the inescapable arbitrariness and
ad hoc limitations of actual connections and the moral possibilities they underwrite and exclude. The moral situation appears to these moral agents en-
tangling, compromising, and permanently unwieldy.[20]

IV

These two versions of the different voice rendered unified are, of course, energetic reconstructions and idealizations. One would not expect a view "systematic" in the philosopher's sense to spring full-blown from any survey of opinion. It must be admitted, finally, that perhaps these reconstructions are too energetic. It may be that similar things many women have to say about morality and responsibility are only contingently related by the fact of women's common situation and social training, and not by some deep conceptual structure a moral philosopher might strive (or contrive) to find. It might be that women's preoccupation with care and relationship and their propensity for concrete over abstract are, if a fact, simply each orientations of thought and feeling which serve their traditional social roles of nurturers, helpers, and keepers of the homely but indispensable material conditions of life. It is this possibility that accounts for much of the ambivalent or hostile reaction to Gilligan's work.[21] It can appear as further depressing adumbration of the apparatus which keeps women in their subservient and private places.[22]

Even if the concerns of the different voices are artifacts of an objectionably limiting social assignment, this does not discredit the view (or views) from that particular set of windows on moral reality. This is not only because any human experience yields matter for moral reflection, nor only because the task of enabling the continuance of human life, to which women's traditional roles and the values these embody are so deeply bound, has now on a global scale become precarious and urgent in ways it has not been for human beings before. It is also because women's social assignments, whatever the local variations, involve the majority of them intimately in quite a special endeavor from the viewpoint of morality: initiation of new members into the moral community. A position of social disadvantage may, on the topic of moral education and moral competence, be one of some epistemic privilege.[23] These voices should be heard, whether they have some large thing to say or many smaller ones.[24]

NOTES

1. Carol Gilligan, *In a Different Voice* (Cambridge: Harvard University Press, 1982), 2. All page references in the text are to this work unless otherwise marked. "Reply," at 324, in L. Kerber, C. Greeno, E. Maccoby, Z. Luria, C. Stack, and C. Gilli-

gan, "On *In a Different Voice:* An Interdisciplinary Forum," *Signs* 11 (1986): 304–33, hereafter cited in the text as R. See also Carol Gilligan and Grant Wiggins, "The Origins of Morality in Early Childhood Relationships," in *The Emergence of Morality in Early Childhood,* ed. Jerome Kagan and Sharon Lamb (Chicago: University of Chicago Press, 1987), for closer discussion of both findings on distribution of moral orientations and their significance.

2. I don't claim that questions about whether certain moral views are significantly gender-related are of no consequence to moral philosophy. They may well be theoretically, methodologically, and sociologically consequential. But one does need to know what those views are before these sorts of consequences may be seriously explored.

3. Since this paper was written a valuable set of papers in response to or occasioned by Gilligan's work has appeared which includes a number of discussions whose aim, like mine, is conceptual exploration of what this work suggests for moral theory. See Eva Feder Kittay and Diana T. Meyers, eds., *Women and Moral Theory* (Totowa, N.J.: Rowman & Littlefield, 1987).

4. Marilyn Friedman, "Abraham, Socrates, and Heinz: Where Are the Women? (Care and Context in Moral Reasoning)," in *Moral Dilemmas,* ed. Carol Gibb Harding (Chicago: Precedent Publishing, Inc., 1985), 25–41, also distinguishes two themes in the different voice. Friedman sees "contextual relativism" as a concern with concrete detail detachable from a relationship orientation, and interprets relationship orientation as special concern with and for relationship as a value or source of norms. For her these features are separable as well as distinct. I find both of these elements more complex and the matter of their connection more puzzling than she does. Neither of the two interpretations I entertain below is identical with her understanding, which she uses to develop a strong criticism of Kohlbergian assumptions and results.

5. *Philosophy and Feminist Thinking* (Minneapolis: University of Minnesota Press, 1986), 210. While Grimshaw finds the claim about distinctive values tolerable subject to critical refinement, she rejects any claim that the structure of women's moral thinking is distinctive as confused and dangerous (204–15).

6. Carol Gilligan, "Woman's Place in Man's Life Cycle," *Harvard Educational Review* 49 (1979): 444.

7. Trenchant critiques (from an Aristotelian viewpoint) of legalistic pictures of moral deliberation in favor of context-sensitive ones are: John McDowell, "Virtue and Reason," *Monist* 62 (1979): 331–50, and David Wiggins, "Deliberation and Practical Reason," in *Practical Reasoning,* ed. Joseph Raz (New York: Oxford University Press, 1978), 144–52.

8. One thinks also of a certain kind of rigoristic, impersonal Christian agapeism that takes a dim view of all partiality and special affection. An echo of this resonates in Kant's famous distinction between practical and pathological love. See Gene Outka's *Agape* (New Haven, Conn.: Yale University Press, 1972), chapter 1, for a discussion of variants of agapeistic care on the issue of love for others.

9. I deliberately use Gilligan's own phrase here for what women are "talking about" from "The Conquistador and the Dark Continent: Reflections on the Psychology of Love," *Daedalus* 113 (1984): 78.

10. Gilligan often invokes this duality, e.g., in "Conquistador," 77–78, and *In a Different Voice* (69). In "Remapping the Moral Domain: New Images of the Self in Relationship," in *Reconstructing Individualism,* ed. Thomas C. Heller et al. (Palo Alto, Calif.: Stanford University Press, 1986), 241–56, she suggests briefly that this duality reflects universal experiences, in childhood, of inequality and attachment. For a fuller treatment, see Gilligan and Wiggins, "Origins" (note 1, above).

11. See J. S. Mill on expediency over justice in Chapter 5 of *Utilitarianism* (New York: New American Library, 1962), 320–21. (Subsequent references to Mill are to this edition.) For a more wistful admission that justice might have to go, see J. J. C. Smart, *Utilitarianism For and Against,* with Bernard Williams (Cambridge: Cambridge University Press, 1973), 69–74.

12. It is not cant when Mill says, "In the golden rule of Jesus of Nazareth, we read the complete spirit of the ethics of utility. To do as you would be done by, and to love your neighbor as yourself, constitute the ideal perfection of utilitarian morality" (*Utilitarianism*, chapter 2, 268). Mill's belief in the "powerful natural sentiment" (284) and "contagion" (285) of sympathy are important grounds of his defense of utilitarianism.

13. Bill Puka, "An Interdisciplinary Treatment of Kohlberg," *Ethics* 92 (1982): 469. Puka provides a clear statement of the basic commitments of "cognitive-developmentalism" in morality.

14. Mill responded early on to criticisms of the demandingness and coldness of utilitarianism (*Utilitarianism,* chapter 2, 269–72). Contemporary critiques on this score include: Bernard Williams, "Persons, Character, and Morality," in *Moral Luck* (Cambridge: Cambridge University Press, 1981), 1–19; Michael Stocker, "The Schizophrenia of Modern Ethical Theories," *Journal of Philosophy* 73 (1976): 453–66. See also, Linda Nicholson, "Women, Morality, and History," *Social Research* 50 (1983): 514–36, esp. 524–25, on how both utilitarianism and Kantianism reflect the same historical location and social organization that yield a certain version of the public vs. private split.

15. Nel Noddings, *Caring* (Berkeley: University of California Press, 1984), hereafter cited in the text as C.

16. Noddings does not put her view forward *as* a representation of Gilligan's different voice, but does identify her view with Gilligan's at points or recruits Gilligan's view in support of hers (e.g., C, 8, 96).

17. See Seyla Benhabib's excellent "The Generalized and the Concrete Other: The Kohlberg-Gilligan Controversy and Moral Theory," in Kittay and Meyers, 154–71.

18. Owen Flanagan, "Virtue, Sex, and Gender: Some Philosophical Reflections on the Moral Psychology Debate," *Ethics* 92 (1982): 499–512, esp. 511, claims Gilligan's "contextualism" is really just a general kind of cognitive sophistication, that of

making subtle discriminations. But this fails to consider that the cognition central to care is understanding *persons; I* do not think intellectual subtlety in, say, mathematics or philosophy indicates cognitive sophistication we should expect to carry over to interpersonal perceptiveness. Nor can Gilligan's claim that the care and justice orientations are "fundamentally incompatible," like two ways of seeing a puzzle picture ("Remapping," 242, 246), be evaluated if the grounding of these two views in different representations of interpersonal relationship and understanding are not fully explored. Yet without considering these different representations at length or in detail, Flanagan and Kathryn Jackson in "Justice, Care and Gender: The Kohlberg-Gilligan Debate Revisited," *Ethics* 97 (1987): 622–37, esp. 626, argue that it is possible to "integrate" perceptions aligned with each into the same episode of moral deliberation.

19. See "Remapping the Moral Domain" (note 10, above) and Carol Gilligan and Eve Stern, "The Riddle of Femininity and the Psychology of Love," in *Passionate Attachments,* ed. Willard Gaylin and Ethel Person (New York: Free Press, 1988).

20. Sharon Bishop, "Connections & Guilt," *Hypatia* 2 (1987): 7–23, explores the implications of a Gilligan-like ethics of responsibility for the inevitability of moral conflict and the resulting affective binds which require working through over time and may leave intelligible but only partly expungeable remainders of guilt.

21. The *Signs* forum (note 1, above) illustrates this amply; beyond criticism, there is resentment, frustration, and distress. I don't mean to imply, of course, there is no basis for dispassionate criticism.

22. Grimshaw, *Philosophy and Feminist Thinking,* expresses this reservation about "women's viewpoint" theories generally. But even so, exposing "female" morality to view may open a mine of insight into the hidden presuppositions and agendae of "male" (read, public) moralities. See, e.g., Annette Baier, "Poisoning the Wells," in *Postures of the Mind* (Minneapolis: University of Minnesota Press, 1985), 263–91, esp. 273–76.

23. Sara Ruddick's excellent studies, "Maternal Thinking" and "Preservative Love and Military Destruction," are exemplars for examining the intelligent structure of "women's work." In Joyce Trebilcot, ed., *Mothering* (Totowa, N.J.: Rowman & Allanheld, 1984), 213–30, 231–62. In a related vein, see Virginia Held, "Feminism and Moral Theory," in Kittay and Meyers, 111–28, on the understanding of human relationship that grows out of the mothering experience.

24. I am grateful for the opportunity to present a shorter version of this paper at the American Philosophical Association Central Division Meeting in April, 1987, in sessions on Carol Gilligan's work sponsored by the American Society for Value Inquiry, organized by Nancy Tuana. In addition to a number of members of that audience, I thank Carol Gilligan, Celeste Schenck, and Arthur Walker for critical comments and encouragement both. I am grateful to Fordham University for a Faculty Fellowship in 1986–87 which provided the time and support that enabled me to write this paper. This author has previously published under the name Margaret Urban Coyne.

5

MORAL UNDERSTANDINGS:
ALTERNATIVE "EPISTEMOLOGY"
FOR A FEMINIST ETHICS

When Annette Baier asked a few years ago what women wanted in a
moral theory, the answer she arrived at was that moral *theory* was just
what women *didn't* want, if a moral theory is a "fairly systematic account of
a fairly large area of morality, with a keystone supporting all the rest."[1] Yet
the latter is what a still dominant tradition of moral philosophy—stretching
from Socrates through Sidgwick to Rawls—*does* want: a fairly compact system of very general but directly action-guiding principles or procedures.
Current philosophical practice still largely views ethics as the search for
moral knowledge, and moral knowledge as comprising universal moral formulae and the theoretical justification of these.

If one asks the somewhat different question of what a *feminist ethics* is,
or should look like, one might have in mind some different things. One is
that feminist ethics is one which clarifies the moral legitimacy and necessity
of the kinds of social, political, and personal changes that feminism demands
in order to end male domination, or perhaps to end domination generally.[2]
Another conception of feminist ethics is that of one in which the moral perceptions, self-images, and senses of moral value and responsibility of women
have been represented or restored. Philosophical ethics, as a cultural product,
has been until recently almost entirely a product of some men's thinking.
There are the usual reasons to suspect that those men will not have represented, or will not have represented truly, modes of life and forms of responsibility which aren't theirs, or which they could recognize fully only at
the cost of acknowledging their interlocking gender, race and class privileges.
While female voices alone may not be sufficient correctives to this, they
promise to be important ones. Here the work of restoration, reconstruction,
and new construction are not sharply divided; all involve suspension and re-
examination of unquestioned assumptions and standard forms.

The reconstructive project has been pioneered in work by Baier, Carol Gilligan, Nel Noddings, Adrienne Rich, Sara Ruddick, Caroline Whitbeck, and others.[3] While the result in each case is distinctive, a lattice of similar themes—personal relations, nurturance and caring, maternal experience, emotional responsiveness, attunement to particular persons and contexts, sensitivity to open-ended responsibilities—has become the object of sharp criticism from *other* feminist quarters. While the criticisms too are varied, they include a variety of cognate concerns about whether the values and paradigms valorized in the reconstructive work are not mistaken and politically retrograde. Jean Grimshaw, Claudia Card, Jennfer Allen, Lorraine Code, Barbara Houston, and others have asked whether maternal paradigms, nurturant responsiveness, and a bent toward responsibility for others' needs aren't our oppressive history, not our liberating future, and whether "women's morality" isn't a familiar ghetto rather than a liberated space.[4] It is fair, if oversimple, to say that some feminists question whether the reconstructive project can meet and nourish the politically normative one.[5]

The many crossing strands of this conversation beg for close consideration, but I will pull one thread loose from the reconstructive project and commend it to our further deliberation as a part, but only part, of an adequate and flexible feminist ethic. The thread I refer to in the reconstructive work is a profound and original rebellion against the regnant paradigm of moral knowledge mentioned in my opening paragraph. Hence, it might be called an *alternative moral epistemology*, a very different way of identifying and appreciating the forms of intelligence which define responsible moral consideration. This view does not imagine our moral understandings congealed into a compact theoretical instrument of impersonal decision for each person, but as deployed in shared processes of discovery, expression, interpretation, and adjustment between persons. Facets of this alternative view which appear repeatedly in reconstructive discussions are: attention to the particular; a way of constructing morally relevant understandings which is "contextual and narrative"; a picture of deliberation as a site of expression and communication.[6]

Here are my limited aims. First, I model this alternative epistemology of moral understandings by describing its three elements and their affinities. Second, I identify how its features challenge the still hardy mainstream universalist tradition on moral knowledge. Finally, too briefly, I indicate some ways this particular result of the reconstructive approach to feminist ethics answers to some concerns of the first, politically normative approach. Refusing the canonical "theory" option does not mean going without guidance in judgements and practices of countering domination. Neither does the alternative moral epistemology by itself require commitments to the specific moral values and paradigms lately in dispute among feminists.

I. ELEMENTS OF AN
ALTERNATIVE MORAL EPISTEMOLOGY

A substantial number of contemporary women writers on morality have sounded the theme of attention to "particular others in actual contexts."[7] Iris Murdoch sets an oft-cited precedent for this theme in her defense of *attention* ("loving regard" or "patient and just discernment") as the "characteristic and proper mark of the active moral agent."[8] In pointed opposition to the emphasis in most moral philosophy on conscientious adherence to principle, Murdoch insists instead on the "endless task" of "good vision: unsentimental, detached, unselfish, objective attention," which she calls *love*.[9] More recent women writers who see acute and unimpeded perception of particular human beings as the condition of adequate moral response concur in Murdoch's epistemological point—her emphasis on a certain kind of understanding as central to morality.[10]

Ruddick, for example, finds in the normative structure of maternal practices a rich display of that openness which allows for revelation of the particular individual. Maternal responsibility to foster growth, on Ruddick's account, requires certain recognitions: of the separate consciousness of another making its own sense of the world; of the common humanity of the other's familiar longings and impulses; of the need to give up expectations of repeatability in order to follow the distinct trajectory of a particular life.[11] Such maternal virtues are ones Ruddick thinks it urgent to cultivate more widely. Whitbeck sees a similar sensibility enabling practices (such as teaching the young, nursing the sick, tending the body) for "the (mutual) realization of people" which are typically considered "women's work."[12] Related themes are sounded by others: Gilligan's reconstruction of the "care ethic" involves "the ability to perceive people in their own terms and to respond to their needs"; Benhabib explores the "epistemic incoherence" of strategies of reversability and universalization once the concreteness of other individuals has been covered over by the "generalized" conception of others in terms of an abstract *status*.[13]

Attention to particular persons as *a*, if not *the*, morally crucial epistemic mode requires distinctive sorts of understanding. Gilligan has usefully described the pattern of this thinking as "contextual and narrative" rather than "formal and abstract," where the latter "abstracts the moral problem from the interpersonal situation," while the former invokes a "narrative of relationships that extends over time."[14] Two elements are at work here: context and concreteness of individuals with specific "history, identity, and affective-emotional constitution," and the special context that is a relationship, with *its* history, identity, and affective definition.[15]

The two are linked by the notion of a narrative, of the location of human beings' feelings, psychological states, needs, and understandings as nodes of a story (or of the intersection of stories) that has already begun, and will continue beyond a given juncture of moral urgency. Conceptually, this means that we don't and can't identify people's emotions, intentions and other mental states with momentary (and especially not momentary inner, private) phenomena. Instead, we identify these features of people by attending to how their beliefs, feelings, modes of expression, circumstances and more, arranged in characteristic ways and often spread out in time, configure into a recognizable kind of story. Practically, this means that individual embroideries and idiosyncracies, as well as the learned codes of expression and response built up in particular relationships, and built up culturally around kinds of relationships, require of us very acute attention to the minute and specific, to history and incident, in grasping cases in a morally adequate way. If the others I need to understand really are actual others in a particular case at hand, and not repeatable instances or replaceable occupants of a general status, they will require of me an understanding of their/our story and its concrete detail. Without this I really cannot know *how it is* with others towards whom I will act, or what the meaning and consequence of any acts will be.

Whitbeck argues for a relational view of persons, of their historical being as "fundamentally a history of relationships to other people," and their actions as responses to the "whole configuration of relations."[16] She connects this view with the essentially responsive, discretionary character of moral responsibilities that relationships generate, responsibilities that cannot then be reduced to obligations and specified in uniform terms. Sharon Bishop has also examined the different light cast on moral responsibilities, problems, deliberation, resolution and guilt when one sees moral response as the attempt to mediate multiple, sometimes conflicting moral claims that arise out of our many actual connections with other people and our needs to maintain them with integrity and sensitivity.[17] This intertwining of selves and stories in narrative constructions which locate what is at stake, what is needed, and what is possible is at the heart of moral thinking for many women and feminist writers. The understanding of such stories requires many forms of intelligence; all are at work in the competent moral agent, according to these views.[18]

One form of intelligence that very often, if not typically, offers crucial resources for the resolution of moral problems is the *ability to communicate* among persons involved or affected. While this avenue to understanding is not always open, it often enough is, and its efficacy is so obvious that it is astonishing how little attention is paid it in most nonfeminist moral philosophy. Even in that strain of theory that postulates or simulates an original agreement or compact, the role of communication in, as it were, the moral event is routinely ignored, and the moral agent on the spot is depicted in lonely cogitations (or sometimes in admirable but solo display of fixed habits of virtue). Given the particularistic paradigm of understanding and the situated conception of responsibility already discussed, it is not surprising that the resource of communication is often stressed in women's writing on morality. Gilligan stresses the commitment in the "care" ethic she describes to "activating the network [of relationships] by communication;" and Bishop's reconstrual of moral response as "offering compensation and mediating settlements" pictures us as engaging those affected by our moral choices in tight places in a common search for constructive ways of answering unsatisfiable or competing claims. Benhabib even more directly challenges the "monological model of moral reasoning" with a proposal for a "communicative ethic of need interpretation," in which actual dialogue replaces hypothetical methods and fixed, prior constraints on "admissible" concerns. Murdoch speaks of a mutual "obscurity" which makes the work of love endless, and urges on us the study of literature as an education in how to "picture and understand human situations."[19] We need not make our obscurity to each other worse by unnecessarily unilateral decision. We might just try turning to each other: talking and listening and imagining possibilities together.

II. FROM MORAL KNOWLEDGE TO MORAL UNDERSTANDINGS

The three elements of attention, contextual and narrative appreciation, and communication in the event of moral deliberation might be seen, in their natural interdependence, as an alternative epistemology of moral understanding, or the basis of one. This view, gleaned from the works of a variety of female and feminist writers, provides an alternative to a now standard and canonical (which is to say: professionally institutionalized) view of the form and point of ethics (or its philosophical elaboration).[20] This view is both old and continuous enough to be called a tradition in the strongest sense, and we might call it the *universalist/impersonalist tradition*. In the words of one of its most explicit proponents, nineteenth-century utilitarian philosopher Henry Sidgwick,[21] its goal is systematization of moral understanding, and its ideal of system is that of "precise general knowledge of what ought to be," (1) encoded in "directive rules of conduct" (2) which are "clear and decisive" (199) and "in universal form" (228). The rationale for pursuing a "scientifically complete and systematically reflective form" (425) in morals is that it "corrects" and "supplements" our scattered intuitions, and resolves "uncertainties and discrepancies" in moral judgement. By useful abstraction it steers us away from, in Sidgwick's words, "obvious sources of error" which "disturb the clearness" of moral discernment (214). For Sidgwick, such distractions include complexity of circumstances, personal interests, and habitual sympathies. Thus, according to Sidgwick, only precise and truly universal principles can provide for "perfection of practice no less than for theoretical completeness" (262).

This capsule description of standard intent and methodology aims to bring into relief its very general picture of morality as individuals standing before the bar of impersonal truth. Moral responsibility is envisioned as responsiveness to the impersonal truths in which morality resides; each individual stands justified if he or she can invoke the authority of this impersonal truth, and the moral community of individuals is secured by the conformity (and uniformity) guaranteed by obedience to this higher authority.[22] From an epistemological angle, one might gloss this view as: adequacy of moral understanding increases as this understanding approaches systematic generality.

The alternative moral epistemology already outlined, holds, to the contrary, that: adequacy of moral understanding decreases as its form approaches generality through abstraction. A view consistent with this will not be one of individuals standing singly before the impersonal dicta of Morality, but one of human beings connected in various ways and at various depths responding *to each other* by engaging together in a search for shareable interpretations of their responsibilities, and/or bearable resolutions to their moral binds. These interpretations and resolutions will be constrained not only by how well they protect goods we can share, but also by how well they preserve the very human connections that make the shared process necessary and possible. The long oscillation in Western moral thought between the impersonal and the personal viewpoints is answered by proposing that we consider, fully and in earnest, the *interpersonal* view.

The result of this alternative epistemology is not, then, an "opposite number" or shadow image of impersonalist approaches; it is instead a point of departure for a *variety* of different problematics, investigations, focal concerns, and genres of writing and teaching about ethics, many of which we have not, I suppose, yet clearly imagined. Some philosophical endeavors are obviously relevant. We might pay greater attention to the pragmatics of communication (of what people mean and do when they address each other, and not just what their words mean). We could explore more fully how moral paradigms and exemplary particular cases are made points of reference for shareable judgements, how they are explicated and how analogies are drawn with them. A lively interest in understanding how various factors (semantic, institutional, political) shape our ability to arrive at shared interpretations is needed, as is a questioning of barriers between philosophical, literary, critical, and empirical investigations of moral life. These endeavors can, however, be carried out in a cheerfully piecemeal fashion; we need not expect or require the results to eventuate in a comprehensive systematization.

The analogue of this on the practical level is the expectation of constant "moral remainders," to adopt a phrase in recent philosophical use. 'Moral remainders' refers to some genuine moral demands which, because their fulfillment conflicted with other genuine moral demands, are "left over" in episodes of moral choice, and yet are not just nullified.[23] Whether this sort of thing is even possible is an issue in contemporary moral philosophy.[24] But if moral life is seen as a tissue of moral understandings which configure, respond to, and reconfigure relations as they go, we should anticipate residues and carry-overs as the rule rather than the exceptions: one's choice will often be a selection of one among various imperfect responses, a response to some among various claims which can't all be fulfilled. So there will just as often be unfinished and ongoing business, compensations and reparations, postponements and returns. Moral problems on this view are nodal points in progressive histories of mutual adjustment and understanding, not "cases" to be closed by a final verdict of a highest court.

III. FROM EPISTEMOLOGY TO PRACTICE

Although I've cast the discussion here in terms of moral "epistemology," my point has been that there is a way of looking at the understanding critical to and distinctive of full moral capacity on which this understanding is *not* really an *episteme*, not a nomologically ordered theory. From the alternative view, moral understanding comprises a collection of perceptive, imaginative, appreciative, and expressive skills and capacities which put and keep us in unimpeded contact with the realities of ourselves and specific others.[25]

It's also true that a picture of moral understanding is not a whole moral view. Indeed, the alternative moral "epistemology" sketched here leaves open to consideration many questions about which sorts of values enable moral agents to express themselves and hear others, to interpret wisely, and to nourish each other's capacities for supple attentiveness. It also leaves open what other values not directly related to these expressive and receptive capacities are those a feminist ethics ought to endorse. It does not promote one kind of relationship as paradigmatic of moral encounter, and invites us to explore the resources and impediments to expression, reception and communication in relationships of many kinds. Yet the priority it gives to voicing and hearing, to being answerable in and for specific encounters and relationships promises, I believe, potent critical resources. The most obvious ones I see are its structural capacity to challenge "principled" moral stances in the concrete, where these are surrogates for, or defenses against, responsiveness in actual relationships; to export an insistence on the primacy of personal acknowledgement and communication to institutional and "stranger" contexts; and on a philosophical plane to pierce through the rhetoric of ethics to the *politics of ethics* as a routine matter.[26]

In the first instance, an ethic based on this alternative picture of moral understanding is set to challenge fundamentally and consistently the way the universalist tradition has institutionalized *indirect* ways of relating as moral *paradigms*. By 'indirect' here I mean ways of appreciating persons and situations mediated through what are typically some few, entrenched parameters of status, right, principle, or duty. The alternative picture discussed here confronts this "policed sociability" of universalism with an alternative ideal of *moral objectivity*: that of unimpeded, undistorted, and flexible appreciation of unrepeatable individuals in what are often distinctive situations and relationships.[27] Morally relevant categories on this view include the full, nuanced range of expressive resources for articulating and constructing interpersonal life. By contrast, the ways of describing and expressing to which universalist morality permits moral relevance are typically limited to those which are "repeatable," "universalizable," "impartial," or "impersonal," i.e., those that embody the forms of detachment that are taken by universalism as constitutive of "the moral point of view."

Universalism presses me to view you, for instance, as a holder of a certain right, or a promisee, or a satisfaction-function, or a focus of some specifiable set of obligatory responses. I am pressed to structure my response or appeal to you in terms which I can think of as applying repeatedly to any number of other cases. If we step into the alternative framework, however, we see universalist morality as thus "curbing our imaginations" by enforcing communicative and reflective strategies which are interpersonally *evasive*.[28] Universalism, for example, tends to regiment moral thinking so that negligent or willful inattention to need and expectation in the course of daily life is readily seen as "mere insensitivity," a non-moral failing, when it is not in dereliction of explicit "duties." Worse, it legitimates *uniformly* assuming the quasi-administrative or juridical posture of "the" (i.e., universal) moral point of view. Yet in many cases assuming that viewpoint may foreclose the more revealing, if sometimes painful, path of expression, acknowledgment, and collaboration that could otherwise lead to genuinely responsive solutions.

A principled appeal to "fairness" or "what one promised" or what "right" one has to something or why "anyone" should expect a certain response may be a summarily effective arguing point. But if it is brought forth in an intricate situation of an ongoing relationship, it may also be the most effective way to stymie or silence your interlocutor—spouse, lover, friend, student, partner, patient—without addressing many questions. The avoided questions may include just the morally relevant ones about the particular needs and harms, the expectations and forms of trust, and the character and future of *that* relationship. Feminists have special and acute needs to fend off this systematic de-personalizing of the moral and de-moralizing of the personal. For on a practical level what feminists aspire to depends as much on restructuring our senses of moral responsibility in intimate partnerships, sexual relations, communities of personal loyalty, and day-to-day work relations as it clearly does on replacing institutional, legal, and political arrangements.

The alternative picture also invites us not to be too tempted by the "separate spheres" move of endorsing particularism for personal or intimate relations, universalism for the large-scale or genuinely administrative context, or for dealings with unknown or little-known persons. While principled, generalized treatments may really be the best we can resort to in many cases of the latter sort, it is well to preserve a lively sense of the *moral incompleteness* or inadequacy of these resorts. This is partly to defend ourselves against dispositions to keep strangers strange and outsiders outside, but it is also to prevent our becoming comfortable with essentially distancing, depersonalizing, or paternalistic attitudes which may not really *be* the only resorts if roles and institutions can be shaped to embody expressive and communicative possibilities. It is often claimed that more humanly responsive institutions are not practical (read: instrumentally efficient). But if moral-practical intelligence is understood consistently in the alternative way discussed, (the way appropriate to relations among persons), it may instead be correct to say that certain incorrigibly impersonal or depersonalizing institutions are too morally impractical to be tolerated. It is crucial to examine how structural features of institutionalized relations—medical personnel, patients and families; teachers, students and parents; case workers and clients, for example—combine with typical situations to enable or deform the abilities of all concerned to hear and to be heard. Some characteristically modern forms of universalist thinking may project a sort of "moral colonialism" (the "subjects" of my moral decisions disappear behind uniform "policies" I must impartially "apply") precisely because they were forged historically with an eye to actual colonization—industrial or imperial.[29]

Finally, this kind of moral epistemology reminds us that styles of moral thinking are not primarily philosophical brain-teasers, data begging for the maximally elegant theoretical construction, but are ways of answering *to other people* in terms of some responsibilities that are commonly recognized or recognizable in some community. Philosophical representations of these styles will both reflect and reinforce the relations of authority, power, and responsibility they encode. Hence, for moral philosophy to be sincerely reflective, it must attend focally to questions heretofore considered "philosophically" inappropriate: questions about the rhetoric and politics of ethics. These are questions about the discursive and expressive formats which have been declared appropriate to the task of representing moral life, and about who has the standing (and the access to institutionalized forums) to make, and to challenge, the "rules" (including substantive assumptions) of the genre. When we construct and consider representations of our moral situations, we need to ask: what actual community of moral responsibility does this representation of moral thinking purport to represent? Who does it actually represent? What communicative strategies does it support? Who will be in a position (concretely, socially) to deploy these strategies? Who is in a position to transmit and enforce the rules which constrain them? In what forms of activity or endeavor will they have (or fail to have) an application, and who is served by these activities?

These questions are hard for philosophers to ask; it flies in the face of the professional self-image of supposedly disinterested searchers after timeless moral truth to recognize that a moral philosophy is a particular rhetoric too, situated in certain places, sustained and deployed by certain groups of people. Its apparent form may belie its real application and meaning. For example, philosophers have long insisted on "the universal" in ethics, and continue, I find, to insist on formal universality of norms, concepts, or procedures as the key moral bulwark against bias and injustice. Yet the rhetoric of universality has been entirely compatible, as feminist philosophers have repeatedly shown, with the most complete (and often intentional) exclusion of women as moral agents from such loftily universal constructs as the social contract, pure practical rationality, or the good life for man, and with bypassing altogether in application whole areas of life that are the province of women (voluntarily or not), such as the rearing of children.[30]

Further, not only the substance and presuppositions but also the standard discursive forms of moral philosophy—its canonical styles of presentation, methods of argument, characteristic problems—require pragmatic evaluation. These forms include stark absence of the second person and the plural in projections of philosophical deliberation; virtual exclusion of collaborative and communicative modes of formulating and negotiating moral problems; regimentation of moral "reasoning" into formats of deductive argument; reliance on schematic examples in which the few "morally relevant" factors have already been selected, and in which social-political context is effaced; and omission of continuing narratives that explore the interpersonal sequels to moral "solutions." These are rhetorical conventions which curb the moral imaginations of academic philosophers drastically. Alarmingly, we visit them on our students as we "refine" their moral thinking, obscuring morally significant features of everyday life, personal relations, and the social conditions which structure them.

There are alternatives to the abstract, authoritarian, impersonal, universalist view of moral consciousness. The picture of direct mutual response and responsibility is not a whole ethics, but it is one way of rotating the axis of our investigation around the fixed point of our real need.[31]

NOTES

1. Annette Baier, "What Do Women Want in a Moral Theory?" *Nous* 19 (1985): 53–63, esp. 55.

2. This view of feminist ethics does not rule out in principle that some currently prominent view in philosophical ethics, properly applied, can be a feminist ethics. Although this possibility seems less promising currently, early feminist discussions of issues like abortion, rape, and pornography often invoked standard notions of rights, respect, or the promotion of happiness. And it is still a fact that in our given political culture appeals to moral standards which cohere with liberal political ideas are potent and indispensable tools in pursuing feminist social and legal objectives.

3. Annette Baier, "What Do Women Want in a Moral Theory?" "Trust and Anti-Trust," *Ethics* 96 (1986): 231–60, and "The Need for More than Justice," in *Science, Morality and Feminist Theory*, ed. Marsha Hanen and Kai Nelson (Calgary, Canada: University of Calgary Press, 1987); Carol Gilligan, *In a Different Voice* (Cambridge: Harvard University Press, 1982); Nel Noddings, *Caring: A Feminine Approach to Ethics*

and Moral Education (Berkeley: University of California Press, 1984); Adrienne Rich, *Of Woman Born* (New York: W. W. Norton and Company, 1976) and *On Lies, Secrets, and Silence* (New York: W. W. Norton and Company, 1979); Sara Ruddick, "Maternal Thinking," in *Mothering*, ed. Joyce Treblicot (Totowa, N.J.: Rowman & Allanheld, 1984); and Caroline Whitbeck, "A Different Reality: Feminist Ontology," in *Beyond Domination*, ed. Carol C. Gould (Totowa, N.J.: Rowman & Allanheld, 1984).

4. Jean Grimshaw, *Philosophy and Feminist Thinking* (Minneapolis: University of Minnesota Press, 1986); Claudia Card, "Virtues and Moral Luck," Working Series I, no. 4 (1985), Institute for Legal Studies, University of Wisconsin, Madison, Law School [now available in *The Unnatural Lottery* (Philadelphia: Temple University Press, 1996)]; Jeffner Allen, *Lesbian Philosophy: Explorations* (Palo Alto, Calif.: Institute of Lesbian Studies, 1986); Lorraine Code, "Second Persons," in *Science, Morality and Feminist Theory*; and Barbara Houston, "Rescuing Womanly Virtues," in *Science, Morality and Feminist Theory*. Grimshaw is specially critical of claims that women's moral *thinking* is characteristically different; Code criticizes "maternalism"; Houston discusses objections by Card, Allen, and others. For critical reactions to Gilligan's work, see Debra Nails, Mary Ann O'Loughlin, and James C. Walker, eds., *Social Research* 50 (1983); Linda Kerber et al., "On *In a Different Voice*: An Interdisciplinary Forum," *Signs* 11 (1986): 304–33; and Meredith Michaels, "Morality Without Distinction," *Philosophical Forum* 17 (1986): 175–87.

5. I don't mean to make this dialogue sound too bipolar. Virginia Held, "Feminism and Moral Theory," in *Women and Moral Theory*, ed. Eva Feder Kittay and Diana T. Meyers (Totowa, N.J.: Rowman & Littlefield, 1987), is cautious on the issue of jettisoning principles to particularism. Marilyn Friedman, "Beyond Caring: The De-moralization of Gender," in *Science, Morality, & Feminist Theory*, combines a plea for the integration of justice and caring values with the view that the character of particularized moral commitments does not combine with rule-based respect. Both Held and Friedman tentatively suggest the application of different moral approaches to different "spheres" of life or different kinds of relationships. But see my section III, below, on the "separate spheres" idea.

6. The characterization "contextual and narrative" comes from Gilligan, *In a Different Voice*, 19.

7. Held, "Feminism and Moral Theory," 118.

8. Iris Murdoch, *The Sovereignty of Good* (London: Routledge and Kegan Paul, [1970] 1985). On "loving regard," see 40; on discernment, 38; on the moral agent, 34.

9. Murdoch, *The Sovereignty*, 28, 65–66. Murdoch herself credits her conception of a "just and loving gaze directed upon an individual reality" (34) to Simone Weil, whose views are complicated enough (and ambivalent enough, from the viewpoint I'm discussing here) to require quite separate consideration.

10. Many may not share the Platonism, Freudian psychology, theory of art, or other views to which Murdoch joins her views on love. One subtle critique of the deep social conservatism of Murdoch's views is provided by Sabina Lovibond, *Real-*

ism and Imagination in Ethics (Minneapolis: University of Minnesota Press, 1983), 189–200.

11. Ruddick, "Maternal Thinking," 218–20.

12. Caroline Whitbeck, "A Different Reality," 65.

13. Carol Gilligan, "The Conquistador and the Dark Continent: Reflections on the Psychology of Love," *Daedalus* 113 (1984): 75–95, esp. 77; Seyla Benhabib, "The Generalized and the Concrete Other," in *Women and Moral Theory*, 164. See also Held, "Feminism and Moral Theory"; "Noddings, *Caring*, chapters 1 and 4; and Martha Nussbaum, "Flawed Crystals: James's *The Golden Bowl* and Literature as Moral Philosophy," *New Literary History* 15 (1983): 25–50, on reviving the Aristotelian notion of perception as "appropriate acknowledgement" of the particular person in the face of the blinding urge to preserve preconceived, harmonious orderings of abstracted value.

14. Gilligan, *In a Different Voice*, 32, 28.

15. The phrase is Benhabib's in "The Generalized and the Concrete Other," 163.

16. Whitbeck, "A Different Reality," 76.

17. Sharon Bishop, "Connections and Guilt," *Hypatia* 2, no. 1 (1987): 7–23.

18. See also Cora Diamond, "Having a Rough Story about What Moral Philosophy Is," *New Literary History* 15 (1983): 155–69, on the importance of grasping the moral "texture" of individuals (an idea she attributes to Iris Murdoch).

19. Gilligan, *In a Different Voice*, 30, 12; Bishop, "Connections and Guilt," 12; Benhabib, "The Generalized and the Concrete Other," 167, 169; Murdoch, *The Sovereignty*, 33–34.

20. The difference between representing morality and "rationally reconstructing" it philosophically is not always clear, and this is itself a source of deep problems, substantively and methodologically. Kathryn Addelson, "Moral Passages," in *Women and Moral Theory*, for example, deeply challenges the appropriateness and moral legitimacy of an academic practice of philosophical ethics (if I understand her correctly). I take this challenge quite seriously, even as I right now continue to do a version of academic philosophical ethics.

21. Henry Sidgwick, *The Methods of Ethics* (Indianapolis: Hackett Publishing, [1907] 1981). Sidgwick's work richly repays study if one wants to see in explicit and self-conscious form the "rules" of the genre of today's philosophical ethics. But one could find the same rules formulated (or implicitly honored) in any number of mainstream twentieth-century authors. Page citations in the text hereafter are to this edition.

22. Since writing this I have discovered a parallel characterization in Anthony Skillen's description of modern bourgeois moral consciousness as a blend of "abstract authoritarianism" and "generalized disciplinarianism." See Anthony Skillen, *Ruling Illusions* (Atlantic Highlands, N.J.: Humanities Press, 1978), 153.

23. A standard example would be that in which two promises, each sincerely and responsibly made, turn out to be contingently incapable of both being kept. In such cases, whichever commitment I fulfill, another will have been neglected. Bishop,

"Connections and Guilt," 13ff., discusses the importance of taking the longer view of such cases.

24. A number of widely known essays which debate the issues about dilemmas and moral remainders are collected in Christopher Gowans, *Moral Dilemmas* (New York: Oxford University Press, 1987).

25. A moral epistemology of the sort described finds common or overlapping cause with a number of other contemporary deviations from dominant views. For critics of impartiality on behalf of the personal life, see Bernard Williams, *Moral Luck* (Cambridge: Cambridge University Press, 1981), Lawrence Blum, *Friendship, Altruism and Morality* (London: Routledge and Kegan Paul, 1980), and Michael Stocker, "The Schizophrenia of Modern Ethical Theories," *Journal of Philosophy* 73 (1976): 453-66. On interrogating moral views for their concrete social and historical conditions, see Alasdair MacIntyre, *After Virtue* (Notre Dame, Ind.: University of Notre Dame Press, 1981). For insistence on the primacy of judgments in particular cases, see the new Aristotelians, Martha Nussbaum, *The Fragility of Goodness* (Cambridge: Cambridge University Press, 1986), and David Wiggins, "Deliberation and Practical Reason," in *Practical Reasoning*, ed. Joseph Raz (Oxford: Oxford University Press, 1978). For other versions of "responsibility ethics" which situate moral claims in relational structures of power and dependency, see Robert Goodin, *Protecting the Vulnerable* (Chicago: University of Chicago Press, 1985), and Hans Jonas, *The Imperative of Responsibility* (Chicago: University of Chicago Press, 1984). On morality as a tissue of acknowledgments and refusals, see Stanley Cavell, *The Claim of Reason* (Oxford: Oxford University Press, 1979), parts 3 and 4. And on morality as constituted by social practices and as expressive of relations of authority in, respectively, a Marxist and a Wittgensteinian-Hegelian vein see Anthony Skillen, *Ruling Illusions*, and Sabina Lovibond, *Realism and Imagination in Ethics*. All these may be, used selectively, resources for a different kind of ethics. Yet feminists might remain wary of unwanted residues and omissions in some of these views

26. On the political aspects of construction and deployment of modes of rationality and styles of thought with respect to gender, see essays by Ruddick, Addelson, and Harding in Kittay and Meyers, *Women and Moral Theory*. See also Cheshire Calhoun, "Justice, Care, Gender Bias," *Journal of Philosophy* 85 (1988): 451–63, for a discussion of the way philosophers' neglect of certain topics reinforces moral ideologies.

27. The phrase is Skillen's, in *Ruling Illusions*, 170.

28. The phrase is Lovibond's, in *Realism and Imagination in Ethics*, 199.

29. In this connection see Skillen, *Ruling Illusions*, chapter 4, on both Kantian and utilitarian disciplinarianism and Bernard Williams, *Ethics and the Limits of Philosophy* (Cambridge: Cambridge University Press, 1985), chapter 6, on Sidgwickian "government house utilitarianism."

30. Annette Baier, "Trust and Anti-Trust" and "The Need for More than Justice," is particularly humane and lucid on this topic.

31. Special thanks to Sandra Bartky for very good suggestions on an earlier and briefer draft of this paper, and to the editors and readers for helpful suggestions.

6

FEMINISM, ETHICS, AND THE
QUESTION OF THEORY

Feminist concern with ethics, as with other areas of thought and culture, has been a concern for how ethics might be other than it is, for how feminists and others might understand moral life in ways different from those represented in the tradition and the present practice of moral philosophy. A considerable body of feminist ethical critique (largely Anglophone and academic) gives reasons to think prevalent representations of morality are marked by gender and other privilege. Worse, it gives reasons to suspect that a good deal of ethics, as it appears in intellectually authoritative and academically legitimated texts and discussions in North American and Western European societies, functions both as an expression and a constituent of processes and ideologies of social dominance. This feminist work on ethics attends specially to the ways in which ethics in "the Western" philosophical tradition is not only not by or about women, but not *for* women either: neither faithfully reflective of women's many different, actual lives nor helpful to their projects of self-discovery and political change.[1] At the same time, it begins to expose how this ethics is not by, about, or for many men either.

Different feminist writers, however, have found different things wrong with mainstream "Western" ethical thought. One cluster of feminist critiques suggests that the moral theories in this tradition are flawed by gender bias that both expresses and reinforces men's domination of social life. This may imply that feminists, at least, need new and better moral theories, framed with an eye to women's experiences and feminist concerns. But another set of critiques raises profound doubts about the legitimacy of moral theorizing itself. On these views, moral philosophizing in North American and European culture(s) is a highly specific social practice involving questionable assumptions of authority and dubious political implications.

I make a case here, within this cultural context and addressed to those who find their impulse to moral critique and reflection situated within this context's terms and traditions, for a third way. Many of the reasons for finding current moral theories inadequate should lead, I claim, not only to the rejection of those theories but to a rejection of a certain entrenched conception of moral theory familiar in twentieth-century Anglo-American moral philosophy. I don't think, though, that giving up moral *theory* (in the quite specific sense of this entrenched model) as the project of ethics means giving up *ethics* as a descriptive and critical understanding of how moral life does and can go on. Yet the recent feminist challenge to the legitimacy of moral philosophizing itself is a deep one. It requires that any ethics done must become politically self-conscious and reflexively critical, and that the impetus to this must be *right in* the kind of ethics any of us do, not an addendum or a postscript to it. I suggest here, in a sketch both brief and rough, an alternative conception of ethics that might begin to meet these demands. But it is not going to be easy for those of us who are "moral philosophers," institutionally trained and certified, to learn to do this kind of ethics, for it is not at all what most of us, professionally, have been trained to do.

I. FEMINIST REACTIONS TO MORAL THEORY

Much Anglo-American feminist ethics to date, quickened and nourished particularly by Carol Gilligan's work in moral psychology, has undertaken an immensely revealing examination of the central preoccupations, key assumptions, and leading images of the moral theories that dominate contemporary philosophical discussion.[2] The results of these investigations substantially converge. Preoccupation (whether in deontological, consequentialist, or contractarian theories) with equality and autonomy, uniformity and impartiality, rules and reciprocity fits relations of nonintimate equals and transactions or contracts among peers.[3] But it ignores or occludes the often unchosen, asymmetrical, and necessarily discretionary responsibilities of those who care for particular (and often dependent, vulnerable) others.[4] These modern theories neglect "the importance of intimacy, relationships, and care"[5] and emphasize abstract problem solving over responses to actual others.[6] They obscure the specificity of situations and moral subjects by emphasizing universality and sameness and excluding or regimenting emotional or sensuous experience.[7]

If this is even roughly right, the main moral theories we have are substantively inadequate to many intimate, unequal, unchosen particular relationships and therefore exclusive or deforming of much of the matter of social life. Since women's socially assigned responsibilities have so often precisely to do with just these kinds of relations, and with many forms of "caring labor" that sustain them, these omissions reveal a "male bias in Western moral theory"[8] that shapes views of morality, sociality, and rationality to fit "masculine affective, sexual, and social histories."[9] But these moral theories are worse than incomplete; they are mystifying and politically malign as well. For the community of freely contracting peers or mutually respecting reciprocators could not exist without the extensive and required labors of the care-givers, whose physical and emotional work cannot be recognized or valued in the moral terms these theories set. As Kathryn Morgan puts it, these theories effect the "invisibility of women's moral domains" and of the understandings of agency and responsibility that go with them.[10]

Might this problem be met by the formulation of better moral theories? Annette Baier has sketched ideas for an "ethics of trust" and Caroline Whitbeck for an "ethics of responsibility," while Nel Noddings has explicated a "care ethic" at book length and Virginia Held envisions a "unified moral field theory" incorporating different moral approaches for different domains of human activity.[11] These projects are apt to be viewed as proposals for new moral theories that are more complete or deliberately inclusive, or that begin from new assumptions that do not privilege characteristically male social positions and experiences, or that privilege female ones instead.

The critics in this first group certainly recognize that the problems feminists find with the moral theories we have are not as simple as "men's theories" versus "women's experience." Rather, assumptions and exclusions shaping dominant twentieth-century theories reflect gender and other hierarchical relations in the setting of specifically modern Western political and social organization, including the pervasive bifurcation of society and social roles into the "public" and the "private" spheres. Opening the question of the social and political situation and uses of moral theory, however, invites another, deeper level of critique.

A second group of feminists argues that fully situating moral theory socially and politically supports the more radical conclusion that the project of moral theorizing itself should be questioned. On this view, moral theories code the viewpoint and preoccupations of a very particular group of privileged people. Further, moral theorizing itself is a specific practice of intellectual authority that legitimates and reproduces the systematic relations, including hierarchical ones, that the theories reflect.

Maria Lugones and Elizabeth Spelman posed the problem of theory generally for feminists in their well-known essay "Have We Got a Theory for

You!" Spelman, in her voice as white Anglo woman, reminds us that "systematic, sustained reflection on being a woman . . . is most likely to be done by women who vis-à-vis other women enjoy a certain amount of political, social and economic privilege because of their skin color, class membership, ethnic identity."[12] Lugones, in her voice as Hispana, warns that "most Hispanas cannot even understand the language used in these theories—and only in some cases the reason is that the Hispana cannot understand English."[13] While acknowledging that "theorizing is integral" to feminism, they severely question the motives and points of view of theorists and ask "whether doing theory is in itself a good thing at this time for women of color or white/ Anglo women."[14] They summarize:

> Speaking to people through theory (orally or in writing) is a *very* specific and context-dependent activity. That is, theory-makers and their methods and concepts constitute a community of people and of shared meanings. Their language can be just as opaque and foreign to those not in the community as a foreign tongue or dialect. Why do we engage in *this* activity and what effect do we think it ought to have? As Helen Longino has asked: "Is 'doing theory' just a bonding ritual for academic or educationally privileged feminist women?"[15]

Addressing the question of moral theory in particular, Kathryn Addelson chides philosophers, feminists included, for failing to ask themselves "by what authority we define the moral institution of life."[16] This authority, she reminds us, is a professional status, politically won and politically maintained. Like social workers and religious leaders, teachers and scholars of ethics have a (usually institutionally seated) power to legitimize and even enforce certain constructions of moral life. But theories freeze and reify categories and patterns of moral thinking and explanation, presenting these as "discoveries" and concealing the production and reproduction of these forms in social interactions, including the socially authorized interactions of teaching, lecturing, and theory making. Without hardier empirical inclinations and refined political sensitivities, philosophers contribute to "the processes and the preservation of systematic gender, age, class, and race divisions" embedded in their uncritical analyses.[17]

Feminist philosophers have exposed politically marked exclusions and deformations in the work of their male counterparts. Recently Marilyn Frye has flatly raised the question whether feminist moral philosophers (usually white, Western, middle-class, formally educated women) ought to be doing ethical theorizing at all. She suggests that they should not, that ethics "perhaps *should* be given up."[18] Frye speculates that the concern with doing right and being in the right that the quest for moral theory projects is something for "those people who must have a foundation for assuming the direction and administration of everything."[19] The need for an ethics, she now thinks, is "race, class and history specific," the need of those in a position to understand their agency "*as* that of judge, teacher/preacher, director, administrator, manager, and in this mode, as decision maker, planner, policy maker, organizer."[20] She notes of the history of ethics in the modern period that it "was evolved by male citizen-administrators, working in a deep historical context of patriarchy, to enable their governing."[21]

Do these more radical critiques impugn not only certain moral theories but ethics itself? I wish to argue that they do not; but my point depends crucially on separating out the project of "theory," in a very specific, historically bound sense, from a much broader project of "ethics."

II. THE IDEA OF MORAL THEORY

That contemporary philosophical ethics centers on a debate about which moral theory is right or best is a familiar fact to philosophers. Most of us were taught ethics and many now teach it with textbooks that divide ethics into theories or that examine "moral issues" by representing the ways different moral theories adjudicate them. Philosophers know what the "main" moral theories are. They are at least Kant's theory and utilitarian theory, and probably social contract theory or rights theory or Rawls's theory. When the likes of Aristotle or Hume get in, they often get in (unhappily) under the title "virtue theory." The refinement and critique of theory are staples of contemporary discussions in philosophical journals, colloquia, and many classrooms. So clear has it been for most philosophers (at least until recently[22]) that ethics is a contest among moral theories that questioning the idea of ethics as moral theory invites incomprehension. Philosophers wonder *what else* ethics might be.

Annette Baier has provided just the right distinction to get at this question. She distinguishes two senses of "moral theory." In one, a moral theory is a "fairly tightly systematic account of a fairly large area of morality with a keystone supporting all the rest."[23] This, she says, is the professionally dominant sense of the term, one that fits those examples recognized as paradigmatic (Kant and Rawls, for example, rather than Aristotle and Hume). But in another, wider sense, a moral theory might just be "an internally consistent fairly comprehensive account of what morality is and when and why it merits our acceptance and support."[24] Baier sees clearly that the constructions philosophers have learned to call "theories" are not distinguished by their *scope* (how much they cover), but rather by the *kind of organization* they would impose on the field of morality, namely, the "tightly systematic" kind. Philosophy in this century has been dominated by a quest for a moral theory not just in any old sense but in a quite particular one.

The regnant model of a moral theory in contemporary philosophy is, in brief, a *codifiable* (and usually *compact*) set of moral *formulas* (or procedure for selecting formulas) that can be applied by *any* agent to a situation to yield a justified and determinate *action-guiding* judgment. The formulas or procedure is typically seen as rules or principles at a high level of generality; application of these formulas is typically seen as something like deduction or instantiation; the formulas and their application hold good and yield the same for all agents indifferently; these formulas model what the morally competent agent does or should know, however implicitly.

This picture of *morality as a compact, impersonally action-guiding code within an agent* results from a powerfully constraining set of assumptions about what morality is. It is assumed that morality is essentially knowledge; that moral knowledge is essentially "theoretical," of an explicitly statable, highly general, and systematically unified type; and that this pure, properly moral knowledge, when brought to bear on incidental "nonmoral" information about a situation at hand, serves to tell us what to do. The emphasis on systematic generality, together with the emphasis on justified judging of what to do or what is done, entitles this model to be called a *theoretical-juridical model*. According to it, the task of moral philosophy is to render clear the pure, systematic core of properly moral knowledge by giving it expression (or rationally reconstructing it) in the right moral theory.[25]

This kind of theory, with its emphasis on the application of general formulas or procedures to determine judgment in particular cases, also involves a particular picture of the logic of moral judgment. Moral consideration presses toward abstraction; only when superfluous detail has been cleared away can cases be sorted into broad types that figure into the formulas or principles that unify the moral field. The most obvious purpose this serves is a guarantee of *uniformity* in judgment and action. This view gives priority to achieving sameness and repeatability by regimenting moral consideration into established paths. Its moral logic might aptly be called a "logic of fair administration," as it approximates the evenhanded application of set policies to all.

Already one can see that some of the feminist critiques of the substance of modern moral theories are not just about the particular versions but confront the theoretical-juridical model itself. The picture of preset generic principles autonomously and impersonally applied by oneself to oneself and others describes participants in a structured game or institution, or administrators and judges disposing of cases in accordance with policy or law. It does not fit well in contexts of personal relationship or responsive care-taking, situations that require sensitivity, flexibility, discretion, and improvisation to find precisely what responds to very particular cases. Such contexts also require awareness of histories of relationship and understandings specific to these histories, for these determine what responses between these particular people mean. Again, these theories do not fail to fit these contexts only because they are about rights, or utility, or contracts; it is because of the *kind* of account they are, namely, theoretical-juridical ones, with a distinctive logic of abstraction, generalization, and uniformity.

Querying the motives behind this logic of the underlying model brings feminist allegations of an authoritarian subtext and an ethos of managerial privilege in ethics into focus. What is such a moral logic for?

A superb case study in this respect, which I can sketch only briefly here, is Henry Sidgwick's massive and influential turn-of-the-century work *The Methods of Ethics.*[26] In it, Sidgwick self-consciously attempts to construct and defend this very model of moral theory, now so widely taken for granted that its specificity escapes notice. The work is exceptionally revealing. Sidgwick is clear from the outset that ethics is "scientific" in pursuing "systematic and precise general knowledge of what ought to be"(1) expressed in "precepts or directive rules of conduct" (3) that "admit of precise definition in a universal form" (228). But Sidgwick is also quite clear that "common sense morality," morality as we actually encounter it among "moral persons of our own age and civilisation," is not like this. Notions here are found "deficient in clearness and precision" and do not give "clear and unhesitating decisions" (215). Scientific ethics, then, seems self-consciously revisionary. If "the aim of Ethics is to systematise and free from error the apparent cognitions that most men have of the rightness or reasonableness of conduct" (77), whom, we might ask, is this revision for?

Sidgwick speaks approvingly of the use of "abstract notions" of conduct and "general rules or formulae" to settle uncertainties and discrepancies in judgment on particular cases (214), and of the value of clarity and consistency for "the perfection of practice no less than for theoretical completeness" (263). This might imply that "scientific" moral philosophy aims at improvement of commonsense moral competence. But it does not, nor does Sidgwick intend it should. Commonsense morality cannot be made scientific; Sidgwick makes a compelling case that many commonsense

virtues and values resist codification. Commonsense moral "principles" retain intuitive persuasiveness just so long as they are vague, and lose it to the
extent that they are sharpened (342). Nor do the vague and multiple principles of common sense reliably form a system, for they are "liable to come
into conflict with each other" (350), and Sidgwick stipulates it as "a fundamental postulate of Ethics" that any conflict of decision methods must be
removed by systematization (6). Yet Sidgwick is content that commonsense
precepts are "sufficiently clear" to give "practical guidance to common people in common circumstances" (361). But then, again, whom is a scientific
ethics for?

   This question is finally answered in the concluding portions of the
Methods, where Sidgwick submits his brief for utilitarianism as "the scientifically complete and systematically reflective form" of ethics, which corrects and completes the "vague instincts" of common sense (425). Sidgwick
does not for a moment think that utilitarian ethics might become the
morality of those "common people in common circumstances." Instead, in
two fascinating chapters, both titled "The Method of Utilitarianism," Sidgwick lays out a kind of strategic and tactical operating manual for a "class
of persons defined by exceptional qualities of intellect, temperament, or
character" (489) whose burden it is to *covertly* deploy this rigorously systematic moral theory for the public weal under the "actual condition of
civilized communities, in which there are so many different degrees of intellectual and moral development" (490). Sidgwick intends this kind of
moral theory as a management tool; it models modern bureaucratic control through rule-bound regimentation. He concludes with the disconcertingly calm observation that "a sincere Utilitarian, therefore, is likely to
be an eager politician" (495).[27]

   This alarming idea of an esoteric morality for a powerful elite charged
with managing the good of the many is not a new one, of course. Its most
famous philosophical predecessor is probably its oldest, Plato's *Republic*. Plato
envisioned the creation of the just society as a bottom-up work of intensive
early education and a stratification of groups based on a publicly disseminated mythology of natural superiority or inferiority. Sidgwick's vision is
that of a top-down form of covert, strategic control. Not myth and *paideia*
but management by utilitarian objective, through theory-based but covert
moral administration, is Sidgwick's idea. I don't say which is worse or better; differences of several kinds between these views beg for closer examination. Sidgwick's, however, seems cast in a peculiarly modern mold of bureaucratic authoritarianism, securing reliability by apparently universal
rule-bound regimentation that bypasses discretion or interaction. This

maintains the appearance of equality procedurally while deliberately obscuring the critical social fact that only some are in positions of making and enforcing rules that may not or do not apply to themselves.

I offer this quick sketch of Sidgwick not as an argument but as a suggestive example of the suspicious convergence of a certain model of moral theory and a distinctly modern disciplinary perspective and managerial outlook. I think it not accidental that the picture of "two levels" of morality applied by one agent—one the direct, intuitive, or naive moral point of view; the other, the indirect, critical, or sophisticated point of view—continues to be rehearsed over and over in *contemporary* defenses of utilitarian and Kantian (i.e., modern moral) views.[28] The older distinction between the moral cognoscenti and their deliberately unenlightened field operatives now seems to have been transposed into a benign split-level moral psychology: moral command central within the agent (the critical or sophisticated view) is distinguished from frontline incidental contact (the naive or intuitive view) that must report back to it.

But has a politically innocent split-level psychology simply replaced an unsavory authoritarian hierarchy? R. M. Hare, eminent contemporary moral philosopher, pictures moral judgments as justified only at a higher, "critical" level of thinking that we achieve only "to the extent that we manage to think like archangels"—like, in other words, those creatures in the Sidgwickian vision defined by "exceptional qualities of intellect, temperament, or character."[29] Hare counsels that the way to ensure "the greatest possible conformity" to what our (imagined) betters would (correctly) have us do is to "try to implant in ourselves and in others whom we influence a set of dispositions, motivations, intuitions, prima facie principles . . . which will have this effect."[30] This unpleasant fusion of images of the superior moral caste, internalized remote control, and manipulative influence should give us pause. So too should we hesitate over John Rawls's suggestion that it "is to be expected" that theoretical accounting of "our sense of justice" will not only involve "principles and theoretical constructions which go much beyond" the standards of everyday life, but "may eventually require fairly sophisticated mathematics as well."[31] We are properly brought again to the question, for what and for whom are such moral theories? Which interests do they serve, and what do they enable doing?

These historical and contemporary examples suggest to me prima facie grounds to explore links between the ascendancy of the theoretical-juridical model of ethics and certain features of modernization: the extended political enfranchisement of white European males, emergence of a production-oriented market economy, colonialism, industrialization, and increasing bureaucratic centralization of political, educational, medical, and other social authorities. A key dymanic of the modern era, as Sandra Harding points out in a provocative paper on "feminine" and "African" moral views, is "the transfer of the conceptualization and control" of bodies, sexuality, labor, and the practical activities of many others to white European privileged males.[32] Whatever relations may obtain in general between privilege, authority, and theory in ethics (and elsewhere), feminist critique of ethics targets something disturbing about theories of a *certain historically specific kind*, modern theories that seem (intentionally or not) to model hierarchical and bureaucratic structures of administrative control.

Does this imply that ethics as simply "a fairly comprehensive account of what morality is"—Baier's second sense of "theory"— is a tainted aspiration? It might, if such an account could only take the theoretical-juridical form. But surely this is not the only form an ethics can take. What follows is my sketch of another.

III. ANOTHER CONCEPTION OF ETHICS

The theoretical-juridical model pictures morality as an individually action-guiding theoretical system within persons. The *expressive-collaborative* conception of ethics (as I'll call it) pictures morality as a socially embodied medium of mutual understanding and adjustment between persons in certain terms, particularly those that define those persons' identities, relationships, and values.[33] The resources of this medium of moral negotiation include shared moral vocabularies, common exemplars, familiar intuitions, and those deliberative styles recognized in some community. These starting points are renewable resources for the continuing construction and definition of social life. Yet they, their authorship, and their continuing acceptability are also contestable within the very processes they frame. On this view, moral problems are not cases to be closed by authoritative verdicts but conspicuous nodal points in histories of attempted mutual adjustment and understanding, both of each other and of the terms of our accountability to each other.

Stanley Cavell suggests that the point of moral assessment, argument, or deliberation is not simply to determine what to do but "to determine *what* position you are taking, that is to say, *what position you are taking responsibility for*—and whether it is one I can respect . . . whether, or to what extent, we are to live in the same moral universe."[34] What makes moral argument rational, then, is "not the assumption that there is in every situation one thing which ought to be done and that this may be known, nor the assumption that we can always come to agreement about what ought to be done on the basis of rational methods," but rather "following the methods which lead to a knowledge of our own position, of where we stand; in short, to a knowledge and definition of ourselves."[35]

The kind of progressive and mutual moral accounting Cavell describes will in fact be a cultural practice already there that we learn from others. We come to any situation of moral assessment with moral concepts, maxims, deliberative strategies and intuitive convictions to some extent given and always shared (even if incompletely) with some others. So too we come with sensibilities, emotional responses, senses of relevance and seriousness invited and shaped by a history of interactions.[36] Not all of these aspects of our moral repertoires are capable of explicit definition or exhaustive statement. Their history and meaning is part of some personal and political environment, and our understanding of them is shaped by our places in that.

They are starting points for a continuing and sometimes hazardous process of revealing and defining ourselves to ourselves and to each other in terms of what we care about, what our responsibilities are, what our commitments and relationships mean. In this way we determine, together and alone, not only what to do but what and how and with whom to be, and how to think about it in ways that can be shared. At the same time, we determine dimensions of criticism and liabilities to blame, what we will "stand for" in both senses of the phrase. There is a presumption in this constant reweaving of the interpersonal fabric that we need to account to others and will try to go on. But this presumption may be defeated in specific cases if we come to lack enough of common, mutually acceptable moral terms or fail to find them with certain others in the first place. That too can be a case of moral understanding, and not always the worst case. More often we will have common terms at our disposal with some or many others, for there are no private moral languages any more than there are others.

Emphasizing that moral deliberation is situated in a particular setting imbued with acquired traditions and terms and trainings foregrounds questions about where these come from and what (or whose) authority and experiences they represent. This view thus supports what Bernard Williams calls the aspiration toward "transparency": that the workings of a society's "ethical institutions should not depend on members of the community misunderstanding how they work."[37] In Sabina Lovibond's broader but nuanced formulation, "a community whose members understood their own form of life and yet were not embarrassed by it" would enable its members to "participate ingenuously, while retaining [their] awareness of it as a specific historical formation."[38]

We might call the moral logic of this alternative conception a "logic of interpersonal acknowledgement."[39] Because persons and their relationships are not uniform and situations are not necessarily repeatable, moral consideration on this view presses toward enrichment of detail and amplification of specific context. Because the moral negotiation of our lives is a continuous process with the coherence of our lives and values at stake, we map fresh situations onto past understandings, or mark their differences, by exploring analogies. We imagine and evaluate possible continuations or revisions of how we go on through narratives of several types: of our own and others' identities, of the nature and significance of our relationships, or of the implications of our commitments, exemplars, and values. These elaborations through *analogy* and *narrative* establish the particularity as well as certain continuities of moral actors and situations. They provide for *flexibility*, rather than uniformity, in adapting existing values and honoring standing commitments. They require, especially when constructed in actual dialogue, sensitivity to alternatives, presuppositions, and ambiguities.

Such a constructive process of moral understanding draws on a variety of perceptive, discursive, and communicative skills, as well as patterns of emotional response.[40] Linked capacities to attend, describe, inquire relevantly, feel appropriately, and respond reliably to situations of a certain kind are the sorts of complex dispositions usually called "virtues." This view calls for close examination of virtues tracing their roots and branches in the specific forms of moral life that sustain and require them. This examination should enhance the transparency and question the habitability of these forms of life from varied points of view within and outside them. It should emphasize that virtues are complex *interpersonal* skills, ones that fit us to appreciate, negotiate, and fulfill our moral positions toward and with others. On this view, the "reflective equilibrium"[41] that counts is one sought *between people* as well as within them, one that is created in shared moral understandings and that creates mutual moral intelligibility.[42]

Morality is thus a medium for bringing our given moral resources to bear in determining how to go on, whether by repetition, reinterpretation, or renovation. Some moral terms already set may render some of us mute, our positions incoherent or inexpressible, our standing as moral agents unauthorized or compromised (as feminist ethics has shown in the case of women and the Western philosophical tradition of ethics). These moral terms may then be contested by appeal to (or invention of) some others. Common moral life is thus renewed or re-created in concrete moral interactions, between individuals or over time in whole communities. Moral philosophy is thus an ongoing description of, and critical reflection on, this

very complex human form of life in its general dimensions as well as its local varieties. It is also a part of it.

IV. ETHICS, POLITICS, AND AUTHORITY

I've claimed here that two distinct strands of feminist ethical critique converge on a common problem with twentieth-century ethics, a certain
defining conception of morality and its allied notion of moral theory. Feminist critique of the content of favored kinds of modern moral theories—
neo-Kantian, contractarian, utilitarian—is in fact homing in on a model
shared by these seemingly very diverse views. At the same time, this shared
theoretical-juridical model of ethics really does seem to code an authoritarian subtext (a presumed top-down model of uniformly administered
policies that can be given either a social or a psychological rendering) that
other feminist critics have argued (I believe mistakenly) might be a politically unsavory feature of ethics itself. My suggestion is that we need new
ethics but not another theory in the theoretical-juridical sense, and that another conception of ethics might unload, or even be an intellectual defense
against, a kind of ethics that models hierarchical control.

   We need ethics because, as I suppose many feminists believe, we need
both constructive and critical ways of thinking about political legitimacy,
social values, and individual and collective responsibilities. But the more
radical body of feminist critique reminds us that the ethics we need must be
a deeply *reflexive* kind of ethics, set to recognize and interrogate its own social impact and intellectual authority. That is, it must look at the ways it itself is a discursive practice that vies or collaborates with others to affirm or
construct certain views of the moral field, and at the ways its practitioners
are a privileged and by no means representative group of people who must
take care concerning the social realities reflected in the accounts they offer
as well as the motives with which they offer them. Addelson is right, I think,
to insist on "proper political and empirical sensitivities," including those that
search out and examine "silences and secrets."[43]

   This goes against the deep and professionally required passion for
"pure practical reason." I mean by this not just an idea of Kant's but also the
more widely shared belief in some pure core of ahistorically true, properly
moral knowledge that largely (or entirely) reflective thought might reveal
and a theory of a certain type might articulate. Baier's suggestion that
"philosophers need to work with anthropologists, sociologists, sociobiolo-
gists, psychologists, to find out what an actual morality is; we need to read

history to find out how it has changed itself, to read novels to see how it might change again" is not a reminder of something moral philosophers just haven't happened to do.[44] It is a challenge to the purity of proper moral knowledge, and to a reflective method that always reflects some kind—but *just* some kind—of experience.

Distinctive to feminist ethics has been a particular emphasis on expressive and relational aspects of specific moral interactions, and a commitment to interrogating the politics of representation involved in philosophers' or others' theorizing ethics, as in other areas. The expressive-collaborative conception I advance joins these in placing all moral thinking in the context of interpersonal recognition and negotiation; this includes the moral thinking of moral philosophers. While *no* kind of moral theory can itself guarantee that its conception of morality cannot function ideologically in exclusive and oppressive ways, moral philosophy on this conception necessarily poses to itself the reflexive questions of privilege and authority just mentioned. Philosophers' own parts in the active reduplication or fabrication of moral life are put on view, situated, and put up for examination and critique.

I don't pretend that this alternative conception is not itself radically situated. It may reflect preoccupations of certain women as philosophers and feminists with breaking silence, talking, and talking back; larger late twentieth-century trends like the prevalence of information-flow models; postmodern fascination with discourse, text, and narrative; and perhaps the author's own obsessions with interpersonal illusions and missed or miscarried communications. This alternative is offered as one way in which ethics might go on for a while with more vitality and less bad conscience.[45]

NOTES

1. A few anthologies that sample these currents are *Women and Moral Theory*, ed. Eva Feder Kittay and Diana T. Meyers (Totowa, N.J.: Rowman & Littlefield, 1987); *Science, Morality and Feminist Theory*, ed. Marsha Hanen and Kai Nielsen (Calgary: University of Calgary Press, 1987); *Feminist Perspectives: Philosophical Essays on Method and Morals*, ed. Lorraine Code, Sheila Mullett, and Christine Overall (Toronto: University of Toronto Press, 1988); and *Explorations in Feminist Ethics: Theory and Practice*, ed. Eve Browning Cole and Susan Coultrap-McQuinn (Bloomington: Indiana University Press, 1992). Additional references are provided in the text and notes.

2. Carol Gilligan, *In a Different Voice* (Cambridge: Harvard University Press, 1982).

3. Most feminist critique has focused on these characteristically modern styles of moral theory. Feminist ethicists have not turned as much attention to the revival of classical virtue ethics. Perhaps some feminists dismiss out of hand the vi-

ability of premodern conceptions or their suitability to feminist purposes. On the other hand, feminist notions of responsiveness and attention to the particular reveal a kinship with ideas of moral judgement more at home with Artistotelian than Kantian ethics. Given my concern here with a conception of moral theory that is the standard *modern* (and contemporary) one, I don't explore the useful points of contact between feminist ethics and virtue ethics.

4. See Annette Baier, "Trust and Anti-Trust," *Ethics* 96 (1986): 231–60, and "The Need for More than Justice," in *Science, Morality and Feminist Theory*; Caroline Whitbeck, "A Different Reality: Feminist Ontology," in *Beyond Domination*, ed. Carol C. Gould (Totowa, N.J.: Rowman & Allanheld, 1983); Virginia Held, "Feminism and Moral Theory," in *Women and Moral Theory*, and "Non-contractual Society," in *Science, Morality and Feminist Theory*.

5. Gilligan, *In a Different Voice*, 17.

6. Nel Noddings, *Caring: A Feminine Approach to Ethics and Moral Education* (Berkeley: University of California Press, 1984), 36–37; Gilligan, *In a Different Voice*, 32–38.

7. Iris M. Young, "Impartiality and the Civic Public," in *Feminism as Critique*, ed. Seyla Benhabib and Drucilla Cornell (Minneapolis: University of Minnesota Press, 1987), 61–62.

8. Annette Baier, "The Need for More than Justice," 45.

9. Sara Ruddick, "Remarks on the Sexual Politics of Reason," in *Women and Moral Theory*, 238.

10. Kathryn Morgan, "Women and Moral Madness," in *Science, Morality and Feminist Theory*, 220.

11. Annette Baier, "What Do Women Want in a Moral Theory?" *Nous* 19 (1985): 53–63, and "Trust and Anti-Trust"; Whitbeck, "A Different Reality"; Noddings, *Caring*; and Held, "Feminism and Moral Theory."

12. Maria Lugones and Elizabeth Spelman, "Have We Got a Theory for You! Feminist Theory, Cultural Imperialism, and the Demand for 'the Woman's Voice,'" *Hypatia* 6 (1983): 573–81, esp. 574.

13. Lugones and Spelman, "Have We Got a Theory," 576.

14. Lugones and Spelman, "Have We Got a Theory," 574, 577.

15. Lugones and Spelman, "Have We Got a Theory," 579. (Helen Longino is quoted by Lugones and Spelman without citation.)

16. Kathryn Addelson, "Moral Passages," in *Women and Moral Theory*, 105.

17. Addelson, "Moral Passages," 105.

18. Marilyn Frye, "A Response to *Lesbian Ethics*," *Hypatia* (1990): 132–37, esp. 133.

19. Frye, "A Response," 135.

20. Frye, "A Response," 133–34.

21. Frye, "A Response," 136–37.

22. In the last two decades, attacks on dominant modern moral theories, or even on the project of moral theory itself, have come from diverse philosophical

standpoints that have nothing to do with feminism: pragmatists and Aristotelians, communitarians and casuists, Marxists and historicists, advocates of personal integrity and partiality. Selections in *Anti-Theory in Ethics and Moral Conservatism*, ed. Stanley Clarke and Evan Simpson (Albany: State University of New York Press, 1989), exemplify some of these trends.

23. Baier, "What Do Women Want in a Moral Theory?" 55.

24. Baier, "What Do Women Want in a Moral Theory?" 54.

25. The impact of the Newtonian paradigm of scientific theory on the conception of moral knowledge and its theory is an important part of the historical story I don't attempt to deal with here. Two good critiques of the scientific analogue and the way it is understood are found in Cheryl Noble, "Normative Ethical Theories," in *Anti-Theory in Ethics and Moral Conservatism*, and Stanley Cavell, *The Claim of Reason* (Oxford: Oxford University Press, 1979).

26. Henry Sidgwick, *The Methods of Ethics* [1907] (Indianapolis: Hackett Publishing, 1981); all page references hereafter in text to this edition. Albert Jonsen and Stephen Toulmin in *The Abuse of Casuistry* (Berkeley: University of California Press, 1988), note that Sidgwick's succession of William Whewell to the Knightsbridge Professorship of Moral Philosophy in fact represented a signal methodological shift as well: from Whewell's piecemeal, casuistical case method and discussion of various different duties to Sidgwick's systematizing theoretical project.

27. See chapter 6 of Bernard Williams, *Ethics and the Limits of Philosophy* (Cambridge: Harvard University Press, 1985), for an illuminating discussion of this.

28. See, for example, R. M. Hare, *Moral Thinking* (Oxford: Clarendon Press, 1981); Peter Railton, "Alienation, Consequentialism, and the Demands of Morality," in *Consequentialism and Its Critics*, ed. Samuel Scheffler (New York: Oxford University Press, 1988); David Brink, "Utilitarianism and the Personal Point of View," *Journal of Philosophy* 83 (1986): 417–38; Thomas Hill, "The Importance of Autonomy," in *Women and Moral Theory*; and Marcia Baron, "Impartiality and Friendship," *Ethics* 101 (1991): 836–57. The contemporary literature on autonomy (a concept linked historically and conceptually to this "covering-law" picture of morality) is also deeply impressed with split-level models of moral psychology. In a variety of accounts well known in this literature, one superior, authoritative part of a person is supposed to superintend or control or give the law to some other lower-order or troublesome part. On these views, good order within the self is some sort of hierarchical order. See Diana Meyers, *Self, Society, and Personal Choice* (New York: Columbia University Press, 1989), part 2, section 1, for a brief, clear summary and critique of such accounts.

29. Hare, *Moral Thinking*, 46–47.

30. Hare, *Moral Thinking*, 47.

31. John Rawls, *A Theory of Justice* (Cambridge: Harvard University Press, 1971), 47.

32. Sandra Harding, "The Curious Coincidence of Feminine and African Moralities," in *Women and Moral Theory*, 309.

33. Aspects of this different view of ethics may be found in otherwise remarkably different philosophical sources. My own debts in this regard are to Stanley Cavell, to the contemporary revival of Aristotelianism, to Sabina Lovibond's nonreactionary exploration of communitarianism, and to the continuing dialogue of feminist moral philosophy.

34. Cavell, *The Claim of Reason*, 268.

35. Cavell, *The Claim of Reason*, 312.

36. On this see especially Annette Baier, "Theory and Reflective Practices" in *Postures of the Mind* (Minneapolis: University of Minnesota Press, 1985) and "Extending the Limits of Moral Theory," *Journal of Philosophy* 83, no. 10 (1986): 538–45, but also Caroline Whitbeck, "A Different Reality: Feminist Ontology," in *Beyond Domination*.

37. Bernard Williams, *Ethics and the Limits of Philosophy*, 101.

38. Sabina Lovibond, in *Realism and Imagination in Ethics* (Minneapolis: University of Minnesota Press, 1983), 158. Lovibond develops a version of moral realism anchored in the language and traditions of particular communities; her treatment of questions about authority and acceptance that arise from this is extremely valuable. See also Cheshire Calhoun, "Justice, Care, Gender Bias," *Journal of Philosophy* 85 (1988): 451–63, for discussion of moral ideology, and the author's discussion of moral rhetorics, in Margaret Walker, "Partial Consideration," *Ethics* 101 (1991): 758–74, reprinted as chapter 3, above.

39. I borrow the term "acknowledgment" from Cavell, *The Claim of Reason*.

40. See Walker, "Moral Understandings: Alternative 'Epistemology' for a Feminist Ethics," *Hypatia* 4 (1989): 15–28.

41. This is, of course, John Rawls's famous term, referring to the goal of bringing well-considered moral judgements into harmony with those general principles that are "the premises of their derivation," *A Theory of Justice*, 20. For Rawls, this is a method of moral theory construction.

42. Martha Nussbaum's work on virtue revives Aristotelian themes within a sensibility both contemporary and interpersonal in the sense just described. See Nussbaum, *The Fragility of Goodness* (Cambridge: Cambridge University Press, 1986), and *Love's Knowledge* (Oxford: Oxford University Press, 1990).

43. Kathryn Addelson, "Moral Passages," in *Women and Moral Theory*, 106.

44. Annette Baier, "Theory and Reflective Practices," 224.

45. Earlier versions of this paper were presented to the Society for Women in Philosophy at the American Philosophical Association Eastern Division Meeting in Boston, December 1990; to a conference commemorating the centennial of the Institute of Philosophy at the University of Leuven, Belgium, in May 1991; and to an NEH Summer Institute on Ethics and the Liberal Arts at Bethany College, West Virginia, in July 1991. I thank those audiences for their comments and also thank Thomas G. Slaughter, Diana Meyers, Cheshire Calhoun, Milton Fisk, and anonymous *Hypatia* referees for helpful comments on earlier readings and drafts.

7

SEEING POWER IN MORALITY:
A PROPOSAL FOR FEMINIST
NATURALISM IN ETHICS

It is often said that the opposition of morality to power is virtually coextensive with canonical Western moral thought. It is supposedly installed as a founding distinction in the dialogues of Plato, where Socrates more than once defeats the view that justice is the advantage of the stronger. But this is not quite right. Socrates opposes not "power" but brute force and the unbridled exercise of rapacious desire upon or in spite of others. Indeed, in Plato's *Republic* the ideal state Socrates envisions can only achieve a true moral order in this world through detailed and extensive coordination of coercive, controlling, and productive powers of several types.

The Platonic root of canonical Western moral theory is really something else: the conviction that morality "itself" is something ideal. Plato's Socrates sees any imperfect, power-dependent worldly realization of moral order as an unstable and shadowy semblance of something itself fully real, true, perfect, and unchanging, not within the plane of ordinary human existence or within the range of those cognitive powers through which we know things of the ordinary world. This Platonic legacy of the *ideality* or *transcendent nature* of morality still reigns. Through most of the canonized Western tradition moral theory has consistently been done as if morality were ideal, and most philosophers today continue to make theory about morality as if it were effectively ideal, even if they do not literally believe that—that is, they treat it is a subject matter largely independent of empirical information about the real histories and contingencies of human relations in society. This legacy underlies many philosophers' boredom with or contempt for too much interest in how human beings actually live and what it has been or is like for them—each of them—to live that way. They think there is little to be learned from what is about what ought to be.

The ideality of morality has enjoyed many formulations: a vision of The Good, a divine command, an unchanging natural moral law, an intuition of non-natural properties, the transcendental logic of pure practical reason, the logic of moral language, the necessary conditions of agency as such, the pragmatic transcendental presuppositions of the ideal speech situation, or what certain imagined beings would have to endorse in certain imagined situations where they mostly cannot know things about actual human beings in actual situations. I do not see strong prospects for any longer defending the view of morality as truly ideal or transcendent. Yet many feminist philosophers, too, share in the tradition that sees the ideality of morality as both inspiring and protective.

A continuing fear is that if morality is too much a matter of what is, and who has the power to make it so, then those without or with less power are left without moral appeal. This fear has real basis: Power unconstrained by moral compunction and unanswerable in fact to standards with moral authority is always something to be feared—and not only by the weakest. But it is a mistake to think that a naturalistic and power-sensitive view of morality itself must "reduce" morality to power or make morality disappear in favor of power. Instead, it should be an instrument for testing the legitimacy of powers that claim moral justification. Still, there is the philosopher's wish, in feminist philosophy serving a political vision, to stand on moral ground that cannot shift. I do not believe the desire for apodictically secured foundations for morality can be satisfied. That is not, however, some problem about the infirmity of morality. In a postfoundationalist era, it is only to say our moral grounds cannot be better, epistemically, than the others that anchor our understanding of the world.

There is an alternative to the idealism of a transcendent view, on the one hand, and on the other, the normative emptiness of a view that rejects morality wholesale in favor of "amoral contests about the just and the good in which truth is always grasped as coterminous with power, always already power, as the voice of power."[1] I cannot defend an entire view of morality here, but I make a proposal for an empirically obligated and politically emancipatory naturalism in ethics that sees the ineliminable roles of power in morality "itself."[2]

MORALITY OF POWER, MORALITY IN POWER

Feminist ethics is inevitably, and fundamentally, a discourse about morality and power. The most obvious way feminist ethics and politics connect morality and power is in examining the morality of specific distributions and exercises of power. Feminism's traditional critique challenges morally the coercive, arbitrary, cruel, and oppressive powers of men over women in many systems of gender. Feminism claims for women on moral grounds economic, political, social, sexual, epistemic, discursive, and symbolic powers denied them by individual, institutional, and cultural male dominance. Feminism must also oppose domination structured by hierarchies or exclusions of class, race, sexuality, age, and ability, for these always partly organize gender even as they are themselves realized in part through specific organizations of gender. To acknowledge this obligation is not, however, to have in hand either the theoretical or political strategies necessary to fulfill it.

Feminist moral theory also continues to produce unprecedented theoretical understandings of the moral meaning of relations of unequal power, especially asymmetric relations of dependency as well as interdependencies that do not even approximate reciprocal exchanges. This theorization of the morality of unequal power, of "power-over," "responsibility-for," "depending-upon," and "trusting-to," reaches to the roots of our conceptualization of human beings as moral beings and requires us to see our moral being in terms of varied relations, both symmetrical and asymmetrical, immediate and highly mediated, to others. The full impact of this reconception on ethical theory and practice is still at the edge of imagination; it remains unclear whether or in what versions some familiar moral and political conceptions can meet the realities of human society as a scene of inescapable connection, dependence, vulnerability, and entrustment.

Feminism's insistent re-examinations of morality and power on these fronts are connected by the need to explore likenesses and differences between legitimate and illegitimate powers, their conditions, and their effects in relations of many kinds. Socially enforced dominance must do quite a lot of things to and with people to make coerced vulnerabilities appear as inevitable ones. Feminist, race, culture, and postcolonial theory continue to reveal this. We cannot distinguish inevitable vulnerabilities and dependencies from manipulated ones until we understand both the manipulated ones in all their subtle and overt varieties, and the inevitable ones from the viewpoints of both those who are vulnerable *and* those who respond to them, as care, ageism, and disability theories show. Works of lesbians, gay men, transsexuals, and sex workers on constructions of sexuality and their implications for identity, citizenship, and family dissect the powers of modern institutions and expert discourses to naturalize norms and to moralize what is natural only for some.

To understand the moral necessity, arbitrariness, or catastrophe of giving some people powers over others or of reserving certain powers for some people rather than others, it seems we need the whole manifold of objects of comparison: people in relations of reciprocal risk and trust; people positioned higher or lower by socially enforced hierarchies of power and privilege, whether legitimately or not; those variously less physically able than most others; the immature and the less mature; the cognitively or socially limited or incompetent; those inescapably or radically dependent. Ours then becomes a question of moral terms for the equivalent political and social membership, the essential material and personal support, and the dignifying care, participation, governance, and representation *of all of us.* It is not clear to me that this question has ever really been set before in the 2,500-year history of the canonical, and usually ostensibly "universalist," Western tradition. Feminist thought has played a crucial role in formulating and pressing this question, showing how tirelessly one must think through ethical problems posed by many relationships and exercises of power.

I suggest now that these mutually deepening insights about the morality of power be joined to another kind of view about the powers of and for morality. This is a naturalist view on which morality "itself" is *a disposition of powers through an arrangement of responsibilities.* In this view the very existence of morality requires many social powers. Powers to control, educate, and influence are required to cultivate and foster senses of responsibility. Powers to govern, persuade, inspire, reward, recruit, and punish are necessary to impose and enforce distributions of responsibility, norms for who may do what to whom, and who must do what for whom, and whose business anyone's welfare or behavior is. Powers to give or pay, to speak, silence, or credit speaking, to rule and punish, to represent, ritualize, and memorialize are needed to nourish relations of responsibility materially, discursively, legally, and symbolically.

But social orders require as well the sustenance of distinctively moral powers: the powers of morality when embodied in the self-understandings of agents and in the structure of discourses and institutions. Even as moral understandings are carried by social arrangements they imbue these arrangements with (ideally) mutually understood importance and depth. Moral understandings thus create meaning for us in reproducing our social arrangements, and sustain pride, gratitude, and trust among us in doing so. They mobilize resentment toward, and shame in, those who deny or undermine them. Where moral understandings command our confidence, they move us in trust and hope to continue or adopt a certain way of living, and we invoke them to move others to do so with us. Social arrangements, limited and enabled by many powers, give body to morality in the world. Morality in turn disciplines many natural human powers of self-direction, expression, attention, reason, feeling, imagination, and mutual responsiveness—in service of a shared way of life whose authority inheres in being understood always as more than *simply* that.

The central point of this view is that morality is *not socially modular*. Morality is neither a dimension of reality beyond or separate from shared life nor a distinct and detachable set of understandings within it. Our moral practices are not extricable from other social ones. Moral practices in particular lifeways are entirely enmeshed with other social practices; and moral identities with social roles and positions. Moral understandings are effected through social arrangements, while all important social arrangements include moral practices as working parts. Moral concepts and judgments are an integral part, but only one part, of practices that attempt to organize feelings, behavior, and judgment in ways that keep people's expectations in rough equilibrium.

This has implications for moral philosophy. In moral theory we abstract moral ideas from social practice, imaginatively varying, simplifying, or idealizing them. This is unavoidable but leaves questions about how the social provenance of ideas shapes what they can mean, and whether novel applications we imagine for them can be achieved, and at what costs. None of us can access by pure reflection necessary moral precepts or pure moral concepts that are not in fact derived from our socially situated experiences of actual forms of social life or our socially constrained imagination of others. If there were a fund of purely moral knowledge accessible to some kind of purely reflective inquiry, then we could do this. But there could be such a fund of purely moral knowledge only if morality completely transcended history and culture, if it were, once again, something *ideal or transcendent*. To speak of morality as a disposition of powers through an arrangement of responsibilities is to say that morality is not like this. Morality is not a norm that either exists independently of human activity and judgment or that remains invariant because it is in no way a function of changes in the course of the histories of human beings in societies. This means that philosophers must ask themselves upon what socially cultured experience of morality they draw in making claims about "morality itself;" or about the presuppositions of being a "person" or an "agent"; or about the intuitions, sense of justice, or concept of responsibility they claim is "ours." It also means that philosophers need to investigate whether and how moral views can be seated in and sustained by actual social arrangements. What disposition of powers do moral views assume and effect, at whose service or expense, with what methods of recruitment and enforcement, and through what ecologies of feeling and attitude? Finally, philosophers will have to acknowledge that many types of empirical information are necessary in investigating the possibility and justifiability of forms of moral life.

No other kind of moral philosophy has explored these issues as persistently and with as profound results as has feminist ethics. A lot of moral philosophy does not explore them at all. My proposal is that feminist and other politically emancipatory ethics adopt the methodological framework that makes sense of this theoretical practice, what I am calling a "naturalistic" one.

WHAT KIND OF NATURALISM?

'Naturalism' is a protean and loaded term that sparks suspicions and resistance of several kinds. '*Naturalism*' may suggest a commitment to natural kinds or natural essences; a presumption in favor of scientific knowledge or a scientific basis for morality; an essentially descriptive and explanatory enterprise that will miss the "normative" character of morality and the critical character of moral philosophy. None of this is what I mean by "naturalism."

I mean by it that morality is a naturally occurring structure of all human social groups. It recruits and produces many powers to shape interpersonal response and self-direction around shared understandings that guide judgment, action, and expectation. Moral theory needs to study this structure in its various forms but also to grasp the characteristic way this kind of structure presents itself to its participants. To investigate how the patterning that constitutes moral relations has the kinds of force and meaning that it does is to ask: What are some distinctive aspects of people's grasp of their social relations that make those relations *moral* ones, that give them the kinds of *authority* that we associate with morality? Moral theory has to use this descriptive and explanatory understanding of the specifically *moral authority of morality* in turn to take up its normative critical task: to investigate whether specific moral arrangements are what they must present themselves to be to have this force and meaning. The descriptive and analytical work constructs a working model of what moral relations are like that can guide the normative inquiry. The normative inquiry, testing how supposedly moral arrangements may or may not turn out to be what their authority requires, in turn refines the model: It reveals more about the ways the various working parts of social arrangements and self-understandings must either pull together or be kept safely apart for a social-moral order to roll (or lurch) on.

My own analytical model of morality is that moral structure shows itself in practices of responsibility. The practices implement and enforce understandings of who may do what to whom, who must do what for whom, and to whom various ones of us have to account. This model directs us to look very closely at how these practices construct and circulate understandings of people's identities, their relations to others (or lack thereof), and commonly intelligible values that sustain a given distribution of responsibilities. Actual attention to our own and others' moral cultures reveals that typically there are different responsibilities assigned to or withheld from different groups of people within the same society. In fact, the differences between groups are defined in important part by the forms and limits of agency these distributions of responsibility impute to them. Practices of responsibility show what is valued (at least by those with most power to define the practices) as well as who is valued by whom for what.

But moral practices are ways of going on together that claim something more for themselves than the inertia of habit and tradition, which are already crumbling as soon as their adherents see them as exactly and *only* that. And moral practices claim something quite other for their specific kind of power over us than main force, coercive threat, or manipulation. At the core of any moral-social order there must be trust that certain basic understandings are common, that the common understandings are the operative ones shaping shared life, and that these operative understandings constitute a way of life that is not only "how we live" but also "how to live," a way worthy of people's allegiance, effort, restraint, or sacrifice. Without this, they really are just ways some people can make others behave.

The "normativity" of morality—the specifically moral authority of morality, whatever powers hold its practices in place—does not descend from someplace outside all human judgment; it inheres in the durability of our understandings and the trust they support under the right kind of tests. The relevant tests are those that reassure us that we do understand how we live and that how we live is indeed worthy, considered in its own conditions and effects or considered in comparison to some other way. So, the tests must tap the experiences and understandings of those who live the lifeway under test. If our way of life in reality betrays our shared understandings, or if these understandings turn out to be driven by deception, manipulation, coercion, or violence directed at some of us by others, where all are nonetheless supposed to "share" in this purported vision of the good, then our trust is not sustained and our practices lose their *moral* authority, whatever other powers continue to hold them in place. They become then nothing more than habits or customs, ways we live that are no longer credible or trustworthy as "how to live." Substantial parts of moral-social orders commonly fail to be credible to, or trustworthy for, many participants who are less valued, protected, or rewarded than others in their orders' differential distributions of responsibility.

This "transparency testing" is both a tool of normative philosophical critique and an actual social process that may be relatively inchoate and undirected or politically accentuated and mobilized.[3] Yet moral understandings in life or philosophy are only ever tested for their worthiness in light of some moral standards or other. We always stand on some moral values as we consider the authority of others; sometimes we stand on certain applications of a moral standard to contest other applications of the same one. This only means that, with respect to moral beliefs, we are not in a different situation than is now widely acknowledged for other empirical beliefs: We are always in the position of using some of what we know to discover whether, and how, we know anything else. So it is for moral knowledge: We never get completely behind or beneath all moral beliefs. And any moral standards we apply in testing others are realized in or abstracted from human practices, discourses, and institutions that are themselves configured and reproduced by power. We cannot get behind or under the powers for and of morality, either.

In this view there is no standpoint completely transcendent to and neutral between all forms of social practice and the conceptions of value and responsibilities they implement. But this does not mean we "lose" the essential dimension of normativity. It means that we never get outside of it, but are never done with reconfirming it, by testing the actual social conditions and effects of the moral practices that claim our trust. Testing the moral authority of our practices means discovering how they actually go, what they actually mean, and what it is actually like to live them from particular places within them. It means examining the power-bound social arrangements which necessarily embody morality. The moral authority of these arrangements, however, is in no way reducible to the fact of their existence.

Scientific knowledge enjoys no hegemony nor even privilege in this critical project. It is one source of our understanding of some features of how we live, but does not trump historical, ethnographic, hermeneutic, cultural, political, and critical studies of lived experience and its meanings; nor can it replace the mutually situating testimonies of all those whose experience of a way of life bears on its claims to authority. Attention to variety in moral practices and appreciation of how they work for people placed variously within them tend to undermine rather than support essentialist generalizations about *how* beings must live to *be* human ones. These studies lead us to explore instead the intricate social architectures that produce specific understandings of ourselves as human beings. This naturalism installs precisely an open-ended and open-minded need to *look and see* how moral ideas materialize in social practices that then constrain at a given time what these moral ideas mean.

A feminist naturalism finds it both too soon and too late for ideal theory. It is too late to turn back from some things we know. We know that past and existing practices of responsibility have encoded oppressive and demeaning social hierarchies covered by deceptively inclusive-sounding ideas like "the good life for man" or "the kingdom of ends" or "our sense of justice." Yet it is too soon to rest confident in what little we know. We may not fully grasp the material conditions and practical constraints under which moral theories and ideals can achieve the emancipatory applications *for all of us* that many of us desire.

RECONSIDERING MODERN UNIVERSALISM

I want to use an example, very briefly, of one such uncertain place to which we are delivered by parallel efforts of feminist theory and critical race theory. Insistently tracking the real intrication of morality and power, feminist and race theory have established a deeply unsettling assessment of one of the most powerful paradigms of modern liberal moral and political theory: the social contract. This conceptual model is still central to moral philosophy today and remains for many feminists a best hope as a model for moral egalitarianism.

Feminist deconstructions of the social contract have uncovered the inescapably gendered conceptual and practical foundations of early modern and contemporary contractarian thinking.[4] The mutually accepted equality of certain Anglo-European men made them free by their own agreement to view *each other* that way. They agreed among themselves to positions for certain women that were defined by their relations to those women—specifically, relations of power over, or access to, them. That is, mutual recognition of these men's rights over certain women is one of the significant respects in which they define themselves as equal. Furthermore, the hierarchical sexual division of labor is a material condition for men's being free to engage in the economic competition, social participation, and political contests that both express and measure their equality in society's public sphere. This pattern continued well into the twentieth century with assumptions that the discourse of justice and equality defines statuses within "public" life of household "heads."

Race theorists have excavated the historical foundations of modern Europe's self-definition as the universe of civilized men. Enlightenment ideals of reason and personhood played central roles in constituting—again deliberately, consciously, and violently—a raced equality that defined white men as moral subjects and political peers in important part by entitling them to power over or access to nonwhite people and what nonwhite people have. As Charles Mills puts it, a "racial contract" has always underwritten the still-invoked social one.[5] Mills, along with other race theorists, makes a compelling case from textual and historical evidence that the equality of Anglo-European men was imagined from the outset in terms of who these men were not, and were not like. More tellingly, separate moral and juridical statuses were explicitly elaborated for nonwhite others in the course of, and for the purpose of, explicitly elaborating and justifying white men's entitlements to work, rule, displace, civilize, own, or kill them.[6] Now the pattern continues in the form of widespread denial by whites of pervasive racism and persisting disadvantage, strategic exclusion, and raced violence in a society organized, politically and epistemically, to sustain this deniability.

Neither of these compelling bodies of critique has yet been joined to the other in a unifying, or at least mutually clarifying, analysis of the contractarian constructions of equality as both Whiteness and Maleness (and perhaps of each in terms of the other). Each of these inquiries, however, powerfully confronts the unsavory historical amnesia and institutional legitimation that allows us to keep thinking about, and circulating, and teaching these views "as if" they "really" proclaimed the universally inclusive freedom and equality, or equal moral worth, of all human beings. In demonstrable and demonstrated fact, they did not. Nor did they intend to. They intended and did the reverse, intentionally erecting the ideal of *equality for equals* to assure mutually the rights of certain people in part by defining them as rights over other people. In all versions of this contract equality was seen as conferred by a restricted class of men on its members, and among the things conferred was the right of those equal to each other to distinguish themselves from the rest, particularly by specific powers *over* those not equal to them.

These historically informed analyses exhibit a central feature of the modern liberal idea of equality *in the context of the actual social arrangements that made sense of it.* This construction of equality requires there to be something *other* than equality. What is other is not merely different but must define and support the equality of equals. Despite claims for its revolutionary nature, the ostensible universalism of modern equality repeats the subsumptive universalism of classical thought. In this conceptual structure, some nature or possible perfection of humanity (usually "Man") was to be realized in the persons of a few human beings suited to it. But the many others are not left out; they occupy *indispensable* roles in relation to the few. Legitimized asymmetrical exercises of power over the many lesser others distinguish the few who enjoy these powers over the many, and not over each other, *as equals*. Concretely, those who are able but not equal supply the wherewithal of common life that is necessary to sustain the "achievement" of equality by some.[7]

This persistent logic of equality (as we have always known it and as it has in fact evolved in tandem with the practices that make sense of it) is that it qualifies some by subsuming or subjecting others. The fundamental problem with the status of women and non-white men in the social contract (and the actual society it images) is *not* capricious and arbitrary exclusion from a status they might just as well have occupied alongside white men if the qualifications were fair, although efforts to "correct" contractarian thought tend to "add in" or "add on" some of those historically excluded. The problem is instead a kind of pointed and invidious *inclusion* in subordinate or diminished statuses that serve to define entitlements of the equals and the nature of equality itself. Equals do not just have different and greater powers and entitlements *relative* to those below; they are defined *as equal* to one another by their shared entitlements *to* and powers *over* those below. The former aspect of unequal status, "distributive" inequality, can be remedied by equalizing "shares" in available goods or access to them. But there is a real puzzle in fixing the latter key feature of equality: If powers *over* others are what defines the equals, then when equality is extended to those below, over whom are they entitled to rule? In other words, the part of the equality status that is defined structurally by "power over Xs" cannot be reduced to any version of "difference from Xs." Yet what we have learned from studies of race and gender oppression shows that it is "power over" that is fundamental; distributive inequality and the social marking of "differences" are *effects* of systemic powers of some over others.

For me, this persistently subsuming and subjecting logic of consensual equality poses the question whether an "association of equals" can in fact be rendered universal. One profound contribution of feminist ethics has been its insistence that moral theory address immaturity, vulnerability, disability, dependency, and incapacity as inevitable, central, and normal in human life. The model of an association of equals does not seem capable of including all of us and will not give the needed guidance, as Eva Kittay puts it, "on our unequal vulnerability in dependency, on our moral power to respond to others in need, and on the primacy of human relations to happiness and well-being."[8] In pursuing an encompassing moral universalism—this time, *for the first time*—we cannot ignore theoretically what we cannot dispense with humanly: many "powers over" are indispensable "powers for," that is, on behalf of, the infant, the immature, the frail, the ill; the occasionally, developmentally, or permanently dependent; the mildly or severely incapacitated. These are not different (kinds of) people. *They are all of us at some times— and necessarily.* It remains unclear to me whether there really can be a single universal and substantive moral status; if there is, I doubt that it can be the status of equality. I do not yet see the deeper logic of moral equality, or a fully inclusive logic beyond equality, that is universal in its moral embrace while it differentiates not only between persons, but fluidly within the lives of persons, over times and contexts, in its assignments of responsibility.

MORALITY, NOT IDEOLOGY

A moral inquiry that reflects on practices of responsibility for an actual social life will not talk about morality instead of power but, rather, will explore the moral authority of some powers and the arbitrariness, cruelty, or wastefulness of others. It is a heavy irony that interrogating the ways power (inevitably) constructs morality so often prompts the charge that one is "reducing morality to ideology." In fact, exactly the reverse is true. In one useful characterization of ideology, it is a practice of presenting claims as existing "above the fray of power and politics," for instance, as being "theoretical, rational, or spiritual and, on that basis, justified in acting as the final arbiter over others,"[9] thus "hiding the social histories and circumstances from which ideas . . . derive their logics."[10] Claims about or within morality are used ideologically when they pretend to operate beyond or above all social powers, rather than as a means of distributing and authorizing social powers and so needing justification as such. The alternative, I have argued, is always to see the power in morality—and to "see through" it to its conditions and costs. This is what I am calling naturalism in moral philosophy. It is something feminist moral philosophers are usually already very good at doing.

NOTES

1. Wendy Brown, *States of Injury: Power and Freedom in Late Modernity* (Princeton, N.J.: Princeton University Press, 1995), 45. Brown argues that "surrendering epistemological foundations means giving up the ground of specifically *moral* claims against domination" (45), but this is true only if moral claims cannot receive an alternative epistemological account, just as other knowledge claims now usually do. Brown repeats the view that the discursive roots of a morality-power antagonism go back to Plato.

2. This is the view I defend at length in *Moral Understandings: A Feminist Study in Ethics* (New York: Routledge, 1998).

3. See *Moral Understandings*, chapters 3 and 9, for fuller discussion of transparency as a moral and epistemic ideal and of transparency testing as an aspect of actual social processes in real times and spaces.

4. Many people have contributed to this analysis. Some examples of sustained discussions of the historical realities include Carol Pateman, *The Sexual Contract* (Stanford: Stanford University Press, 1988); Linda Nicholson, *Gender and History: The Limits of Social Theory in the Age of the Family* (New York: Columbia University Press, 1986); Patricia S. Mann, *Micro-Politics: Agency in a Postfeminist Era* (Minneapolis: University of Minnesota Press, 1994); and Brown, *States of Injury*. Exposures of the continuing occlusion and exclusion of women in Rawls's thought include Susan Moller Okin, *Justice, Gender, and the Family* (New York: Basic Books, 1989), and Eva Feder Kittay, *Love's Labor: Essays on Women, Equality, and Dependency* (New York: Routledge, 1999).

5. Charles W. Mills, *Racial Contract* (Ithaca, N.Y.: Cornell University Press, 1997), 93.

6. Two incisive accounts are those of Mills, *The Racial Contract*, especially chapters 1 and 2, and Lucius T. Outlaw Jr., *On Race and Philosophy* (New York: Routledge, 1996), especially chapter 3. A provocative collection of classical modern philosophical texts that construct race distinctions is Emmanual Chukwudi Eze, *Race and the Enlightenment: A Reader* (Cambridge, Mass.: Blackwell Publishers, 1997). On the specifically American construction of black/white distinction in the context of Anglo-European philosophy and culture, see Winthrop D. Jordan's massive study, *White over Black: American Attitudes toward the Negro, 1550–1812* (Chapel Hill: University of North Carolina Press, 1968). Richard H. Popkin provides an interesting account of the intertwining histories of biblical and philosophical thinking about race in "The Philosophical Bases of Modern Racism," in *Philosophy and the Civilizing Arts*, ed. Craig Walton and John P. Austen (Athens: Ohio University Press, 1974), 126–53.

7. In the *Doctrine of Right* Kant distinguishes "passive citizens" who do not have the same schedule of rights as "active" ones. As Tamar Shapiro explains, passive citizens include not only the "natural" ones, women and children, but those economically dependent, including apprentices, domestic servants, domestic laborers, private

tutors, and tenant farmers. Shapiro explains that Kant distinguishes this restricted citizenship from the "freedom and equality *as human beings*" shared by all and disallows the treatment of passive citizens as things or as members of a permanent underclass, although the possibility for women to work their way up remains doubtful. See Tamar Shapiro, "What Is a Child?" *Ethics* 109 (1999): 715–38. Shapiro's discussion illustrates how the category of those subsumed as "dependent" has encompassed all those whose labor materially supported the "independence" that qualifies relatively few as equals. This "independence" is an amalgam of entitlement to, power over, and exemption from the labors of others. It also dramatizes the question of what moral conceptions like "freedom and equality" mean divorced from actual social implementation of these statuses. In one straightforward sense, they *do not* mean "freedom and equality." Tellingly, Shapiro reconstructs childhood as a "moral predicament," an unfortunate situation to be overcome.

8. Kittay, *Love's Labor*, 113.

9. E. Doyle McCarthy, *Knowledge as Culture: The New Sociology of Knowledge* (New York: Routledge, 1996), 31.

10. McCarthy, *Knowledge as Culture*, 7.

8

SOME THOUGHTS ON FEMINISTS, PHILOSOPHY, AND FEMINIST PHILOSOPHY

I do three things here. First, I offer some "generic" anecdotes, familiar and perhaps troubling to many of us, but about the meaning of which we may not agree. I use them to evoke assumptions, presumptions, confusions, and pressures, which I like to think of as opportunities as well as problems. I draw no single moral from them, but mention some problems they suggest to me. Second, I offer and lightly defend some distinctions I think are useful for understanding some of these problems, although the distinctions are ones I would expect to attract argument. But I will use them, third, to identify some proprietary attitudes about feminist philosophy, and about women and feminists in philosophy, that trouble me. Here are the anecdotes:

A female philosopher is asked to teach a course in feminist philosophy in her department in response to student interest. Feminist philosophy has not been a field of previous training or research for her.

A female philosopher at a feminist philosophy conference tells other women who like herself identify themselves as feminist philosophers that she works in feminist bioethics. They respond, "You mean you work on reproductive issues, that kind of thing?"

A female philosopher who is a feminist works in analytic metaphysics. Some feminist philosopher colleagues say or imply that this kind of philosophy is questionable for a feminist to be doing.

A male job candidate in an historical field is asked whether the philosophy he's discussing needs critical examination as a gendered discourse. He agrees that views about women must be critically examined, not understanding how discourses themselves can be organized around tropes of gender and gendered imagery.

A female job candidate who is an Aristotle scholar uses Aristotle's views on human reproduction in a paper to illustrate incoherences in his metaphysics of matter and form. The question period is largely spent pressing her on her views of the nature and impact of sexism on Aristotle's philosophy. She does not get to talk about matter and form.

A male graduate student in philosophy asks a professor about the graduate course in Feminist Theory she'll teach the following term. He wants to know whether men take this course.

One problem in these examples might be called the "feminization of feminist philosophy," the idea that it's "about women" or something "for women" (in both senses). Women used sometimes to be called "the sex"; sometimes it looks as if feminism has been received (and in some cases written and practiced) in such ways as to make women "the gender." Some of these examples touch on the absorption of feminist philosophy into curricular and professional arrangements as a kind of academic or departmental "women's work," reproducing gendered divisions of labor by means of feminist philosophy. These tendencies are linked to the "ghettoization of feminist philosophy," to ideas that it's not quite or just or really philosophy. At a non-feminist philosophical meeting, some people think you wouldn't want to have many (if any) feminist philosophers at a session not so designated; people might show up for cognitive science or deconstruction or metaphysics and end up getting feminism. Students not infrequently react this way to feminist materials in a course that is not a course on feminism. Editors may assign reviews of feminist philosophy to women philosophers (because they are women) or to male philosophers (because they are philosophers) whether the reviewers are well-schooled in this complex set of literatures; this would not typically be done with aesthetics or semantics. There are questions here about the recognition and legitimacy of feminist philosophy as a family of skilled philosophical discourses and critical methods.

Here's a set of distinctions I think might usefully inform understandings and expectations. Consider the differences among: philosophers who are women; philosophers who are feminists; and philosophers who do feminist philosophy.

The phrase "feminist philosopher" courts confusions, in that it might refer to people in either the second or third categories. Philosophers who do feminist philosophy (that is, who use it, and not just mention it) are going to be feminists at least in some of their self-conscious political views, in the same way that elaborators of liberal theory are going to be liberals. (And in both cases, it's not simply "up to" someone to decide she's a feminist or a liberal.) But those who are feminists and philosophers may not be doing feminist philosophy. So, I'm inclined to add a fourth distinction: philosophers who want to express their feminism as philosophers.

One way to express one's feminism as a philosopher is to write in or otherwise directly contribute to feminist philosophy. That's *one* way. Other ways include one's pedagogical practices, one's patterns of scholarly acknowledgement, one's support for or opposition to curricular measures, hiring polices, and institutional or professional practices, as well as other social and political commitments.

I assume in these distinctions that there really is something called feminist philosophy now, as there was not twenty-five years ago. I assume that this kind of philosophy, like other kinds of philosophy, involves literatures, vocabularies, problematics, terms and postures of criticism, and evaluative standards; that these have histories, meanings, and applications which can only be told by explaining the development of feminist philosophies. These literatures, vocabularies, etc. are in fact diverse; this proliferation is a fact about feminism and feminist philosophy. Given that there is feminist philosophy, a lot of things are feminist philosophy and a lot of things aren't. Some marks of the things that aren't include: not acknowledging or not reasonably representing the literatures, vocabularies, etc. as points of reference or departure; not to accept that one invites evaluation and criticism in some of the going terms of feminist philosophy, even if one finds fault with those terms; not to acknowledge the audiences that feminist philosophy has recruited, not to understand what it is they have been bothering to become skilled in learning and hearing about. Doing feminist philosophy badly is something (at least in many cases) recognizably different, which is again not the same as doing feminist philosophy in a way that some discursive networks of feminist philosophers don't value or agree with.

Here are three proprietary assumptions—assumptions about what belongs to whom, or who or what belongs where—which trouble me, because they seem to me mistaken where not disrespectful.

One is that women and/or feminists who do philosophy *are* doing feminist philosophy. Being a feminist does not make such philosophy as one does feminist philosophy, any more than being a woman makes the philosophy one does feminist philosophy. And neither does addressing issues about women or about feminism make the philosophy one does feminist philosophy.

Another is that women and/or feminists who do philosophy *should* be doing feminist philosophy. There are lots of ways of being a feminist, and of being a philosopher. For example, I believe theorizing is a practice, and feminist philosophy is one feminist theoretical/intellectual practice. But using certain examples, referring to certain texts, asking certain questions, imposing certain forms of organization at a conference or in a volume, or experimenting with certain written or oral styles can also be feminist theoretical practice *in certain contexts, for certain audiences, on certain occasions.* And needless to say, most feminist actions and practices are not theoretical ones.

One way it is disturbingly disrespectful not to recognize the extant reality and the particular and skilled nature of feminist philosophies is that it ignores the costs and works of those women who created and nurtured feminist philosophy, often by exhausting commitments of time and at great personal or professional risks. But due and seemly respect for feminist philosophy as philosophically skilled intellectual work should combine with due and seemly respect for feminist practices (theoretical and otherwise) that are not the doing of feminist philosophy, as well as for feminist philosophy done in many different ways. On the last score, I'd rather see feminist philosophers have the confidence to regard more work as bad feminist philosophy (subject to the usual treatments for bad philosophy—if it's hopelessly or stupidly bad ignoring it, and if it's interestingly or dangerously bad, showing how it is and drawing the morals), than getting caught up in assuming or trying to establish *in advance or in general* that certain styles or methods or subject matters couldn't be feminist philosophy. I'd like to see more work done on what I call "feminist stylistics," studies of the effects and limits both of many varieties of feminist philosophical writing and of other feminist theoretical and rhetorical practices. I'd like to see us *not* disciplining, but *making* more feminist philosophies and feminist intellectual practices.

III

INSTITUTIONAL AND
SOCIAL CONTEXTS

9

KEEPING MORAL SPACE OPEN: NEW IMAGES OF ETHICS CONSULTING

Thinking about "moral expertise" and the idea of ethics "consulting," I asked some physician friends about their experiences working with ethicists in the large urban medical centers in which they teach and practice. One replied that he had found ethicists helpful; they encouraged him to consider issues of autonomy and paternalism, for example, to which he might not otherwise have attended in those terms. After a thoughtful pause, he offered another evaluation. With all the personal and institutional pressures of medical practice in such environments, he suggested, it was important to have a place to go for that kind of thinking; having done it allowed him to feel more confident or more responsible about the decisions taken.

While not mutually exclusive, these two responses are importantly different. The first response corresponds closely to a prevalent picture of ethics consultation as a kind of expert input. Specifically, moral theories or concepts, either global (utilitarianism, rights, vulnerability) or local (patient autonomy, strict advocacy, quality of life), constitute the domain of the ethicist, that *for which* and *about which* the ethicist is charged to speak as one specialist among others. The second response captures something less easily pegged. It is about a kind of interaction that invites and enables something to happen, something which renders authority more self-conscious and responsibility clearer. It is also about the role of maintaining a certain kind of reflective space (literal and figurative) within an institution, within its culture and its daily life, for just these sorts of occasions. I want to explore the second answer here, for it could represent not just another feature of ethics consultation but a significantly different view of it.

Literature of the last fifteen years on moral expertise and ethics consulting shows a shift in emphasis from issues of content to those of *process*—from what the ethicist knows, to what the ethicist does or enables. This shift parallels two others, one practical and one philosophical. The establishment of institutional ethics committees accelerated rapidly in the 1980s, spurring questions about whom these committees serve and who should serve on them, what they should be doing, and how it should be done.[1] Philosophical ethics in the academy has also been a scene of change in the last two decades; the project of constructing and refining moral theories (in a quite limited and particular sense) has been ever more criticized, while moral philosophers of diverse stripes attend more closely to the languages and practices of actual moral communities and to the constructive process of renewing common moral life. I want to link these parallel shifts in practical medical ethics and general philosophical ethics from thinking of ethics as a "what" to thinking of ethics as a "how." I do this in order to consider the *difference* this makes in conceiving the nature of ethics consultation and the role of ethicists.

FAMILIAR SUSPICIONS ABOUT A FAMILIAR IDEA

A certain familiar conception of ethics is that it is the attempt to articulate and justify the right or the best moral theory. This conception is familiar because it has been the prevailing definition of academic philosophical ethics for most of the twentieth century. It is also thoroughly embedded (although not uncontested) in medical ethics. On this view a moral theory is *not* merely any comprehensive, reasoned, and reflective account of morality, of the ways and means, point and value, of a moral form of life. (A classic example of such an account is Aristotle's *Nichomachean Ethics*.) On this dominant modern view a proper moral theory is instead a highly specific kind of account of where moral judgments come from: a *compact code* of very general (lawlike) principles or procedures which, when applied to cases appropriately described, yield impersonally justified judgments about what any moral agent in such a case should do. Invocations of theory and principles in practical medical ethics have tended to reproduce this conception. "Theories" are impersonally action-guiding formulations, like versions of utilitarianism or Rawls's theory of justice; principles are lawlike directives of high generality, like those giving autonomy, or sanctity of life, or beneficence absolute or relative priority.

This conception of ethics directly constructs a particular and familiar picture of moral expertise. If the core of moral understanding from which particular judgments flow is theory *in this sense*—a compact impersonal system of action-guiding directives—then it seems clear what moral expertise is. It is being specially learned about the epistemic foundations, internal structures, relative merits, and types and limits of application of the most currently promising theories. This special, subtle, and refined knowledge qualifies one as expert in ethics (as opposed to nephrology or hospital administration); this expertise in turn qualifies one as a technically equipped specialist in moral input or intervention. The consulting ethicist represents and is expected to supply expert moral opinion as an additional component of the process of evaluating or making decisions.

As familiar as this picture is, so is a battery of suspicions about it, either about its conception of ethical competence, or about the relevance to the clinical setting of the abstract kind of moral-theoretic knowledge it features. Could full moral competence really consist entirely in intellectual mastery of codelike theories and lawlike principles? What of skills of attention and appreciation, of the practiced perceptions and responses that issue from morally valuable character traits, of the wisdom of rich and broad life experience, of the role of feelings in guiding or tempering one's views? Philosophers within and outside medical ethics have questioned the equation of expertise in state-of-the-art theory deployment with superior or specially reliable moral insight.[2]

Furthermore, can philosophers' abstract constructions of morality be brought into contact, sensitively and usefully, with problems in the clinic? What of the typical complexity of clinical decisions, and of the inevitably *ad hoc* nature of real-time decisionmaking? Philosophers' lawlike principles seem remote from the typically vague maxims nonphilosophers (and philosophers when they're not philosophizing) actually use in moral deliberation.[3] Aren't abstract principles often given (sometimes new) meaning under the impact of concrete cases, rather than cases being simply "decided" by the "application" of principles? And who or what decides what *is* a "case"—a moral problem—in the first place, as well as what sort of case— subject to what principle or principles—it is?

These objections are as familiar to medical ethics as the paradigm of expertise to which they object. Arthur Caplan's frequently cited critiques of this model of ethics and experts have given it a handy name: the "engineering model." Caplan and others in the medical ethics literature have homed in on how misleading, if not harmful, this engineering or application model of clinical ethics is.[4] Yet it is the natural companion of a certain very specific view of what you know when you know, specially or expertly, about ethics; you know codelike theories and how to apply them.

Sometimes attacks on the application idea are understood as salvos against having theories in ethics at all, and some ethicists respond to the perceived attack on theory with a kind of incredulity. "If ethical theories are useless," asks Ruth Macklin, "is it not likely that all attempts at rational analysis and systematic resolution of moral problems are doomed?" In the same volume of essays Robert Veatch warns that without the "systematic approach" to problems that ethical theory provides the alternatives are "an intuition, gut feeling, appeals to authority, or just blatant inconsistency."[5]

The term 'systematic' is an important marker in these arguments. 'Systematic' solutions can mean 'rationally ordered' or 'considered' as opposed to 'whimsical,' 'inexplicable,' or 'unjustified' ones; *or* systematic solutions can mean solutions generated by a *system*, 'by the rules,' 'by the book,' or 'according to the theory.' To criticize the engineering model is to raise suspicions, not about logical, intelligent, informed moral judgment for which consistent and persuasive reasons can be given, but about judgment which is supposedly yielded by deducing conclusions from codelike moral theories. If there are *other* kinds of moral theories, or better, *methods* of moral deliberation that do not travel through top-down application of codelike theories, then to reject the engineering model is not to abandon rationality or consistency. It might just involve abandoning the neat but suspicious view of essential moral knowledge as captured in moral "systems," those codelike theories mastery of which makes someone an "ethical expert" on the engineering view.

Suspicions about codelike theories or their application within medical ethics mirror diverse critiques of specifically modern codelike theories within philosophical ethics generally. Is morality obviously best represented by something *like* utilitarian, or Kantian, or contractarian—i.e., codelike—theories? In the last few decades a remarkably diverse collection of moral philosophers— Aristotelians and Wittgensteinians, casuists and communitarians, pragmatists and feminists, Hegelians, postmodernists, and assorted others—have thought not.[6] Certain themes have been widely (though not universally) repeated across these "antitheory" critiques, despite profound differences and outright antagonisms among them.

One recurrent theme is the *social situation* of morality: moral understandings are always embedded in and make sense of a particular social setting and its characteristic relationships, problems, and practices. This warns us off trying to abstract some pure all-purpose core of moral intelligence from the historically specific assumptions and circumstances that give moral conceptions their point and meaning. Another theme is the importance of specific ways and means of bringing morality to bear on the *particular* occasion. General moral maxims or principles can often be connected to particular instances only by a thick tissue of perceptions and interpretations; these are fed by diverse skills and rooted in varied habits of thought and feeling. Moral competence is thus not reducible to a codelike decision instrument (much less an algorithmic one) any more than carpentry is reducible to a saw. A third theme (more controversial, but easily implied by certain versions of the other two) is that moral deliberation and decision are often (and in novel or hard cases are always) *constructive*. Communities, relationships, and moral ideas themselves are often not left where they were, but are renewed and revised as the process of interpersonal negotiation and interpretation in moral terms goes on. Moral concepts, principles, values, and argument forms may be starting points and reference points for moral deliberation, but that process is progressive and once traversed may not leave everything as it was at the outset.[7]

One idea has reappeared so often in recent views which stress the social, the particular, or the constructive dimensions of morality that it's become a sort of buzzword in the checkered terrain of recent moral philosophy. It's the idea that deductively modelled theory-and-application in ethics should give way to a *narrative* understanding of moral problems and moral deliberation. I'll use this central idea of narrative as a way to shift perspectives: from thinking about morality as a theory applied to cases, to thinking about morality as a medium of progressive acknowledgement and adjustment between people in (or in search of) a common and habitable moral world. This will lead us back to the ethics consultant, who will have undergone a parallel metamorphosis, from engineer to *architect* and from technical expert to *mediator*.

ANOTHER IDEA: NARRATIVES AND NEGOTIATION

Emphasis on narrative as the pattern of moral thinking is, first, a way of seeing how morally relevant information is organized within particular episodes of deliberation. The idea is that a story, or better, *history* is the basic form of representation for moral problems; we need to know who the parties are, how they understand themselves and each other, what terms of relationship have brought them to this morally problematic point, and perhaps what social or institutional frames shape or circumscribe their options. Emphasis on narrative also captures the way moral resolution itself takes the form of a *passage* conditioned but not completely determined by where things started, and indefinitely open to continuation. Different resolutions will be more or less acceptable depending on how they sustain or alter the integrity of the parties, the terms of their relationships, and even the meaning of moral or institutional values that are at stake. A narrative approach reminds us that "moral problems" are points in *continuing* histories of attempted mutual adjustments and understandings between people.

A narrative picture of moral understanding doesn't spurn general rules or broad ideals, but it doesn't treat them as major premises in moral deductions. It treats them as markers of the moral *relevance* of certain features of stories ("But isn't that lying?"); as guidelines to the typical moral weight of certain acts or outcomes ("Surely we ought to avoid lying."); as necessary shared points of *departure* ("We've got a problem here with undermining the patient's trust in the physician's candor."); and (with any luck) as continuing shareable points of *reference* ("Might the patient not still see that as misleading?") and *reinterpretation* ("Withholding isn't necessarily deception, though.") that lead to a morally intelligible resolution.

So narratives in moral thinking come before, during, and after moral generalities (whether of theory, principle, or basic moral concept). They permit and invite full exploration of what often seems neglected or devalued on the engineering model: specific histories of individual commitment, of relationship and responsibility, of institutional practices and evolving moral traditions. The need to "apply" principles at the level of abstraction typical of codelike moral theories creates pressure to shear off complicating, possibly "irrelevant" details and to magnify "repeatable," even "universalizable" features general enough to map cases on to available theoretical categories. Emphasis on narrative construction pulls in the opposite direction—from premature or coercive streamlining of cases toward enrichment of context and detail.

Specific values and commitments (personal, religious, professional or cultural) may matter crucially to individuals' maintaining integrity and coherent moral self-understanding over time.[8] Determining our responsibilities in the concrete usually involves a grasp of the history of trust, expectation, and agreement that gives particular relationships distinct moral consequences. To know what general values or norms mean in situations now requires appreciating how these have been applied and withheld, circumscribed, and reinterpreted before within individual, social, or institutional histories. So adequate moral consideration needs to follow these stories of identity, relationship, and value, to see how they can go on, and whether it is better or worse that they do so. Principles and theoretical concepts mark broad areas of value or define generic priorities. But only the content of these specific histories can define what in an actual case is owed—by whom, to whom, and why—and what different moral resolutions of cases will mean (and will cost) for involved parties. The determinations we make on their basis may alter our grasp of principles and concepts with implications for future moral reasoning as well.

Consider the case study of Carlos and Consuela.[9] Carlos, a young man who is HIV-positive, is to be discharged from the hospital to complete his convalescence from a gunshot wound under the care of his twenty-two year old sister, Consuela. Medicaid will not pay for nursing because a caregiver is available in the home. Consuela is willing, but is ignorant of Carlos's HIV status; Carlos refuses to inform her, fearing that she, and worse, his father, will learn of his homosexual orientation. Two commentators arrive at different conclusions about how to reconcile respect for confidentiality with a duty to warn.

One models the case in a way which approximates the application or engineering model; the issue is whether a duty to warn could outweigh a duty to keep the patient's status in confidence. Considering degree of risk and possible alternatives and harms (couched in terms of physician's telling or not telling Consuela, and inferring how Consuela might behave if told or not told), this commentator concludes that three general conditions which would justify elevating the duty to warn are not met. Therefore, the physician is morally obligated to respect confidentiality. Unless Carlos can be persuaded to reconsider telling his sister, the physician's duty to warn will be reasonably fulfilled by providing Consuela with serious training and the equipment for universal precautions.

The second discussion embodies more fully a narrative approach. This commentator foregrounds the relationship between Carlos and Consuela, as well as the history, both personal and social, that places the latter in the caregiver role. Consuela has cared for Carlos and another sibling since their mother's death ten years before; the health care system deems her (a woman in the home) an available caregiver, thus relieving itself of the expense of providing professional care. But, asks the commentator, would a private nurse or other health-care worker not be told of Carlos's HIV status? Is access to Consuela's caregiving taken for granted by that system, by the physician, by Carlos? Is Consuela not seen as a responsible party who chooses to give care? If so, must she not be respectfully allowed to consider possible risk and assume her responsibilities with clear understanding of what she must do both for Carlos and to protect herself? Is Carlos mindful of what he asks of Consuela, and should he not be willing to assume some responsibilities and risk some trust if he expects her to do so? This ethicist agrees that the physician should not breach confidentiality, but also concludes that unless Carlos will deal forthrightly with his sister, the physician should not risk exploiting Consuela's good will under conditions of ignorance. If Carlos will not tell her, he must do without her nursing care.

Although both ethicists (inevitably) draw on stories of the origins and possible outcomes of the problem, the second features Consuela and Carlos as moral actors whose history and future of moral responsibilities are intertwined in specific ways, and who need to respond to each other *as such*, within a larger web of family relations and societal pressures. The physician is, appropriately, dealing with a problem of medical management and norms of professional ethics. But Carlos and Consuela are at a juncture of prior and continuing moral stories that tell who they are, what they expect of and owe to one another, and what forms of trust and what commitments they are willing to undertake.

Moral generalities on the narrative view are ingredients rather than axioms. They are ingredient to stories that reveal how problems have come to be the problems they are, that imagine what ways of going on are possible, and that explore what different ways of going on will mean in moral terms for the people involved and for the values at stake. In the case of Carlos and Consuela, the general duties to warn and keep confidence are immediately apparent from the physician's point of view. But Carlos's and Consuela's stories, in social perspective, draw other general concerns of self and mutual respect, filial obligation, exploitation, gratitude, and trust into the picture. The second ethicist's rendering not only enriches the "circumstantial" detail of the case, it induces a more complete view of the moral values at stake, and this in turn defines more sharply what the different parties must acknowledge and take responsibility for.

The fuller narrative construction also highlights the situation's dynamic potential. The deductive relation of validity (invoked by the model of applying principles to cases) either holds or it doesn't, and when it holds, holds under the impact of all further additions of information. In narratives, however, what comes later means what it does in part because of what preceded it, while what came earlier may also come to look very different depending on what happens later. Narratives are *built* or *constructed*, and remain open to elaboration, continuation, and revision; they make more or less sense, and may be more or less stable as they unfold. In Carlos's and Consuela's situation, there are (at least) three moral actors who have powers and unfolding opportunities to influence each other and to determine how well the resolution they effect responds to the values at stake.

NARRATIVES AND MUTUAL ACCOUNTABILITY

The narrative picture of moral deliberation I've outlined implies that the resolution of a moral problem is often less like the solution to a puzzle or the answer to a question than like the outcome of a negotiation. But this does not mean that anything settled on is right, nor that a resolution is right only if everyone can settle on it. A narrative view can be just as committed to holding that certain kinds of things are *really* better or worse for people, or certain requirements are *really* deeply obligating, as any other. In the case of Carlos and Consuela, I argued that the fuller narrative account was more adequate because it uncovered real values and obligations which had to be reckoned with in a morally justifiable resolution.

The narrative approach addresses the question of *how* values and obligations can guide particular people facing complex problems to solutions that are morally justifiable. There are usually multiple parties and multiple values to be acknowledged and (ideally) reconciled in cases that require any serious deliberation at all. (Cases which provoke discussion in clinical ethics are invariably of this kind.) There is no reason to assume these sorts of moral problems have unique right solutions, rather than ones which are more or less responsive to the values at stake. And there is every reason to think that competing claims posed by agents' integrity, their valued commitments, and the moral ideals they and their communities recognize may not be smoothly reconcilable in many instances. Elaboration through narratives opens moral deliberation to fuller consideration of these claims, and so to better, more responsive solutions. But whether uniquely compelling and universally satisfying resolutions are possible—and especially where they are *not*—fuller consideration serves the larger end of *keeping us morally accountable* to each other, renewing common moral life itself.

Moral deliberation and its enabling stories have to make sense to and stand up within some moral community. We deliberate in order to act justifiably, in a way we can convincingly account for in moral terms. This requires that we share (enough of) a common moral medium (moral languages, moral paradigms, deliberative strategies) and familiarity with the social terrain of interactions, roles, and relationships to which it belongs. Prior moral understandings do not have to be unanimous; imperfect understandings, conflict, and incomprehension provide opportunities for critical and constructive moral thinking. They can propel close rethinking and the search for mediating ideas or reconciling procedures. They challenge complacency, superficiality, parochialism, and groupthink. Even when disagreement is intractable, rendering it articulate may be a moral passage, pressing deliberators to acknowledge what commitments they are taking responsibility for and which understandings they refuse, foreclose, or silence.

Moral narratives are (ideally) authored and judged by those whose moral stories they are: those *by* whom, *to* whom, and *about* whom these moral accounts are given. Mutual moral accounting *presupposes* and *seeks* a continuing common life negotiated through, and so intelligible to its parties in those terms. By accounting to each other through a moral medium, parties to a common life (or the hope of one) recognize each other as agents of value, capable of considered choices, responsive to value, and so responsible for themselves and to others for the moral sense and impact of what they do. They invoke their shared moral resources not only to achieve solutions, but to achieve solutions which at the same time protect, refine, and extend those very moral resources themselves—ones which keep the moral medium alive and available, that keep the moral community itself going. Morality, philosopher Stanley Cavell reminds us, "provides *one* possibility of settling conflict, a way of encompassing conflict which allows the continuance of personal relationships."[10] Fully personal relations are ones in which we provide for continuing mutual acknowledgement of our status as agents of value. Disagreements may be settled and communities regimented in other ways, some of them involving fists and weapons, propaganda and censorship, forced medication or detention. "Morality is a valuable way," Cavell remarks, "because the others are so often inaccessible or brutal."

The larger aim of continuing moral relationship and mutual moral intelligibility moves us to look at not only what we are doing in moral deliberation—solving problems, setting policies, invoking moral norms and notions—but at how we are doing it. It prompts self-consciousness about the moral means we conserve, renew, or invent, and our responsibility for keeping our individual and communal moral lives vital and coherent by means of them. It also shifts attention to the important question of who "we" are. If moral accounts must make sense to those *by* whom, *to* whom, and *about* whom they are given, the integrity of these accounts is compromised when some parties to a moral situation are not heard or represented. If chances for different perspectives which open critical opportunities are missed, moral community is doubly illserved: alternate narratives go unexplored, and some members are in practice disqualified as agents of value. If some positions in a deliberation in fact carry greater authority, it is important to acknowledge this, so the legitimate grounds of that authority are commonly understood.

In these ways the narrative conception of moral thinking shifts attention to the *process* of interpretation, negotiation, construction, and resolution required by any complex deliberation as well as to the *roles* of deliberators. If this sketch of the structure of moral deliberation is even roughly right, knowing specially about ethics and moral thinking can no longer be seen simply as knowing about ethical theories, principles, or concepts and some standard patterns of argumentation in which they are put to work. It is not only knowing what the theories, concepts or arguments are, but knowing what they are *for*, and understanding under what conditions they can be made to serve.

ETHICS CONSULTING RETHOUGHT

Recent literature on ethics consulting shows a shift. Discussions from the mid-1970s through the mid-1980s were largely preoccupied with *what the ethicist knows*, and figured the consultant as a logical superintendent who sharpens concepts, upholds standards of rigorous argument, and polices fallacious thinking. These were the moral engineers, needed to service the engines of ethics (the theoretical hardware) through purely conceptual maintenance routines.[11]

Since the mid-1980s concerns about *what the ethicist does* have moved to the fore.[12] Matters at issue include: different institutional functions of ethicists; the differing kinds of responsibility, authority, and accountability that should accompany them; how the ethicist fits with the criss-cross of relationships among health care providers, patients, families and caretakers; and how moral deliberation within health care institutions connects to larger social arenas of moral consensus and conflict.[13] Terrence Ackerman models the ethicist's role as that of *facilitator* in an inherently social process of moral inquiry which identifies norms and problem-solving plans of action that evoke "shared and stable social commitments."[14] The ethicist is one *within* a community; the ethicist's privilege in hypothesizing plans of action is warranted to the extent of the ethicist's currency in the dialogue of the larger moral community. In a similar vein, recent discussions of institutional ethics committees emphasize "their ability to facilitate the process" of moral decision through "pluralistic exchange of values," and to move ethical discernment "from the realm of private judgment to the arena of discourse and communal review."[15]

These recent views capture the interactive, constructive, and open-ended character of moral inquiry and decisionmaking in clinical and other settings. What views of the ethicist's capability, authority, and responsibility fit this picture? If the ethicist is not a technical expert who strategically "inputs" ethics, but rather a participant who "facilitates" a social process of moral negotiation and mutual accountability, how might we remodel the ethicist's role? Indeed, is there a well-defined and justifiable role left specifically for ethicists under this change in perspectives?

Arthur Caplan questions whether "society should create a social role that accords power and authority to moral experts,"[16] however moral expertise is understood. But when we consider the site at which most organized ethical consultation occurs, there are strong reasons to think an institutionally specified and authorized role of ethicist is necessary. That site is the acute care setting of the medical center/teaching hospital, a "quintessentially communal world" where "bureaucratic procedures essential to mass production of services" prevail. In such settings "hierarchically structured health care teams . . . administer their responsibilities collaboratively," and "patients are fortunate if they can assert any autonomy at all."[17]

Some early essays about ethicists as "strangers" or "outsiders" to professional and institutional cultures of medicine recognized the crucial *representative* role of the ethicist. For Larry Churchill, "what makes the ethicist truly a stranger is his *advocacy for normative inquiry.*" In William Ruddick's words, "The short-term goal is to make moral discussion professionally acceptable, even routine, among medical students and clinicians . . . [to] encourage current and future clinicians to think of moral questions about therapeutic decisions as a matter of public analysis, rather than a matter of intuition or private conscience protected by professional authority."[18] The role of the ethicist marks the institution's recognition of the ever-present moral dimension of its works and ways. The presence of the ethicist shows the institution's acceptance, in fact sponsorship, of a visible and authorized process of communal moral negotiation as part of its life. The ethicist's role is an emblem of that institutional commitment. But the ethicist is not a repository of the institution's ethics, nor is she or he its conscience. The ethicist's special responsibility is to keep open, accessible, and active (and if necessary to create and design with others) those moral-reflective spaces in institutional life where a sound and shared process of deliberation and negotiation can go on.

It is precisely in busy, bureaucratized, and balkanized acute care settings where the maintenance of those spaces in institutional life will be most urgent. In multiple and fleeting contacts, the moral force of ongoing relationship never builds or is easily depleted or never builds at all; the collaborative nature of treatment can render individual responsibility confused or skewed; the parade of patients and press of cases fragment and blur whatever institutional moral memory there may be; an asymmetrical web of communications makes it difficult to get a clear view of who has been heard from and what has been heard. Given a setting "steeped in routine and hierarchy,"[19] institutionalization of the ethics consulting role is probably the only way reliably and authoritatively to mark and open moral-reflective spaces. These will be actual spaces—places and times—where there are regular discussions, consultations, conferences, lectures, meetings, rounds, and so on, that animate and propel the moral life of that institution and link it to the larger communities of moral discourse in which it nests and to which it must account.

To be effective in creating these spaces and in enabling the shared process of moral deliberation within them is a different authority than the authority to decide cases, deliver ethical verdicts, or set policies. Continuing concerns about whether ethicists (or institutional ethics committees, on which ethicists now often serve) should be decisionmakers, rather than educators and facilitators, are appropriate. Ethics consulting, whether by individual or committee, should serve the ends of clarifying the responsibility and accountability of patients, proxies, and professionals, not pre-empting, erasing, or diluting it.

The ethicist is neither a virtuoso of moral theory nor a moral virtuoso, but is one among other participants in a process. All will be concerned with making responsible decisions. All will be recruited to the distinctly human and humanizing task of keeping moral community and traditions alive and meaningful—each being at once, in Kant's moving and durable phrase, a "legislator," both member and sovereign, in a moral "kingdom of ends." Yet different participants will have distinctive interests in the process. Ethicists will want to discover the potency and limitations of our moral resources as they stand, measured by all the complexity and intensity of clinical practice. Patients will hope not only for medically sound therapy, but for enhanced dignity, comfort, and peace of mind. Medical professionals will want, among other things, "to remain therapists, despite professional and institutional pressures to become functionaries."[20] The ethicist does, however, have the special responsibility as ethicist to foster and nurture a collective and collaborative moral process. What aptitudes and attitudes does this role require?

The orchestration of moral collaboration will be complex. Parties will share morally problematic situations but may have different senses of relevance and understandably different personal stakes. The ethicist has special responsibility to enliven a process in which these common moral concerns stay in focus while differences are recognized and, ideally, mediated. The old staples of conceptual and analytical skills, honed specifically for medical and clinical contexts, remain important tools. They are necessary to keep track of how the discussion has (and has not) been going. But knowing where the discussion might or could go, and how the process is shaped not only by ideas but concretely by actors and environments, requires other sorts of preparation as well.

One sort of preparation is very wide (and critical) conversance with the actual terms, usually diverse and not tightly systematized, of moral assessment in the society the institution takes as its community—conversance with what Howard Brody calls "the broadest and most inclusive conversations in the area of medical ethics over a reasonable period of time." Ackerman calls it being current in the "reflective social dialog," embodied in "a myriad of academic journals, books, newsletters, government publications, and public discussions."[21] Whatever one calls it, it is very different from familiarity with those breathtakingly streamlined artifacts of philosophical texts and textbooks, moral "theories" in the characteristically modern sense.

This wide conversance calls for an understanding historically and sociologically (as well as conceptually), of the community's moral resources and current state of discussion within institutions and outside them. Long-term ethicists within institutions may encourage the institutional moral memory of hard cases. They may also be well placed to track "housekeeping" problems—ongoing practices and assumptions, norms and authority relations which are so familiar they are hardly remarked, but which may nonetheless be moral sore spots.[22] At the same time the moral culture of institutions must respond to larger academic, legal, and social currents in moral discussion, and the ethicist must be sensitive to relations and significant differences among these contexts. Wibren Van der Berg, in a recent analysis of the "slippery slope argument" so common in applied ethics, warns, for example, that "too often, ethicists simply assume that a sound argument in the context of morality is also sound in the context of law, and vice versa."[23] He reminds us that applied ethicists themselves need discrimination and agility in keeping straight the moral, conventional, legal, and political dimensions of problems, policies, and practices.

Another part of the institutional ethicist's critical equipment must be alertness to differences between the conceptual weight of certain moral considerations and the social authority that may or may not be behind them. If an ethicist has a special responsibility for the moral-reflective space, this includes sensitivity to configurations of authority and dynamics of relationship that can either help structure that space or deform it. Interest in and practice with professional norms, typical role-structured perspectives, and particular institutional folkways is vital. This is not only because ethicists won't be respected if they don't know "the nuances and complexities of moral life as it is lived in a hospital,"[24] although they probably won't if they don't. It is also because without this kind of nuanced understanding the ethicist may not be effective in encouraging *critical, reflective,* and *collaborative* moral thinking. This includes moral thinking in which the unselfconscious exercise of power or expression of role-bound interests is replaced by conscious acknowledgement of legitimate authority and justified interests, and accepting the responsibilities these entail.[25] Differences "ideally" will be mediated, reconciled, or blended in fruitful compromise; but even in cases where they cannot be clarification of roles, values, and responsibilities is an achievement and a resource for future deliberation. This is exactly one of the things the moral space must provide for.

Ideal ethicists, then, would be equipped with broad cultural and philosophical understanding of morality as living social medium. They would cultivate perceptions and skills that help them to help others move deliberations along in ways that both arrive at resolutions *and* produce mutual recognition and clarifed responsibility along the way. One important qualification for this role is appreciating its very complexity, its ideal requirement of very broad intellectual and social culture combined with keen interpersonal perceptiveness.

These attitudes and aptitudes are not easily mapped back on to existing disciplinary models in higher education. Graduate education in academic ethics in American universities today aims at a far narrower form of intellectual preparation than that discussed here. (This philosophical training in elegant theory-construction "tested" largely against hypothetical cases and ingenious counterexamples was, after all, the root of the engineering model.) As momentum builds for certifying or credentialing practical medical ethicists it is well to consider how limited and limiting are current disciplinary definitions. It seems clear that training for ethics consultants would need to be both interdisciplinary (by present definitions) and interwoven with intern- or apprenticeships which rehearse ethicists in the ways of the clinical world. It is also true that the idea of "the" ethics consultant (reflecting the idea of some one individual as a repository of expert or privileged moral knowledge) is questionable. Flexible networks of inside and outside ethicists, linking the moral space of particular institutions to other sites of "the reflective social dialog"—in universities, policy centers, government, patient activist organizations, and other places—need to be explored.

FROM ENGINEERS AND EXPERTS TO ARCHITECTS AND MEDIATORS

It's not surprising that when the idea of ethics consulting caught on, academic ethicians were recruited to defining and executing the task, and not surprising that many of them would tend to envision it in the prevailing mode of mid-twentieth-century ethics as quasi-scientific theory building and testing. It's also unsurprising that a promise of expert input would help to insert them into settings thoroughly organized in terms of professional specializations and the prestige hierarchies. But while ethicists gained access, the center of the original model does not seem to be holding, either in philosophical or in applied medical ethics. The picture of morality as construction and negotiation offers some new images.

Try thinking of a consulting ethicist from one angle as like an *architect*, someone who designs a structure to fulfill a function at a given site. Architects must have certain kinds of genuinely technical expertise—in basic engineering principles, for example. But they must also draw on social and psychological fact and on aesthetic sensibility, both programmatic and vernacular, to relate structure to function in workable and satisfying ways. A consulting ethicist needs conceptual tools and training, but also a sense of where moral space needs to be created or sustained, and of how to structure that space for an integrated and inclusive process of moral negotiation within the constraints of a particular institution.

Now try thinking of the consulting ethicist acting within the moral space as a kind of *mediator*. A mediator actively participates in a situation (usually one of actual or potential conflict of viewpoint and interest) with a primary commitment to a fruitful process of resolution. The mediator isn't "value-free," because the mediator is deeply interested in good resolution. A *good* resolution is the kind that might come from stakes being clearly assessed, parties becoming clear on their own and others' legitimate positions, compromises being achieved that will stand up satisfactorily to later review because of the care with which they were constructed. The process itself becomes a constituent in the good of the product.

These two images might be further explored in reviewing the concept and the practice of ethics consulting.[26]

NOTES

1. Joan McIver Gibson and Thomasine Kimbrough Kushner cite a 1985 survey by the American Hospital Association's National Society for Patient Representatives showing that as many as 60 percent of hospitals nationwide may have established IECs, a figure double that for 1983. See "Will the 'Conscience of an Institution' Become Society's Servant?" *Hastings Center Report* 16, no. 3 (1986): 9–11.

2. See Gilbert Ryle, "On Forgetting the Difference between Right and Wrong," *Essays in Moral Philosophy*, ed. A. I. Melden (Seattle: University of Washington Press, 1958); Robert W. Burch, "Are There Moral Experts?" *Monist* 58 (1974): 646–58;

Bela Szabados, "On 'Moral Expertise,'" *Canadian Journal of Philosophy* 8 (1978): 117–29; Francoise Baylis, "Persons with Moral Expertise and Moral Experts: Wherein Lies the Difference?" in *Clinical Ethics:Theory and Practice*, ed. Barry Hoffmaster, Benjamin Freedman, and Gwen Fraser (Clifton, N.J.: Humana Press, 1989), 89–99.

3. See Daniel Dennett, "The Moral First Aid Manual," *The Tanner Lectures on Human Values*, vol. 8, ed. Sterling M. McMurrin (Salt Lake City: University of Utah Press, 1988).

4. See Arthur L. Caplan, "Mechanics on Duty: The Limitations of a Technical Definition of Moral Expertise for Work in Applied Ethics," supplementary volume 8, *Canadian Journal of Philosophy* (1982): 1–18.

5. Ruth Macklin, "Ethical Theory and Applied Ethics: A Reply to the Skeptics," in *Clinical Ethics:Theory and Practice*, 102–24; Robert M.Veatch, "Clinical Ethics, Applied Ethics, and Theory," in *Clinical Ethics:Theory and Practice*, 7–25, at 8–9.

6. One handy collection that represents some of these critiques is Stanley G. Clarke and Evan Simpson, *Anti-Theory in Ethics and Moral Conservatism* (Albany: State University of New York Press, 1989).

7. Abraham Edel, "Ethical Theory and Moral Practice: On the Terms of Their Relation," in *New Directions in Ethics*, ed. Joseph P. DeMarco and Richard M. Fox (New York: Routledge and Kegan Paul, 1984), 317–35, provides a good discussion of all these factors.

8. On the bearing of individual's moral histories, see Margaret Urban Walker, "Moral Particularity," *Metaphilosophy* 18 (1987): 171–85, reprinted as chapter 1 in this volume.

9. "Please Don't Tell!" case study, with commentary by Leonard Fleck and Marcia Angell, *Hastings Center Report* 21, no. 6 (1991): 39–40.

10. Stanley Cavell, *The Claim of Reason*, part 3 (New York: Oxford University Press, 1979), 269.

11. Two early and interesting exceptions to this are Larry R. Churchill, "The Ethicist in Professional Education," *Hastings Center Report* 8, no. 6 (1978): 13–15; and William Ruddick, "Can Doctors and Philosophers Work Together?" *Hastings Center Report* 11, no. 2 (1981): 12–17, which explore the roles of ethicists as "strangers" or "outsiders" to professional medical culture and to the institutional cultures of their consulting locales. I return to these important insights below.

12. See Bruce Jennings, "Applied Ethics and the Vocation of Social Science," *New Directions in Ethics*, 205–17, esp. 208–9, on this "second stage" in applied ethics.

13. In a recent Humana Press collection which focuses on the consulting role, fully seven out of ten papers deal primarily with these issues. See Hoffmaster et al., eds., *Clinical Ethics:Theory and Practice*.

14. Terrence Ackerman, "Moral Problems, Moral Inquiry, and Consultation in Clinical Ethics," in *Clinical Ethics:Theory and Practice*, 141–60, esp. 150–56.

15. Janet E. Fleetwood, Robert M. Arnold, and Richard J. Baron, "Giving Answers or Raising Questions? The Problematic Role of Institutional Ethics Committees,"

Journal of Medical Ethics 15 (1989): 137–42; Sisters of Mercy Health Corporation, *Hospital Ethics Committees* (November, 1983), 8, quoted in Gibson and Kushner, "Will the 'Conscience of an Institution' Become Society's Servant?"

16. Arthur Caplan, "Moral Experts and Moral Expertise," in *Clinical Ethics: Theory and Practice*, 59–87, at 85.

17. Robert Baker, "The Skeptical Critique of Clinical Ethics," in *Clinical Ethics: Theory and Practice*, 27–57, at 44–45.

18. Churchill, "The Ethicist in Professional Education," 15; Ruddick, "Can Doctors and Philosophers Work Together?" 15.

19. William Ruddick and William Finn, "Objections to Hospital Philosophers," *Journal of Medical Ethics* 11, no. 1 (1985): 42–46, at 45.

20. Ruddick, "Can Doctors and Philosophers Work Together?" 17.

21. Howard Brody, "Applied Ethics: Don't Change the Subject," in *Clinical Ethics: Theory and Practice*, 183-200, at 194; Ackerman, "Moral Problems, Moral Inquiry, and Consultation in Clinical Ethics," 156.

22. Virginia Warren, "Feminist Directions in Medical Ethics," *Hypatia* 4 (1989): 73–87, discusses how preoccupation with "crisis" cases in medical ethics persistently occludes "housekeeping" issues. In the same special issue on medical ethics and feminist critique, see also Susan Sherwin, "Feminist Medical Ethics: Two Different Approaches to Contextual Ethics," 57–72, and Susan Wendell, "Towards a Feminist Theory of Disability," 104–24.

23. Wibren Van der Berg, "The Slippery Slope Argument," *Ethics* 102 (1991): 42–65.

24. Caplan, "Moral Experts and Moral Expertise," 84.

25. See Fleetwood et al., "Giving Answers or Raising Questions?" 139–40.

26. Many thanks to the editors of the *Report* for initial encouragement and invaluable editorial judgment. Thanks also to Drs. Caroline Kalina and James Whalen, who provided the conversation for the opening anecdote. I am grateful to Fordham University for a Faculty Fellowship in Spring, 1992, during which this essay was written.

10

INELUCTABLE FEELINGS AND
MORAL RECOGNITION

In his famous essay "Freedom and Resentment" Strawson tries to "keep before our minds something it is easy to forget when we are engaged in philosophy, especially in our cool, contemporary style, viz. what it is actually like to be involved in ordinary inter-personal relationships, ranging from the most intimate to the most casual."[1] Strawson reminds us "how much we actually mind, how much it matters to us, whether the actions of other people—and particularly of *some* other people—reflect attitudes toward us of goodwill, affection, or esteem on the one hand or contempt, indifference, or malevolence on the other."[2] He calls our attention to attitudes and emotional responses that embody and express our "minding"—how we react to—others' attitudes and emotional responses of this kind. Resentment, gratitude, love, forgiveness, and, I would add, trust and mistrust are among "personal" reactive feelings and attitudes to expressions of others' wills toward us. The larger family encompasses "moral" or "impersonal" reactive attitudes felt in response to someone's injury, insult, or benefaction to others, such as indignation, moral hatred, admiration, respect; and there are "self-reactive" attitudes too that embody our reactions to our own attitudes toward others and toward their expression in action: guilt, shame, remorse, compunction, contrition.

Some contemporary philosophers seem to have warmed to the idea that proneness to certain feelings about others matters very much indeed. They argue that certain feelings about others betray a recognition of their moral claims on us whether or not we wish to acknowledge them, or a stronger recognition than some of us might be willing to admit. I will examine four philosophers' hopeful arguments that a certain kind of emotional response to another constitutes a recognition—and in the kinds of contexts imagined, an unwilling concession—of another's humanity, and so

141

another's claim for moral recognition comparable to that which the recognizer expects for herself or himself. The first two arguments I consider, by Christine Korsgaard and Martha Nussbaum, do not explicitly invoke an emotional response as constituting moral recognition, while the latter two, by Patricia Greenspan and Laurence Thomas, explicitly do so. But the former two, I will try to show, do so implicitly; it is hard to see what they are supposed to turn on if not, in crucial part, that someone "can't help but feel" something that once felt constitutes or forces recognition of humanity in another just like the recognizer's own.

Whether or not my claim about the implicit emotional appeal is persuasive, however, the first two examples illustrate one point I want to make about moral recognition that applies as well to the clearly emotion-based arguments. It is the mistake of thinking of moral recognition as essentially uniform and so symmetrical: to recognize someone morally is to see him or her as deserving the same moral regard one would have for oneself, or even to have that moral standing that applies to everyone if it applies to anyone. While this view is philosophically popular, even canonical in modern ethics, it is dangerously false if one wants to understand actual human social and moral relations.

The mistake is to fail to note the real and very commonplace phenomenon of asymmetrical and unequal but nonetheless clearly moral recognitions that lie at the heart of many human societies and their interpersonal relations. It is one thing to hold that asymmetrical or unequal recognition of others' claims on our restraint or goodwill is *inadequate* or *flawed* or the *wrong kind* of moral recognition. It is another to pretend there is no such thing as this, to overlook it, or to rule it out "conceptually" as not what is meant by "moral" recognition. For it appears to be the rule among human beings. It *is* their way, in many different versions at actual places and times, of recognizing each others' humanity and taking responsibility for certain shared expectations of proper treatment: assigning human beings (and only human beings) to distinct and proper, but not necessarily equal or symmetrical, places in a moral and social world. Without seeing this one can easily go wrong about the roles that interpersonally loaded reactive attitudes play in structuring and expressing moral relations. If one further holds certain doubtful views about the discrete, uniform, and minimally discriminating operations of emotions, it is easier still to be misled. If moral recognition is not all or nothing and homogeneous, however, neither will be the operation of reactive attitudes; they will operate contextually, nonsymmetrically, selectively, and on sliding scales. They are not a royal road, or a uniquely quick or true one, to *uniform* and *symmetrical* moral recognition. They are a learned repertory of highly discriminating responses that embody very different attitudes to different sorts of people. The formation of these responses and feelings is one way to entrench and propagate unequal, and unequally advantaged, moral standings that reflect social ones.

FOUR HOPEFUL ARGUMENTS

"We are strangers and you are tormenting me. . . ."

Christine Korsgaard imagines that "we are strangers and that you are tormenting me" and that I call upon you to stop, asking how you would like it if someone did that to you. This, she says, obligates you in the following way. You would not merely dislike being tormented, but would *resent* it, would take the tormentor to have a *reason* to stop that springs from your own objection. She explains:

> "You make yourself an end for others; you make yourself a law to them. But if you are a law to others in so far as you are just human, just *some-one*, then the humanity of others is also a law to you."[3]

The argument, she notes, does require that you "see yourself . . . as just someone, a person, one person among others who are equally real" and that you could not see this if you failed to see "what you and the other have in common."[4] Korsgaard claims that the argument *cannot* fail by your failing to see this. For your failing to see this amounts to hearing the words of the other as mere noise: "In hearing your words as *words*, I acknowledge that you are *someone*."[5] I either see you as "someone" (like me) or see you as no one at all.

Only if I fail to see what I and another have in common, viz. our bare humanity, our being "just someone," could I fail to see that I am one person among others, including you, who are equally real. But if I so much as understand you to be speaking, then I take you for what I am, a human being. So I cannot fail to see that I am "just someone" like you, and seeing that is just *enough* to "force you to acknowledge the value of *my* humanity."[6] But is it?

Korsgaard says that I force you to acknowledge the value of my humanity "*by making you think these thoughts.*"[7] In fact, though, I have to care about what I imagine when you ask me "how I would like it." When I realize I would *resent* your doing to me what I'm doing to you, this does more than register a sort of third-person observer judgment, or a disinterested thinking of thoughts. It registers my first person experience of the wrongfulness of your treatment of me in the form of angry wronged *feeling*, for that is what resentment is.[8] It is important that Korsgaard has chosen an example of "torment"—painful treatment—as the scene in which one person challenges another to imagine "how they would like it." If the imagined scene were, for example, one in which the recipient of possibly unjustified treatment were not suffering, the honest answer to "how would you like it?" might be "I wouldn't mind." We mind being *tormented*; what is not painful or distressing is not "torment."

Yet even with the assumption that the tormentor cannot evade the painfulness of what he or she inflicts, the argument fails to get the grip it needs. For what the argument finally turns on is the unavoidability of the tormentor's understanding the victim's words as words, and so the recognition of the victim as a human speaker. And it is supposed to be this recognition of bare shared humanity, of "being someone," that compels the tormentor to acknowledge that the victim's suffering has the same moral significance as the tormentor's own. I know I'm "someone" and am forced to admit you are "someone" too, and knowing you are "someone" is all that I need to know. But this assumes just what is to be proved. What is to be proved is indeed that some other human beings' suffering (or, for that matter, expectation, hope, need, etc.)—just in being that of a *human* being—constrains me at least as much as, and in those ways that, I see my own suffering to constrain them. Korsgaard supposes that I already see my claim on others' restraint (or assistance) as constituted by my "being someone"—being a human being—and no more. But if there is a question of whether human beings count *just as such* morally for the tormentor (and for the victim), and count *uniformly* morally just as such for them, the argument hangs.

Suppose I see another I am tormenting as "just someone," that is, as unquestionably simply another human being. I might think "Oh, just another human being, just someone," meaning that he or she is not *more* than merely a human creature, not one singled out for particular kinds of respect or regard, for example, not one of us; not one who matters; not one I must honor or trouble about. For example, someone's bare humanity might present itself, unless bare humanity just as such is already a morally compelling reason for one, as presenting a *strategic*, rather than moral, problem. If one has to deal with a someone, rather than a something or another kind of animal, one has certain distinctive options and problems in exerting control or extracting behavior from this someone. This is the way of regarding a human being that Strawson called the "objective attitude," not because in it one takes a person for a thing, but because in it one takes in a person with the object of purely manipulative control of that person, in which the controlled person's own thoughts and attitudes are of concern only as means or impediments to ends determined independently by the controller.[9]

Or, in another case, another's being just someone and nothing more—lacking a certain standing or membership—might be exactly the reason I take the other to be eligible for treatment which would be unacceptable, even outrageous, in the case of others who are more than merely human beings. I might see myself as among these more-than-merely-human others. Then the response to the challenge "how would you like it?" might be amusement, irritation, or outrage at the very suggestion that our positions could be reversed, or resentment that I, who am certainly not just "someone," would endure what I now inflict on you.

It is unsettling that the image conjured up by Korsgaard's featureless example is that of a torturer and victim. If the victim is already "reduced" to screams, groans, or unconsciousness, there is no question of the torturer's being obligated by "words," that is, by something that can only be human speech. Yet pick any case of face to face, hands-on torture you choose: could we imagine that the torturer does not fully grasp that the victim is another human being? If we imagine a torturer dispassionately attempting to achieve a goal, such as extracting information, then the victim's humanity is primarily a strategic consideration. On the other hand, I find it difficult not to imagine that it is precisely the humanity—the punished, subjugated, helpless, or degraded humanness of the victim—that drives the torturer. Whether the torture is strategic, sadistic, or both, it is not the other's humanness that the torturer does not see.

It is even possible that those administering policies of torture in official roles feel some compassion for their charges. Maria Rosa Henson was the first woman in the Philippines to accept a Japanese reparation payment and government apology for her torment as a "comfort woman," held captive at age fifteen for sexual use by ten to thirty Japanese soldiers a day. Mrs. Henson says of her captor Captain Tanaka, who also raped her but stroked her hair and kissed her cheek: "I was always asking him, 'Let me go, Tanaka,' but he answered: 'I cannot do that. It is against my Emperor'...I realized that the vow of Tanaka to his Emperor was very great, greater than my plea."[10] It is not easy to know what the "recognition" of the "humanity" of "someone" comes to, even when it takes the occasional form of appropriate feelings of sympathy. But it is by no means deeper or more compelling than many role-defined responsibilities, which may be specified precisely as things one is required to do to particular human beings in certain circumstances.

Seeing in otherwise very differently situated (and sexed, and colored, and powerful) people their "common" bare humanity, seeing that bare humanity *as* a moral status, and seeing it as the *same* one in each of its instances regardless of other features they have or lack, is seeing someone's "simple" humanness in a very special light. There is reason to think people have to learn to see this, and that the process, cultural and individual, in which people are seen in their simple, fully comparable, and morally fundamental humanness is not a simple process. The reason to think it is not so simple is that it has seemed so often, so long, among human beings so hard to see. It has been hard to see even at close, indeed intimate, quarters, and even when the intimacy is that of fond attachment and not terror.

"He has acknowledged her humanity already . . . "

Martha Nussbaum conjures up a different image for a parallel argument. Her argument for the necessity of symmetrical recognition—that one must recognize the moral value in, or the standing of, another as essentially like one's own—turns on a more detailed scenario and on a relatively "thick" conception of an individual's humanity. Nussbaum resuscitates an argument of the Roman Stoic Musonius Rufus. It "uses a conception of the human being for feminist ends,"[11] to conclude that women are morally entitled to a liberal education that, like men's, is necessary to develop their intellectual and moral capabilities. The first premise is that the very presence of capabilities in a human being for certain central human functions "exerts a claim" on society that the capabilities be developed to the point that the functions might be chosen by that human being. The second premise is that women do have, experience shows, the basic capabilities to perform "a wide variety of the most important human functions."[12] Nussbaum describes the second premise as puzzling: why does "the imaginary recalcitrant male interlocutor" accept it? The puzzle, notice, is not: what evidence shows that the second premise is true? but: what would compel a recalcitrant male interlocutor's acceptance of it? Here she refers, apparently along with the Stoic, not to general observation of women, but to the experience of a husband who "interacts with his wife in a number of areas of life," including childraising, household management, intentionally monogamous sexual relations, companionship, and broader social and political life.[13] His own personal experience reveals that "he tacitly acknowledges, in fact strongly relies on, his wife's capability to engage in practical reasoning and ethical distinction making. . . . So, in his daily life he acknowledges her humanity, her possession of the basic (lower-level) capabilities for fully human functioning."[14]

It is Nussbaum's explanation of the force of this argument that puzzles me. She explicitly appeals to the beliefs of the interlocutor about his wife as evidenced in his expectations and in her behavior that satisfies them. These beliefs constitute the husband's tacit acknowledgment. Of what is it the acknowledgment? What is described is, in fact, precisely what a good wife of a certain social class at a particular time and place does. No doubt there are at that time and place, as at many others, many good wives. And even women who are not very good wives exhibit basic recognizably human behaviors and cognitive functions; they are recognizably human females. But it cannot be this that is only tacitly conceded and so needs to be made explicit. What must need admitting is that the good wife's performance shows that she has a basic humanity *in no way different* from her husband's. But that is what husbands, then and now, have often denied; for the fact is, she is a wife because she is a *woman*. It is just that which has been so enduringly seen as marking a basic distinction among human beings. What is curious is that Nussbaum sees Musonius as scoring a decisive point by calling the husband's attention to exactly this woman's *wifely* excellence: this is just the kind of thing, after all, at which *women* (where that term often refers not just to females, but to females of certain classes or categories) are believed distinctively or uniquely to excel.[15]

Perhaps this is why Nussbaum flavors (it seems following Musonius) the description of shared conjugal life with more than flat description of a wife's speech and other purposive behavior. She adds parenthetically that "(. . . he observes, or imagines, her in labor, enduring risk and pain for the sake of the family . . .)"[16] and emphasizes the warm and cooperative companionship that the couple enjoy. What is pictured is not a detached observer, but a fond, proud, and devoted husband. One might fairly conjecture that this husband does not only "strongly rely" upon his wife, but trusts and admires her. He might cherish her and feel grateful not only that he has such a wife but feel grateful *to her* for the life they enjoy owing in part to her competence and good character. When Musonius asks "How . . . can he consistently deny her what would be necessary in order to develop and fulfill that humanity?"[17] there is, then, a tug on the imagined feelings of the imagined husband. I think he is (we are) supposed to *feel* her claim, to be claimed by the feelings that are drawn out by her valuable, admirable self.

But why should this help? The proud and devoted husband is proud of and devoted to his good wife, grateful for her seemly decorum, her fidelity, her loyalty, her good sense in performing her wifely duties. Need this inspire the thought, much less the wish, that the capacities that allow her to be this ought to be otherwise or further developed? Should her head for household

accounts be turned to geometry, her physical courage to martial arts, her pru-
dence to commerce, her ideals of shared life to politics? Could we assume
the unfolding of her capacities in these novel ways would prompt more affection, admiration, trust, or gratitude in turn? Neither the beliefs that his
wife's distinctly human capacities allow her to function in a way he so approves, nor the feelings of approval themselves, suggest that he will see in her
another human being exactly like himself finding fulfillment in housekeeping. Much less is he likely to be struck by how he might use his basic human
capabilities to be a good wife. One need not deny that husbands and fathers
may sometimes experience at least the former epiphany. One needs only to
note that they do not do so invariably, or even typically. This is because there
is no incompatibility between seeing one's wife as human and continuing to
believe that certain things are better for human beings *of her kind*, where the
relevant kind is "women." This view can include, and historically has often
included, the belief that certain things are best for human females to be and
do because these are the things human males need or want them to do, or
find it attractive that they do.[18] Neither did slave masters in the antebellum
South of the United States think that slaves' aptitude for religious instruction
and for the faithful performance of duty without direct supervision showed
a *kind* of humanity that demanded personal autonomy and political liberty
like their own. Christian divines in fact appealed to the *humanity* of slaves in
exhorting slave-owning whites to be *good slave masters*.[19] The curiosity of
Nussbaum's claim that this argument about sex equality demonstrates "the
power of a universal conception of the human being"[20] is that it is not clear
how it is supposed even to generate the universal conception of the human
being exactly the same in all cases, much less a uniform standard of fair treatment for all those who are human, whatever else they are.[21] Again, it is as if
a closer look and a little reflection are supposed to reveal an insight that history and society show us repeatedly is hard won and still mostly resisted: that
the sex of human beings is, or can be, or should be, irrelevant to the ways
they display some common humanness that all human beings have.[22]

 In the arguments of Korsgaard and Nussbaum, I have claimed that the
insinuation of certain feelings is in fact meant to pull weight in bringing the
conclusion of comparable or symmetrical moral recognition home. Even if
this is not so, these arguments seem strangely innocent about the availabil-
ity of what is apparently a difficult achievement: the conception of simple
common humanness with a uniform moral meaning all its own. They make
it seem easy. Two other arguments introduce greater complexity and bring
emotions explicitly into an analysis of interpersonal relations in which some
are not accorded equal or comparable recognition to others.

"Social exclusion pulls against our natural response tendencies."

Patricia Greenspan defends a view of morality as shaped from the bottom up by emotions. She assumes that "despite the social sources of our adult stock of emotions, ethics . . . has to rely on the shape given to behavior by our natural emotion tendencies," and in particular a "tendency to identify emotionally with others."[23] She argues that exclusive caste systems, which "put some subgroups beyond the moral pale," run up against a "barrier" in the natural emotional tendencies of human beings. While the barrier is "not insuperable" it imposes "a social cost."[24] The argument is this.

Moral emotions "seem to be formed from other responses on the basis of natural identificatory processes that are not directly sensitive to social or socially marked distinctions among people—or even to differences in natural endowment of the sort that might be used to support social stratification according to function."[25] Instead, inculcation of moral emotions "presupposes sensitivity to personal and behavioral similarities and relationships such as contact and personal dependency."[26] Since "behavioral similarity would seem to be enough to set off the mechanism," "the attempt to limit it to members of a social subgroup—or to check it with some opposing tendency . . . might be taken as yielding an unstable combination," a persistent tension between elements that "tends to undermine moral code construction." It is not a question of impossibility, but of "social and psychological costs."[27]

It is obvious that there are matters here for empirical research into the acquisition or enculturation of moral emotions or their affective antecedents. Greenspan does not in fact appeal to empirical studies. But this much seems clear. If there are natural, that is, spontaneous, identificatory processes that are indiscriminate (Greenspan's example is the contagion by which infants cry in response to the sound of another infant's crying), moral emotions must be considerably "formed" beyond these responses. Greenspan herself notes that moral emotions involve complex intentional structures; the result of emotional learning is emotion "directed toward fairly sophisticated sorts of propositional objects, including moral act-requirements."[28] If the moral emotions we acquire are sensitive to socially marked differences among situations that define which acts are required or forbidden, why would we assume that these discriminating, conceptually complex responses are indifferent to socially marked distinctions among people, which after all are among the more salient features of interpersonal situations?

Children clearly master the arts of tact and white lying, or appropriate trust, or obedience to authorities, for instance, by learning to attend to special features of situations in context.[29] These features include kinds of relationship (like dependency, familiarity, and responsibility), or relative standings (like that of elders and children), or roles (like police officer, schoolteacher, or priest). Why then suppose they do not learn to discriminate among various salient relations of authority and subordination, or of symmetry or complementarity, and many different kinds of those? Learning to resent wrongful injuries by responsible parties includes learning which parties are responsible, to whom, and in what matters, and learning which things it is wrong for certain people to do to others. In actual social worlds, this means learning which things it is not wrong for certain people to do to certain others (e.g., to give them orders, impose punishments, restrict behavior), and grasping differences in accountability between people in different relations and statuses.

Moral emotions, or their appropriate form and occasions of expression, including resentment, indignation, shame, guilt, vengefulness, gratitude, remorse, disapprobation, respect, trust, or forgiveness, might be learned in some contexts at some points *without explicit attention* to socially marked distinctions. A child might begin to learn to identify and express these responses to different kinds of people or people distinctively positioned in situations without being instructed explicitly in all the differences of their applications. Yet it does not follow even then that the child is not learning paradigms of trust, respect, or contempt *in* particular relations, and perhaps learning *different* ones in different relationships. And even if a child is learning some very general things about sympathy, resentment, or distrust, it does not follow that this "generic" learning will not be further refined as the child confronts a fuller spectrum of situations in which socially marked difference are standardly held to imply different grounds for resentment or compassion with respect to differently placed people in certain kinds of situations. In caste systems, or other social systems which require significant hierarchy or segregation between groups identified by sex, skin, marking, or costume, the relevance of distinctions to what is appropriately felt about or for people of different groups will be part of a child's social initiation and experience from early years. A crucial part of that social learning will be learning with whom one should identify (and so feel with, or feel like) and with whom one should or must not. As Lillian Smith said plainly of a twentieth-century childhood in the southern United States, "The mother who taught me what I know of tenderness and love and compassion taught me also the bleak rituals of keeping Negroes in their place."[30]

Greenspan seems to want to establish that the cost to a society of "allowing or encouraging indifference to the welfare of a certain subclass of its members" is not a negligible one.[31] The cost she alleges seems to be one of individual psychological strain or conflict. Agents, she says, will "risk acting at cross purposes in not taking adequate moral account of the sufferings of people they understood to be human."[32] And this is supposed to threaten the possibility or stability of moral code construction because of an oscillation in the motivational structure that supports adherence to the code.

Yet most human societies have embodied and continue to require significant hierarchy or segregation among groups they comprise. Often societies institutionalize the marginality or stigmatization of some groups by others. In most cases these practices serve the welfare of members of some groups directly to the detriment of others, place undeniably different values on the welfare of people of different groups, and often place very little value on the lives or happiness of people of some (social) kinds.[33] Patriarchal, hereditary caste, racist or ethnic nationalist, and other hierarchical and inegalitarian societies do this. It has been the rule, not the exception, among human beings. The fact seems to be that moral norms of actual human societies serve to regulate behavior, distribute responsibility, and shape and direct feeling *through* these forms of social differentiation, rather than alongside them or in spite of them.[34] It appears that early learning and continuing experience do reinforce different kinds and levels of trust, sympathy, antipathy, indignation and resentment, and do teach complementary, rather than symmetrical ("identificatory"), expectations and responses among people of different social "kinds."

Greenspan's argument pictures a world in which each learns to feel X for "human beings" in Y—say, to feel sympathy for human beings who are suffering. The learned responses are generic responses to "human beings" in states and situations, and are mediated by one's "identification" with other human beings in those situations. She thinks people must then experience conflict, tension, or confusion when incompatible social directives ruling out identification with, or certain feelings for, some human beings collide with the original lesson. It is as if, say, one found out later that one need not feel sympathy for the outcast (slave, lower orders, women), because it is her fate (need, role, nature) that makes her live as we would shudder, or bitterly resent, or find it an indignity, to live.

This view partakes of the assumption, already noted in the arguments of Korsgaard and Nussbaum above, that there is an obvious kind of moral recognition that simply goes to human beings *just as such*, providing a uniform standard or baseline of acceptable or obligatory treatment. This assumption, I have already argued, makes the point of view this recognition embodies seem easy to achieve. Greenspan, too, treats moral recognition as if it were *a* (that is, one, uniform) point of view on or kind of response to "someone." But she also holds that this recognition includes or is shaped through a repertory of *emotional* responses that are not typically or normally sensitive to socially marked differences. She represents uniform or symmetrical emotional responses (which include or are mediated by emotional identification) as "normal," when these are clearly not typical among all people in many societies. In patriarchal societies men do not resent or feel grateful for the same things in or done by women as they do those done by other men, and conversely. In white supremacist societies whites do not feel pity, indignation, or admiration for the same things done by non-whites as they do those done by whites, and conversely. In caste societies, the circumstances of contempt, shame, respect, or mercy are different for those of lower and higher caste, both with respect to each other's kind and within their own.

Selective and discriminating distributions of responsibility and obligation, and the rich repertories of selective and discriminating feelings that support them and respond to them, are more common than not, and relatively sturdy. It may not be welcome to some of us, but it is so. Differentiated social systems house and implement differentiated moral ones. Since Greenspan herself sees morality as actual humanly fabricated codes that seek community flourishing, her speculative psychology cannot stand up to the overwhelming evidence that actual, longstanding codes tend to implement precisely the calibrated and selective emotional responses that she wants to say constitute a serious barrier to them. I believe distinctive psychological and social costs are paid by systems that must reproduce hierarchy, segregation, marginality, or exclusion. Distinctive psychological and social costs are born by egalitarian social arrangements, too.[35] Whose costs these are, and how great they are, remains to be determined. It is not obvious that inegalitarian or even oppressive societies under varied social conditions entail special difficulties in meeting their "costs." Most human societies are like this; it is clearly a possible type of social world and not obviously more difficult to sustain than the alternatives. Within our social worlds we acquire the moral feelings that fit that world and our places in it.

> *"Slaveowners could not delight in the goodwill of slaves and show no gratitude."*

Laurence Thomas is acutely aware of the complexity of actual moral arrangements, the variety of ways they can be deformed by oppression, cruelty, or exploitation, and the pathologies of community, relationship, and individual character that result from this. I believe, though, that while this is a central theme of Thomas's work he still sees the emotional fabric of relationships that he considers so important to morality as more homogeneous than it is, or even than his own views suggest it is.[36]

Like Greenspan, Thomas argues that ongoing oppressive social relations where the dominators rely upon their subordinates but do not acknowledge their full humanity, such as those between white masters and African slaves in American slavery, give rise to incongruities that entail psychological strain and demand psychological maneuvering. While Greenspan appeals to a (questionable) kind of "thin" generic emotional identification and a uniform tendency to symmetrical response, Thomas explores a thicker tissue of emotional responses that support specific types of interactions between people in ongoing relations of unequal power. Thomas is interested in how people negotiate the complex network of feelings inevitable in "expectations-generating power arrangements" in which subordinates are integrated into the lives of dominators, rather than being simply objects of coercive force.[37] He thinks what dominators *feel* in such relations gives the lie to the assumption that these are indeed *rightful* forms of domination. And he thinks that dominators' inability to recognize, or their need to stave off, the implications of what they feel requires that they be or become psychologically damaged or warped. What they feel, in particular, is trust and resentment. Thomas argues that " . . . certain forms of oppression and hostility carry in their wake moral sentiments which, far from denying the humanity of the oppressed, logically presuppose the humanity of the oppressed."[38]

These daily relations involve *trust* between dominators and subordinates, and so, Thomas argues a "moral relationship between the agents and subjects": "Whenever we desire that another believe that she or he can trust us, then, given compliance behavior on the person's part which is recognized as such, we acknowledge that person as a moral agent, if only minimally."[39] For example, slaveowners entrusted the bodies and lives of their children to slaves, and slaves trusted masters to acknowledge slaves' obedience with goodwill and restraint of masters' power. So "pockets of trust" are parts of the fabric of what is nonetheless in the overall a coercive and immoral, even brutal, form of social life.[40] But this introduces *incongruities*. Thomas says "slaveowners certainly viewed slaves as belonging to the category of beings capable of at least some form of deep moral trust."[41] But beings so capable are distinctly—Thomas prefers to say "manifestly"[42]—human beings, and this is precisely what makes their enslavement impossible to justify, and what therefore cannot be acknowledged by their masters.

Nor, it seems, can masters keep coherent their feelings of resentment at slaves' insolence, rebellion, or disobedience, since to experience resentment is to hold oneself intentionally wronged, that is, injured or insulted wrongfully by a person. And if a dominator recognizes resentment operating in those she dominates, then she recognizes them as full-fledged human beings, precisely what puts her domination in question. While Thomas does not fully amplify these points, I think I can reconstruct this more fully.

Masters can resent the ingratitude of slaves who, like Harriet Jacobs's brother in her narrative *Incidents in the Life of a Slave Girl* (1861),[43] run away despite (comparatively) kind treatment and repeated promises of future manumission. The very interpersonal responses that make sense of masters' resentment (that they have earned the slaves' trust by forms of restraint and benevolent intentions that acknowledge the slaves' loyalty) are the reasons the masters' resentment does not make sense. If what you have enslaved is a person, you not only might expect him to run away when he can, but you must see that he is right to do so, and therefore that you are not injured by his doing so. And what else can the slave be but a person, if the slave is assumed to understand the master's trust—to grasp the expectation of goodwill from the slave that the master expects to be elicited by the slave's awareness of the master's expectation?[44] These complex, iterated awarenesses and responses require forms of thought and feeling that are distinctively human. Indeed, the more deeply the resentful, indignant, or outraged master becomes embroiled in his resentment that the slave has betrayed his trust, even that the slave invited or accepted trust in return for goodwill, the more incoherent the master's feelings become. It is worse still if the master feels outraged at the slave's resentment and lack of gratitude; for beings who are capable of resentment and gratitude must have the same basic capacities as resentful masters do. The nuances and complexities of understanding and feeling the master ends up attributing to the slave, and the master's own complex reactions to the slave, betray just how deeply implicated in the slave's humanity are the master's attitudes, expectations, and reactions. The incongruity then is this. It is just the slave's humanity that establishes that the master had no right to any expectations of the slave's acceptance of his or her slavery.

I have already rehearsed with respect to the three foregoing arguments the problems with assuming that there is a self-evident bare humanity seen as just the same whenever human beings encounter and interact with human beings in distinctively human ways, and with supposing that if one does acknowledge a common bare humanity that this automatically counts as morally relevant, and morally relevant in the same way whatever else is true about the human beings who possess this bare humanity. Here, I want to note the way an assumption of uniform, and so symmetrical, feeling creeps into Thomas's discussion of specific relations or occasions of trust and gratitude, or mistrust and resentment.

Thomas prompts us to think that any forms of trust or resentment felt between people show something about their perceptions of each other's functioning, and show essentially the same thing in each case: if I trust you, I see you in the same way I see myself insofar as I see myself as a candidate for your (or someone else's) trust. Thomas does not investigate the ways trust relations can be nonsymmetrical, selective, contextual, and sliding-scale.[45] That is, I might very well trust you, all the while making very different assumptions about what is expected of you, why you will be moved to performance, and what capacities in you are presumed necessary and what conditions surrounding you are presumed salient such that my expectations and reliance make sense. Trust relations need not be symmetrical, even if they are reciprocal: A and B may be bound together by relations of trust, but that in which and with which A trusts B may not be that in which and with which B trusts A. Nor must A trust B on the same grounds, for the same reasons, or with the same assumptions of ability and motivation that B trusts A. Nor can we assume that trust relations between individual masters and slaves were similarly, much less uniformly, defined and based.

A slave might trust his master to forebear cruel treatment in certain cases and feel gratitude to a master for meeting these optimistic expectations; another slave might trust his master to forebear cruel treatment in confidence that he has demonstrated to the master the ineffectiveness of lashing, with gratitude quite out of point.[46] A master might trust her slave to obey and be loyal, where the thought of gratitude to the slave for being loyal is preposterous. The master expects deferential and (realistically) fearful obedience: masters in antebellum slavery did have to trust their slaves to a great extent, but they still used hard overseers and almost all had recourse to the lash. Although masters expected the prospect of punishment, as well as the promise of restraint, to instill loyalty and obedience in their slaves, we should not for that reason think that this is not a case of trust. It seems masters indeed trusted slaves to behave in desired ways on the basis of optimism about how little likely slaves were to see disobedience or disloyalty as an option, and confidence that slaves would act in response to their expectations. But the likelihood of slaves seeing mayhem, disobedience, or escape as an option was bounded by the use of lashing and other physical and psychic punishments, as well as a comprehensive system of legal ownership rights and institutionalized white supremacy and racial caste that rendered effective rebellious action extraordinarily risky. Slaves literally, in multiple senses, had almost no place to go, for escape, relief, or redress.

The presumption that slaves would respond to masters' expectations of them very likely rested on masters' self-flattering assumptions about the slaves' perceptions of the masters' benevolence or rectitude, as well as masters' wishful assumptions about their personal authority, fearsomeness, or grandeur in the eyes of their human chattel.[47] People in socially inferior positions are usually believed by their superiors to be less intelligent, self-controlled, responsible, mature, and, in some departments of life, less competent than their betters. They are often believed to believe the reverse about their betters. Masters and patriarchs have often believed their own mythologies about the greater credulity, trustingness, or natural responsiveness to authority of their charges (at least when it was not convenient to believe for certain purposes in the greater cunning, deceitfulness, and willfulness of them). It is very unlikely that masters' assumptions about the capacities and psychologies of their slaves, including the ones that made the grounds and kinds of trust they invested in their slaves reasonable, were similar to masters' beliefs about their own personalities and capacities, or even to that of others of their inferiors or subordinates. Finally, since what is trusted in and entrusted between masters and slaves is by no means similar, the assumption that masters and slaves in trusting each other attributed to each other similar capacities, motives, or options is implausible. Masters seemed vastly more likely to trust some slaves with their children and with the intimate details of their personal lives than they were to trust any with their money. The last thing with respect to which slaves trusted masters were their children or their real thoughts and feelings about their captors, themselves, or those they loved.

Thomas's claim that the master's feelings are riddled with incongruity prepares the way for his view that people's unconflicted ability to abuse others is explained by "a corrosive failure" of psychological functioning, in particular a failure of some "affective component."[48] He argues that normal human development requires parental love that necessarily engenders self-love, and that self-love necessarily involves a strong conviction that one must not be treated "as less than one among others."[49] Whatever merit this view has with respect to individual psychopathologies, it does not fare well in the context of oppressive systems. I have already said that human beings learn from early years in stratified societies that some *are* more and some *are* less among certain others. Thomas's view further shields from examination precisely how the sense of one's value sets one's own thresholds for insult and resentment, trust and gratitude, as well as one's perception of the thresholds of others. In stratified societies these thresholds will vary among people of different standing. It obscures precisely how much a sense of one's value engendered by parental love may turn on a well and early learned sense of the superiority of one's blood, or skin, or sex, or caste, or class, or alternatively on the fulfillment of demeaning or disabling roles that one has learned to accept, and in which one has even learned to take pride.

I view much of Thomas's work on abusive power arrangements and moral psychology as right and important, and I am far from denying that human relations in such contexts are riddled with inconsistency, incongruity, and absurdity. I think, however, that we need a closer look at specific positions and interactions between similarly and differently placed participants in these usually complexly orchestrated social worlds to see where the incongruities and contradictions emerge. Otherwise one might be tempted to assume there is some human-to-human baseline of recognition that is merely covered over, "hiding out" as it were beneath or behind the outward show of very different and unequal terms of relationship.

PARTICIPANTS AND THEIR ATTITUDES

What fascinates me about these four similar arguments, drawn from the works of philosophers with significantly different ethical views, is their hopeful implausibility. They try to make a direct and powerful connection between certain kinds of affectively hinged interaction and the recognition of another as fully morally akin to oneself. Yet it is a sad, frightening, and unavoidable fact that experiencing or participating in many emotionally charged interactions (including ones of intense intimacy and vulnerability, even mutual vulnerability) is and ever has been wholly compatible with many people's failure to see others as worthy of regard similar to what they expect for themselves, if they see those others as worthy of significant regard at all in some or most respects. This is true, and it is obvious, in cases of institutionalized systems of unequal standing and entitlement (slavery, caste, patriarchy, apartheid, or other exploitative or oppressive arrangements). It may also be true of discrete episodes of "opportunistic" injury or violation that intends to demean and degrade the victims (rape, hate crimes against persons, torture). There is the further problem that in some cases of injury and insult, perhaps of the former and especially of the latter kind, it may be precisely the recognition of another person's humanity that fuels the injury or insult, or makes it rewarding to the aggressor. It is ugly, but it is true. If the conclusions of these arguments did follow from premises that are true as stated in these arguments, it seems we would live, and human beings would ever have lived, in a different and vastly better world than the actual one we know. These arguments seem to aim to show that a situation *must* obtain that pretty evidently does not.

To be fair, these arguments do not try to show that certain interactions between human beings *produce* proper moral recognition. Rather, they claim these interactions commit their parties to *tacit* acknowledgment of each others' moral standing, such that the parties' then pay a price for not recognizing this standing explicitly. Those who turn away from, stave off, or bury what is already implicitly there are on the hook of inconsistency, conflict, or strain as a result. The point is then that it is in some way uncomfortable, unstable, or painful on that hook for those who refuse proper moral recognition. I do not see that making the point subtler in this way makes it more plausible. It does make more evident the powerful appeal of the hopefulness in this line of thought. It implies that the generous distribution among human beings throughout their history of enslavements, oppressions, torture, slaughter, or garden variety domination has been a kind of uphill psychological battle against a resilient natural current of equal moral regard.

Again, this view seems very unlikely. But worse than unlikely, it seems to me harmful. It may have its place in explaining strain, even agony, in episodes where an *already* accepted kind of regard for another is, suddenly or episodically, required to be jettisoned; this might happen to people not raised in a warrior culture who are sent to war, for example. But applied to ongoing and often institutionalized patterns of relations in societies, it starts from the wrong end. It assumes egalitarian ideals and practices that *make* the criterion of moral regard "simply" our common humanity are a naturally occurring default position of human relations. In saying this I do not mean to imply, on the other hand, that cruelty, domination, or abuse are the spontaneous or default tendency of human relations, either. Instead, I think it is dangerous not to notice that all human societies elaborately construct patterns of relationship and specific norms for them. These *are* their ways of responding to human beings, more often than not differently to human beings seen as in some way different from some other human beings. These patterns and norms are learned and reproduced (inevitably with changes and drift) bottom up, top down, and across the breadth of social life. Early trainings and ongoing practices shape thought, behavior, and feelings at once, shape each by means of the others, and shape all to make sense of the patterns of relationship that prevail, whether egalitarian, symmetrical, and reciprocal, or hierarchical, complementary, or unilateral. The dangerous, if alluring, idea is that there is some natural human response to what is simply human, that people understand what they respond to as the distinctive property of simple humanity, and that this is *at the same time* a recognizably moral (or proto-moral) response. I cannot prove that there is not such a thing, but I have tried to suggest reasons that shift the burden of proof to those who think there is. It is not, at any rate, something that one can assume without turning a blind eye to much of human history and present society. I suspect there is a wish at work here that telltale feelings could be relied upon to announce what sophistications of reason might deny.

I sympathize with the spirit of arguments that, at least in the cases of Greenspan and Thomas (and explicitly, in her other work, Nussbaum[50]) urge us to recognize the degree to which morality is embedded in our lives in the form of feeling and emotional response. I agree that morality is as much resident in the feelings that move us as it is shaped by our abilities to understand and reason about what is felt or done. Both feelings and understanding are educable, either at once together or each by means of the other. For this reason it is important to get right what moral weight might be—and cannot be—borne by the tissue of feelings that binds human beings together, for better or worse, in forms of relationship and society. I believe these unpersuasive arguments get a certain appeal from mistaken assumptions about both moral recognition and emotions.

I have argued that it is too easy to assume that there is just one point of view or form of regard that is moral recognition, and that one either receives it or does not. In fact the rule among human beings, whether one approves of it or not, is different social standings that define and are elaborated by different moral ones—different responsibilities, obligations, entitlements, and prerogatives—where some of the latter may be defined precisely by what some people may do with or to others that others may not do with or to them. Human beings have a way of expressing precisely their sense of the meaning of the humanity of different people through slavery, caste, purdah, patriarchy, race privilege, and class entitlement as much as through universal dignity. There are different kinds, contexts, and levels of moral recognition.

Not only thoughts but powerful feelings of pride, disgust, resentment, and outrage are recruited to this social work of creating proper places for human kinds and keeping human beings in them. So I have argued that we ought not to be complacent that people very differently placed with respect to each other feel essentially the same things in essentially similar situations on essentially similar grounds when we say of them that they "trust," "resent," "respect," "are grateful to," "feel contempt for," "pity" or "sympathize with" one another. There may well be differences in conditioning assumptions, motivations, expressions, and grounds of feelings that track different social positions, privileges, and vulnerabilities. Comparative ethnographies of emotion, not only across but within societies, are important alongside, or as materials for, philosophical analyses of emotions.[51]

In addition, as Michael Stocker and Elizabeth Hegeman persuasively argue, individual *character* and *personality* mediate between judgments that characteristically figure in kinds of emotions and the occurrence of the emotion. Whether, for example, someone is moved to sympathy by recognizing, even identifying with, another's vulnerability or suffering will depend on what kind of interest that person takes in the sufferer, whether the observer likes himself, or whether she is prone to affiliate with or differentiate from others. Whether one is shamed by seeing oneself from a perspective one endorses in which one falls beneath what one should be depends, for example, on whether one is more likely to look at oneself as a nurturing care-giver might or as a stern judge. Often, to know where and if a feeling like shame fits, "we must examine people—not the concept of shame."[52] Stocker and Hegeman emphasize the ways individual psychological differences determine to what and in what way people are apt to respond emotionally. I have emphasized the social place at which the individual finds herself, and the understandings of her own and others' places that can determine whether and how she responds emotionally to situations and to other people in them. Of course, these will interact.

Finally, considering the ways that richly interpersonal emotions like trust, resentment, admiration, or gratitude vary with the structures and definitions of relationships in which they occur, we might notice how much these emotions, and perhaps others, are not only motive springs of action within persons, but leads and prods to response between persons. While arguments continue about the relative importance of phenomenological experience (literally, feeling) and cognitive content (constitutive or conditioning beliefs) in the analysis of emotion, the *expressiveness* of emotions has received less attention.[53] The fact is, *our emotions show*, and this is very likely one of their most important functions. In addition to whatever beliefs they involve, however they make us feel, and whatever they make us do, they are signals to others: leads, prompts, warning flares, distress calls, entreaties, invitations, assurances, and threats. When directed at people, the messages emotions convey are not only to those at whom they are directed. They display to anyone who correctly identifies them how we take people, what we take them for, and how we take ourselves to be related to them. Is it surprising, then, that they incorporate and express many of the calibrations and differentiations of relationship and position that social orders produce and demand?

It has been noted that those emotions Strawson called "reactive attitudes" are a kind of *moral address*. They call on ones at whom they are aimed, and often call out to others, to recognize the existence or possibility of a kind of relationship.[54] That is why they constitute a kind of recognition. They are, as Strawson said, the attitudes *of* participants *toward* participants.[55] But the attitudes of participants vary with the specific practices and relations in which they participate and with their specific standings within them. These attitudes will be as familiar as are the practices they serve, and the practices will serve them in turn by making sense of the attitudes, at least on the whole and for the most part. It is hard to imagine how it could work otherwise. But it is also hard when we are doing philosophy to remember how such things work as they familiarly do.[56]

NOTES

1. P. F. Strawson, "Freedom and Resentment," in *Studies in the Philosophy of Thought and Action*, ed. P. F. Strawson (New York: Oxford University Press, 1968), 77.

2. Strawson, "Freedom and Resentment," 75.

3. Christine Korsgaard, *The Sources of Normativity* (New York: Cambridge University Press, 1996), 143.

4. Korsgaard, *The Sources of Normativity*, 143.

5. Korsgaard, *The Sources of Normativity*, 143.

6. Korsgaard, *The Sources of Normativity*, 143.

7. Korsgaard, *The Sources of Normativity*, 143.

8. See Jeffrie Murphy and Jean Hampton, *Forgiveness and Mercy* (New York: Cambridge University Press, 1988) for illuminating analyses of resentment.

9. Strawson, "Freedom and Resentment," 79.

10. Quoted in Seth Mydans, "Inside a Wartime Brothel: The Avenger's Story," *New York Times*, November 12, 1996.

11. Martha Nussbaum, "Human Capabilities, Female Human Beings," in *Women, Culture, and Development*, ed. Martha Nussbaum and Jonathan Glover (New York: Oxford University Press, 1995), 96.

12. Nussbaum, "Human Capabilities," 97.

13. Nussbaum, "Human Capabilities," 98.

14. Nussbaum, "Human Capabilities," 98.

15. For acute analysis of ways the category "woman" does not always apply uniformly to females in societies stratified in other ways than by gender, see Elizabeth V. Spelman, *Inessential Woman* (Boston: Beacon Press, 1988).

16. Nussbaum, "Human Capabilities," 95.

17. Nussbaum, "Human Capabilities," 95.

18. A study of three motifs—woman as partial man, anti-man, and helpmeet of man—that recur monotonously in the history of Western thinking about sex and gender is found in Caroline Whitbeck, "Theories of Sex Difference," in *Women and Philosophy*, ed. Carol Gould and Marx Wartofsky (New York: Putnam, 1976).

19. See John Blassingame, *The Slave Community: Plantation Life in the Antebellum South* (New York: Oxford University Press, 1979), 89, 269–70.

20. Nussbaum, "Human Capabilities," 98.

21. Nussbaum goes on in the next section of her paper to consider separately the question of whether there should be a single or different standards for human functioning, corresponding to the differences in male and female 'natures.' This makes it unclear what the Stoical argument was to have accomplished. It looks like an idle wheel, which I have argued that it is.

22. Thanks to Michael Byron and Peggy DesAutels for helping me formulate the problem here more clearly.

23. Patricia Greenspan, *Practical Guilt* (New York: Oxford University Press, 1995), 199.

24. Greenspan, *Practical Guilt*, 199. Greenspan also argues that there may be certain norms of "social rationality" that constrain moral code viability as well (93–94), but I deal here with her point about emotions, which she herself treats as more important.

25. Greenspan, *Practical Guilt*, 95.

26. Greenspan, *Practical Guilt*, 95.

27. Greenspan, *Practical Guilt*, 96.

28. Greenspan, *Practical Guilt*, 194.

29. A study of the discriminating nature of children's obedience to authority is found in Marta Laupa, Eliot Turiel, and Philip A. Cowan, "Obedience to Authority in Children and Adults," in *Morality in Everyday Life: Developmental Perspectives* (New York: Cambridge University Press, 1995).

30. Lillian Smith, *Killers of the Dream* (New York: Norton, 1949, 1961), 27, is quoted in Elizabeth Spelman, "The Virtue of Feeling and the Feeling of Virtue," in *Feminist Ethics*, ed. Claudia Card (Lawrence: University Press of Kansas, 1991).

31. Greenspan, *Practical Guilt*, 92.

32. Greenspan, *Practical Guilt*, 96.

33. Iris Young, *Justice and the Politics of Difference* (Princeton, N.J.: Princeton University Press, 1990) gives a comprehensive view of different forms of social domination and oppression. Young examines the distinctive operations, interactions, and deployments of these, including discourses that "scale" the normality and acceptability of different "kinds" of human bodies.

34. I treat the relevance of social position to moral standing extensively in Margaret Urban Walker, *Moral Understandings: A Feminist Study in Ethics* (New York: Routledge, 1998).

35. Walker, *Moral Understandings,* chapter 6, considers costs and pressures in creating mutually recognizing "autonomous" peers.

36. Thomas develops different aspects of his views about the conditions and effects of systems of extreme domination or destruction of groups of people in different writings. I don't do justice to a great deal of what he says, and I agree with much of it. I focus here on the theme of incongruous feelings that runs through Laurence Mordekhai Thomas, *Vessels of Evil* (Philadelphia: Temple University Press, 1993); Laurence Mordekhai Thomas, "Power, Trust, and Evil," in *Overcoming Racism and Sexism*, ed. Linda A. Bell and David Blumenfeld (Lanham, Md.: Rowman & Littlefield, 1995); and Laurence Mordekhai Thomas, "Evil and the Concept of a Human Person," in *Midwest Studies in Philosophy XX*, ed. Peter A. French, Theodore E. Uehling, and Howard K. Wettstein (Notre Dame, Ind.: University of Notre Dame Press, 1996). The diagnosis of psychological failure is found in Thomas (1996).

37. Thomas, "Power, Trust, and Evil," 154.

38. Thomas, "Evil and the Concept of a Human Person," 51.

39. Thomas, "Power, Trust, and Evil," 157.

40. For Thomas, part of what is perverse about such orders is that a moral good—the interpersonal affirmation involved in trusting relations—is pressed into service of immoral institutions. I share his view, but want to bring out here instead a questionable assumption about the uniform or symmetrical character of trust relations in the kinds of cases he emphasizes.

41. Thomas, "Power, Trust, and Evil," 162.

42. Thomas, *Vessels of Evil*, 90; and "Evil and the Concept of a Human Person," 51.

43. This narrative offers many illustrations of incongruous outrage, especially on the part of the protagonist's master, Dr. Flint, and the white father of her children, Mr. Sands. Jacobs's story is collected with other slave narratives in Henry Louis Gates Jr., ed., *The Classic Slave Narratives* (New York: Penguin Books, 1987). For the episode concerning "Linda's" brother in the story, see Gates, 453–56.

44. See Karen Jones, "Trust as an Affective Attitude," *Ethics* 107 (1996): 4–25, for a persuasive analysis of trust that features both cognitive and affective components.

45. Here I follow roughly the analysis of trust in Jones 1996; see also several essays in Annette Baier, *Moral Prejudices* (Cambridge: Harvard University Press, 1995) on trust. The points I raise here, though, make me hesitant about the level of generalization these analyses of trust assume, without considering how the forms and bases of trust available between people in or across very different situations and statuses might be different. Some discussions of emotional possibilities linked to distinct social positions are Diana Tietjens Meyers, "Emotion and Heterodox Moral Perception: An Essay in Moral Social Psychology," in *Feminists Rethink the Self*, ed. Diana Tietjens Meyers (Boulder, Colo.: Westview Press, 1997); Maria Lugones, "Hard to Handle Anger," in *Overcoming Racism and Sexism*, ed. Linda A. Bell and David Blumenfeld (Lanham, Md.: Rowman & Littlefield, 1995); Sandra Bartky, "Shame and Gender," in *Femininity and Domination* (New York: Routledge, 1990); and Alison Jaggar, "Love and Knowledge: Emotion in Feminist Epistemology," in *Women, Knowledge, and Reality*, ed. Ann Garry and Marilyn Pearsall (Boston: Unwin Hyman, 1989).

46. Frederick Douglass's decisive fight with an overseer is famous in this regard, but not, apparently, unique. See Douglass's life narrative (1845) in Gates, *The Classic Slave Narratives*, and see Blassingame, 318–20, on the term-setting some slaves did, especially with respect to lashing. See also Orlando Patterson, *Slavery and Social Death* (Cambridge, Mass.: Harvard University Press, 1982) for the extraordinary variety of master slave relations throughout all times and many cultures.

47. For a more contemporary earful about perceptions of white people by black people familiar with twentieth-century segregation and racism, see John Gwaltney, *Drylongso: A Self Portrait of Black America* (New York: Random House, 1980).

48. Thomas, "Evil and the Concept of a Human Person," 53.

49. Thomas, "Evil and the Concept of a Human Person," 48.

50. See especially Martha Nussbaum, *Love's Knowledge* (New York: Oxford University Press, 1990).

51. See essays in Richard A. Shweder and Robert LeVine, *Culture Theory: Essays on Mind, Self, and Emotion* (New York: Cambridge University Press, 1987), and Richard A. Shweder, "Menstrual Pollution, Soul Loss, and the Comparative Study of Emotions," in *Thinking Through Cultures* (Cambridge, Mass.: Harvard University Press, 1991), on the cultural shaping of emotions.

52. Michael Stocker, with Elizabeth Hegeman, *Valuing Emotions* (New York: Cambridge University Press, 1996), 209–42.

53. See Stocker with Hegeman, *Valuing Emotion*, on the argument for feeling; see Gabriele Taylor, *Pride, Shame, and Guilt* (New York: Oxford University Press, 1985) for discussion of constitutive beliefs. An anthropological analysis that stresses an expressive and communicative role for emotions is Robert I. Levy, "Emotion, Knowing, and Culture," in Shweder and LeVine, *Culture Theory: Essays on Mind, Self, and Emotion* (New York: Cambridge University Press, 1987).

54. See Jonathan Bennett, "Accountability," in *Philosophical Subjects*, ed. Zak Van Straaten (New York: Oxford University Press, 1980); Gary Watson, "Responsibility and the Limits of Evil," in *Responsibility, Character, and the Emotions*, ed. Ferdinand Schoeman (New York: Cambridge University Press, 1987); and Barbara Houston, "In Praise of Blame," *Hypatia* 7 (1992): 128–47 on reactive attitudes as forms of address. The phrase seems to be Watson's. More could be said about Strawson's own treatment of reactive attitudes in "Freedom and Resentment" as a prototype of the arguments I criticize here. Strawson does not make the kind of claim I criticize here, but his treatment of "the participant attitude" invites this kind of error.

55. Strawson, "Freedom and Resentment," 80.

56. This essay was written while on a Frances Elvidge Fellowship at The Ethics Center of the University of South Florida, and a Fordham Faculty Fellowship from Fordham University. I am grateful to these institutions for their support of my research. Colleagues at The Ethics Center provided discussion of the paper and suggestions for its improvement; thanks to Peter French, Stephen Turner, Peggy Des-Autels, Michael Byron, and Mitch Haney. Additional thanks to Michael, as well as to Hilde Nelson, for suggesting numerous improvements in style.

11

NATURALIZING, NORMATIVITY, AND USING WHAT "WE" KNOW IN ETHICS

The provenance of "naturalized epistemology," so called, is too recent for the hand of Quine not to be still heavily upon it. But like its older relative, "naturalism," it is an idea rich enough to be coveted, and protean enough to be claimed, by diverse comers with different things in mind. While Quine's version of naturalized epistemology of science inevitably furnishes the backdrop for current discussion of naturalizing moral epistemology, it is important to pause over what "naturalized epistemology" can and should mean in ethics. To what extent is Quine's example of an epistemology *of* science that helps itself *to science* the model for understanding knowledge of and in morality? Does it require a view of moral knowledge as reducible to, or in a fundamental way furnished by, science? Or a view of moral theory as science-like in some way? I argue that the appropriate analogy is instead a holistic and reflexive epistemology of morality that helps itself to moral judgments and standards seen as answerable to the experience of the kinds of shared lives they make possible and necessary. This approach neither privileges nor rejects wholesale what scientific inquiries might have to say. In the spirit of naturalized epistemology, the importance of science to moral understanding is held subject to what else we think we know, including what we know morally.

My aim is to show that there are choices here that are deeply enmeshed in views about science, knowledge, and morality. I take morality, and hence the object of moral theorizing and moral epistemology, to be real-time, culturally embedded practices of responsibility. I see moral philosophy as a reflective but (for that reason) empirically burdened theoretical practice that is epistemically reflexive and normatively critical.[1] There is no question here of trying to defend the view as a whole; instead I want to illustrate how it exemplifies some features of a naturalized conception, with the effect of steering attention in directions that moral philosophers have been slow to go, and perhaps resistant to going.

My specific, interested, and constructive appropriation of naturalized epistemology is as loaded as anyone else's is going to be. But this is only "natural," in the relevant epistemological sense: there is no epistemic position outside (a great deal of) our knowledge. But *where*—that is, on what knowledge—we stand as we seek new understanding or revisions in the understanding we possess, and what some of "us" think of as "our" knowledge, is a question that must be opened. I am going to suggest our response to it should be morally and politically self-conscious, as well as epistemologically freewheeling.

1. HOW QUINE "NATURALIZED" EPISTEMOLOGY

In "Epistemology Naturalized," Quine argued that, with the failure of reduction programs that promised firm foundations for mathematical and scientific knowledge, science might just as well explain itself.[2] "Epistemology, or something like it, simply falls into place as a chapter of psychology and hence of natural science" (82), whose job is to study the actual construction of a picture of the world from scant sensory inputs. Quine is unconcerned about the circularity of using empirical science to validate empirical science, since there is no alternative knowledge of our knowledge. "We are after an understanding of science as an institution or process in the world, and we do not intend that understanding to be any better than the science which is its object" (84).

This move immediately and persistently raised the question whether Quine's naturalized epistemology recaptured the *normative* mission of traditional epistemology to explain what constitutes *adequate* justification and *real* knowledge. The role of norms in scientific knowledge in Quine's naturalized epistemology is debatable.[3] Quine's view seems to be that the cognitive equipments of human creatures disciplined by "pragmatic" inclinations, like conservatism in theory change, simplicity of laws, and of course the ultimate "empiricist discipline" of predictive success, are quite good enough. Our inquiry into "how it is done" *in science* will reveal what it is like for it to be done *well*, for science is our best case of natural knowledge. Its practice embodies what is *to be done*, as well as what is done, in this pursuit.

In the conclusion of another essay from the same period, Quine's triumphal teleology of natural science emerges unabashed. As he has it there, we pass from reliance on our innate similarity sense, through intuitive understandings of similarity, and then on to the scientific definition of theoretical kinds with explanatory significance, which need not owe anything to the innate similarity sense. So, "the animal vestige is wholly absorbed in the theory," providing us a "paradigm of the evolution of unreason into science." It is also an example of natural knowledge that spurs further knowledge which in turn rejects or corrects the original knowledge, or puts it into its newly discovered place. Yet this looping process by which what we (think we) know is corrected as we go farther on its very basis, has for Quine a *direction*. Even as we "live by bread and basic science both," it is science to which human sapience "rises."[4]

In naturalized epistemology as Quine first styled it under that name, we have the usually remarked elements of holism (the "web of belief" vs. foundationalism), fallibilism (any of our previously credited beliefs could be found in need of rejection or revision) and naturalism (there is knowledge of the world only through its limited sensory impacts on us, no knowledge *a priori*). These together disqualify an *indefeasibly privileged epistemic position* that epistemology as normative tribunal of all knowledges would have to occupy. But there is also the *scientism*, the vision of science as the mature culmination of all natural knowledge, science as that knowledge in and of the world than which there is not any better.[5] This makes science the operative normative tribunal for other kinds of knowledge of the world as well as all of its own parts (but never, of course, all at once).[6]

2. THE SCIENCE QUESTION IN MORAL EPISTEMOLOGY

Quine's founding discussion of naturalizing epistemology suggests a certain prototype of that enterprise: a global scientifically regimented holism and a particularly scientific naturalism. I argue now that this is but one option, and not the best one, for naturalizing *moral* epistemology. Here is a generic prototype version (NE) of a broadly "Quinean" argument for naturalizing the epistemology of scientific knowledge. Without vexing the question about Quine's views, I build into this prototype the demand that epistemology have a *normative dimension*. I build this in because I think even philosophers who place themselves far distant from the search for foundations of knowledge are nonetheless reasonably disinclined to view anything as an epistemology that does not issue in at least, to use Hilary Kornblith's generous phrase, "constructive advice on the improvement of our epistemic situation."[7] Of course, in a naturalized epistemology, normative insight must be compatible with epistemology's being a kind of natural knowledge within the world, available through uncontroversial human cognitive capacities; the normative dimension must not interject itself from somewhere else, or enter through claims to insight prior to or beyond all experience. A normative dimension does not require that epistemology introduce some *sui generis* constraints, values, or standards from somewhere outside actual epistemic practices of several kinds. It might, for example, reflectively retrieve standards immanent in epistemic practices and try to understand relations of those standards to the practices themselves and to other standards of those practices, as well as to standards of other practices. I also use "real knowledge" as a dummy expression for whatever conditions for beliefs' being warranted one wants to plug in.[8] I am interested in exploring a structural parallel here, and I try to leave this schematic prototype extremely general. This will allow us to study some options for naturalizing moral epistemology in extremely simplified and broad form, as well as to see where the "normative" element reappears differently in the case of moral understanding.

NE: The epistemology of science seeks to tell us under what conditions we have real knowledge of the world.

So, epistemology must have a normative dimension, its inquiries must distinguish conditions under which we are likely to have genuine knowledge of the world from those under which we have something else (belief that is not warranted).

There is no kind of purely nonempirical knowledge that could validate scientific knowledge.

There is no empirical knowledge with validity superior to scientific knowledge.

So, there is no kind of knowledge that does not include scientific knowledge that can be used to establish the validity of scientific knowledge.

So, the account of how we have real knowledge of the world must itself become another application of science. That is, we will have to use (presumptively genuine but always in principle fallible and revisable) scientific knowledge (our best knowledge and its methods) to explain the conditions under which we come to have such a thing as genuine scientific knowledge.

Now let's explore straightaway one direct extension of this prototype for naturalizing epistemology in the case of moral knowledge (NME1).

NME1:   The epistemology of moral knowledge tells us under what conditions we have real knowledge of how we ought to live.

Moral epistemology must have a normative dimension, its inquiries must distinguish conditions under which we have genuine knowledge of how we ought to live from those under which we have something else (beliefs about how to live that are not warranted).

Moral knowledge is one kind of knowledge about the world (rather than about a transcendent or non-natural realm).

Moral knowledge is knowledge about which understandings of how to live are "valid" (true/right/acceptable/deserving of authority).

So, there is no kind of purely nonempirical knowledge that could validate moral knowledge.

There is no kind of empirical knowledge about the world, including moral knowledge, with validity superior to scientific knowledge.

So, there is no kind of knowledge outside of scientific knowledge that can better be used to establish the validity of moral knowledge.

So, the account of how we have real knowledge of how we ought to live becomes another application of science. That is, we will use some (presumptively genuine but always in principle fallible and revisable) scientific knowledge (our best knowledge and its methods) to explain how we come to have such a thing as genuine knowledge of how we ought to live.

I have represented the matter of moral knowledge here under the generic idea of "how we ought to live." I assume this place holder can accommodate views with deontological, consequentialist, virtue and other elements, so long as these are views about how we ought to live. I have for the purposes of this discussion assumed that people express, defend, wonder and argue about, and teach their children beliefs about how to live, and that the question about moral knowledge involves asking whether such beliefs are or could be warranted.[9] I have included the "naturalistic premise" that moral knowledge is a kind of knowledge about this, our actual, world. Although a naturalist need not go in for naturalizing epistemology in morals or elsewhere, it is hard to imagine anyone interested in naturalizing moral epistemology not being some kind of naturalist about morality. But the idea that moral knowledge is in and of the world is meant in a fairly undemanding sense. It does not imply narrower naturalist commitments about moral properties or facts; it only suggests, on a parallel with NE above, that such knowledge as we may have of how to live is gotten in the world by ordinary cognitive capacities from our experiences of the world, which include our experiences of living with others and thinking about how we and others act and live.[10] Finally, I leave open the characterization of the validity of beliefs about how to live in order to leave open the possibility that multiple ways in which to live might be "validated" by inquiries into morality, and that there are different forms that this "validation" might take. Again, I think this allows for the structural parallel to emerge at a high level of generality.

This model raises a problem widely associated with scientifically natu-ralized moral epistemology, the "loss of normativity." Scientific theories with explanatory power and predictive value may tell how morality arises, is seated in our native capacities, and is transmitted in communities with more or less continuity, *without* being able to say whether any extant forms of morality are *morally* better or worse than others.[11]

Naturalized epistemology of science might at least plausibly claim to have recaptured epistemology's normative role from *within* science, to the extent that sciences are *successful* practices of knowledge of how the world in fact is in some respects. In their respective domains with respect to the kinds of explanatory and predictive powers for which we want that kind of knowledge, sciences deliver what we want. We want to know how things work, in particular how the structures of things explain how they work; where applicable, we hope by knowing how things work to anticipate what they do, and make them do what we want them to, and not what we don't. Well-developed bodies of scientific theory deliver this, and deliver more of it as they are extended and refined. Thus many of us are already as sure as we can be (having given up on Cartesian certainty) that we have some of what we want and it will pay to follow the patterns by which we got it, at least if we want more of *that.* This is why, except to the philosophical skep-tic, proposing to vet claims to knowledge by appeal to the ways we get such knowledge as science gives does not simply jettison the pursuit of norms, but supposes that much of science as practised embodies the relevant norms. That is, the several sciences embody such norms as conduce to obtaining the kinds of knowledge at which they respectively aim. (And that the norms in play at any given time are revisable does not mean that at any given time there are not norms.)

The relevant norms for moral knowledge, however, would have to be the ones owing to which moral knowledge delivers what is wanted from *it.* We want moral knowledge in order to know how to live. This is what be-liefs embodied in actually practiced morality or the simplified theoretical constructions of normative moral theory tell us: the necessity, importance, or superior value of, for example, human dignity, eternal salvation, the great-est happiness, harmony with nature, the preservation of natural hierarchies, proper respect for ancestors, nonviolence and universal compassion, or more or less coherent combinations of these or others. If the going moral norms (what we think we know morally, theoretically or on the hoof) *successfully* produce what is wanted in their respective forms of life, the question nonetheless remains open: is this a form of life we should want? This version of naturalized moral epistemology seems to have no way to supply the kind of normativity involved in people's living as they really ought to live. And if moral inquiry in either its philosophical or nonacademic versions is to retain its *normative* identity as an inquiry into what is *really* right or good, into how human beings get right how they *ought* to live rather than how they variously in fact do, it seems that moral inquiry must be something other than a purely scientific investigation.

This is not to deny that empirical findings of a scientific sort might fulfill a part of the empirical burden of moral philosophy. Insofar as moral epistemology needs, as it does, to understand what people know in understanding how to live *as they in fact do morally*, to that extent the parallel holds. Scientific studies of several types, for example, might well help us understand how people come to master the moral concepts in use, recognize the patterns of behavior their extant morality requires or suppresses, and cultivate the perceptions and feeling responses that enable people to bring expression and action into morally appropriate play, both in fulfilling moral demands or ideals as well as in understanding the terms of deserting or defying them. A very important part of moral epistemology is the investigation of the actual conditions of moral competence of various kinds. Naturalized moral epistemology should be eager to reap the benefits of whatever scientific studies of individual capacities or group processes successfully explain how we are able to share a way of life and to learn how to live within it (which does not always consist in living in accordance with it).[12] But this robustly empirical study, ripe with potential for scientific contributions, leaves us one question short of philosophical ethics. The missing question is: no matter how successfully some group of people sustain a way of life they happen to live, is the way they live how they *ought* to live? A naturalized moral epistemology that has been absorbed into scientific studies might give us the best accounts we can have of how they do it, without yet touching in what sense they should.

Just here, though, there is more than one way to understand the normativity problem. It might seem as if the kind of knowledge that comes in with asking whether a given moral way of life is *really* how to live cannot be any kind of empirical knowledge, and so must either be knowledge of something nonempirical ("transcendent moral reality," "non-natural properties"), or nonempirical knowledge of something ("pure practical reason," "the logic of moral language"). But these moves to transcendence or to knowledge *a priori* throw in the towel on naturalized epistemology for morality. Alternately, we might hold that aside from what we know about how to get around in a "local moral world," there is no kind of moral knowledge left over to have. This idea, however, can be taken in more than one way. It can be taken to say that there is nothing that could be an answer to that "normative question."[13] Or, on the contrary, it could be a starter for naturalizing moral epistemology. There is no knowledge "over and above," but there are further uses of the *same* kinds of naturally acquired moral knowledge we already have, together with whatever else about the world we think we know, to assess our and others' moral beliefs and our or others' ways of arriving at them.

3. NATURALIZING MORAL KNOWLEDGE

In line with this idea, now try a different naturalizing model, one that does not so much "extend" the naturalizing of science to ethics as take up the structural analogy for ethics.

NME2:   The epistemology of moral knowledge tells us under what conditions we have real knowledge of how we ought to live.

Moral epistemology must have a normative dimension, its inquiries must distinguish conditions under which we have genuine knowledge of how we ought to live from those under which we have something else (beliefs about how to live that are not warranted).

Moral knowledge is one kind of knowledge about the world (rather than about a transcendent or non-natural realm).

So, there is no kind of purely nonempirical knowledge that could validate moral knowledge.

Moral knowledge is knowledge about what understandings of how to live are "valid" (true/right/acceptable/deserving of authority.)

There is no kind of knowledge that can assess the moral validity of a way of life that does not include moral knowledge, no knowledge of the validity of values that does not include evaluative knowledge.

So, there is no kind of knowledge that without moral knowledge can be used to establish the validity of moral knowledge.

So, the account of how we have real knowledge of how we ought to live becomes another application of moral knowledge. That is, we will use our best (presumptively genuine but always in principle fallible and revisable) moral and other knowledge of how to live to explain how we can come to such a thing as knowledge of how to live.

If we take seriously this approximation to a prototype for naturalizing moral knowledge, other facets of naturalized moral epistemology have to configure compatibly with it.

A naturalized moral epistemology will be holistic. But if we take (NME2) seriously, we need to rethink what kind of holism about knowledge it is plausible to endorse. "The" web of belief is a powerful image that retains the pleasing picture of knowledge as all of one piece, even as it jettisons the older architectural metaphor of a single structure with *fixed* foundations. But what is the status of the idea that knowledge *is* all of one piece? Surely an *a priori* conviction of the necessity of the unity of knowledge does not comport with a naturalized epistemology. Furthermore, (NME2) incorporates a commitment to natural moral knowledge. But if moral knowledge introduces a kind of normativity and forms of normative question open to natural investigation that some other types of natural knowledge cannot answer or explain, then it seems that moral knowledge (and perhaps other types of evaluative, practical, and craft knowledge) is a distinct type of knowledge, and we should not suppose that methods of discovery or patterns of validation are simply identical to or continuous with ones that obtain in other contexts. Finally, the image of "science" is apt to play a mystifying role in these discussions: is there a unified theoretical web of "science"? The "unity of science" represents a regulative ideal invested with philosophical hopes (akin, interestingly, to the reduction programs whose failure Quine remarks in introducing of the idea of naturalizing epistemology), not the known reality of a web of seamlessly interconnected theory, or even methods entirely homologous (much less uniform) in detail.

So it seems we have not enough reason to affirm a single web of belief, and some reasons not to. I suggest that a naturalized moral epistemology should opt for a *contextual holism* about knowledge. Instead of the view that every belief in the web is linked by some connections to all others, contextual holism would affirm only what we know: every belief is linked in some network of beliefs to indefinitely many others, including to normative standards that may be context-specific.[14] How and to what extent "webs" of belief overlap or intermesh is itself *open to inquiry*. Whether the "web" idea with its pleasing connotations of lithe transparency, springy flexibility, and tensile strength is apt for imaging the organization of our knowledges is *to be explored*. There is something after all very "unpragmatic," in its way, about Quine's web: it pictures a tissue of belief holistically hovering outside diverse action-repertoires, practices, relations, techniques and institutions that are involved in making available and vetting the status of beliefs. Open-ended contextual holism neither seals "morality" and "science" off from each other as separate language games nor pre-emptively unifies moral and scientific belief into a single field.

Of course, one approach to naturalism in ethics tries to preserve the autonomy of morality precisely by getting it off the secure path of science, lest it be "secured" (as in NME1) by the disappearance of ethics as a normative inquiry.[15] This can be done by making morality something natural that is other than knowledge. In this category come noncognitivist and expressivist views. I sympathize with this move in that I think it a distortion to picture morality as only, essentially, or even primarily a matter of knowledge. This slights the complex economy of feelings and the expressive and directive aspects of our moral practice and discourse. But I consider ethics as pursuing an understanding of morality, which provides *understandings* of ourselves as bearers of responsibilities in the service of values.

Instead, I reject two equations. One is the identification of "natural" or "empirical" knowledge exclusively with what can be known from within the world about the ways the world in fact is. The other is the equation of knowledge about how the world in fact is with scientific knowledge of the world. We sometimes know from within the world how the world might or could be *for* us, that is, how the world could be *better* or *worse* for us in some ways. Indeed, our knowing this is a condition for our understanding many ideas basic to morality, such as cruelty, suffering, and humiliation, or dignity, gratitude, and trust, and for identifying the states and relations these ideas represent. It is also true that much of our understanding of how the world in fact is and could be is available not only through commonsense knowledge, but through refined and methodic inquiries that are not scientific, or are of the more dubiously scientific sorts. Humanistic and critical disciplines, like history, philosophy, critical social theory, historical and critical studies of scientific practice, institutional genealogies, literature, literary studies, cultural studies, and semiotics, as well as in those scientifically lower-ranking social sciences and their still lower ranking parts, such as social psychology, sociological theory, ethnography, and their like, illuminate ways people live and how these ways are understood by those who live them. In sum, for moral knowledge and its improvement we must always use some of what we know about the world, and some of what we know that bears most crucially on moral knowledge and its refinement is not scientific knowledge. For a suitably generous naturalism, we and our experiences of the world and each other are in the world; how our world is, could be, and would be better or worse are among the things we can know from within our world about it.

In casting off global holism and scientifically regimented naturalism, I have pulled out the main struts of a "scientism" that can prop up some visions of naturalizing epistemology. Scientism is not (any) science, but an ideological vision of the cultural role and human significance of scientific knowledges. "Scientism" is a vision of a mythicized entity "science" as the ultimate source of valid answers to anything worth knowing and the tribunal of what could possibly be taken seriously as a question. Scientism is really a full-blown normative view; it is an ethics and a politics, not exclusively of knowledge, but inevitably of culture, authority, and society. That, however, is not something wrong with it. What's wrong with it is its spurious regimentation of scientific practices into mythic "science," and its *a priori* imposition of incontestable and pre-emptive closure on our pursuits of understanding. What renders scientism ideological is its obscuring the variety, complexity, and fallibility of scientific practice, its claiming strictly universal (and necessary?) dominion in the realm of knowledge, and its borrowing the mantle of "scientific objectivity" when it is itself not science. Scientific inquiries don't need scientism. And naturalized epistemology should avoid the embarrassing irony of putting "science" in the place of an incontestable and universal epistemic tribunal, which was exactly what classical epistemology is usually understood to have hoped itself to be. It will be necessary to repeat: I am not criticizing scientific inquiries or saying that scientific method is an ideology. It is scientism, not science, that has no place in a fallibilist and naturalized approach to epistemology.

Freed from confining and reductive pictures of knowledge, it becomes easier to acknowledge what is essential to a naturalist and naturalized knowledge of morality. Moral knowledge needs all the reliable and useful empirical information of any type that it—or rather we—can get. Part of the point of seeing morality naturalistically is to dig into the idea that there is no prior restriction on what we could come to know about ourselves in our world that might not have implications for our beliefs about how to live. By the same token, moral knowledge is as open-ended, revisable, and ultimately fallible as any other kinds of natural knowledge. Here, as elsewhere, we use what we know, and accept that we are likely at any time to be wrong about something. And we must rest on some presumptive knowledge in order to examine where knowledge itself comes from, while this very examination may reveal that what we thought was knowledge was not what it appeared. A naturalized epistemology needs to be freewheeling and fallibilist, which is to say *open* to the best and most contextually useful fruits of all inquiries and experiences. And the naturalized epistemology of morality, in particular, seeks an understanding of moral knowledge that is necessarily both epistemically and morally reflexive.

4. NORMATIVE QUESTIONS

What now of that "normative question," not a question of simply explaining the causes, organization, and effects of any individuals' or communities' moral behavior, but a question of establishing whether we *must* or *should* do what our going morality demands? This is a question about morality's *authority*, not merely its de facto power but its *rightful dominion* over us. It is easy to start thinking that "the normative question" is one big jackpot question about "all" morality that arises from some reflective standpoint outside of or beyond morality. It can seem as if this is a sort of super-question that requires a sort of super-answer, that is, an answer to the question "Is it *really* right (obligatory, good, etc.)?" that is of a different order from answers to those garden variety questions of "must I really. . . ?" and "would it really be wrong to. . . ?" or "how much does it really matter if I. . . ?" that arise about different matters and at different levels of generality in people's lives. I suspect that the idea that there is a separate, external question about morality's authority is rooted deeply in non-naturalist, and perhaps supernaturalist, thinking about morality that yearns for its validation by something "higher," be that God, human nature, the natural law, pure practical reason, or perhaps "science." Even theories of ethics that understand it as a human construction, like a procedure, or a contract, or a discursive situation, still often think that the construction that could answer the normative question must be an *ideal* construction. This is the idea that nothing any group of people is doing at a place at a time is—indeed, could possibly be—our touchstone in ethics when we ask whether a way to live *really* has authority.

But there cannot be *just one* normative question. For one has to stand on some part of morality to pose a normative query about some other; and there is always at least the possibility (although it is not inevitable) that the moral judgment on which one stood for those purposes at that time might come in question at some other. "The" normative question is not one question, but a kind of question that recurs applied to different matters or reapplied to earlier answers. And there is no way for it to be posed "outside" some moral assumptions or other.

The situation is no different for moral theorists. As naturalists, we do not hesitate to look at the facts about the formation of moral beliefs. The fact is that what and how we can think about morality depends on what we have learned in the context of our places within particular ways of life, questions within them, and perhaps comparisons between them and other ways more or less comparable. In *fact*, then, "reflection," in moral philosophy or outside it, is *on* or *of*, or better *from*, some bits of (putative) moral knowledge, some already familiar forms of moral reasoning, some extant norms of responsibility, that allow us to know that it is *morality*, what is right and good, that we are thinking about here. Moreover, a large mass of critical work in the late twentieth century maps the deliverances of "reflection" in moral philosophy onto specific locations in a given social field: moral theorizing "reflects" characteristic roles, expectations, and life-experiences or the absence of experiences that track race, education, national culture, religious heritage and practice, economic status, gender, age, sexuality, physical ability and other factors that account for different social worlds or very different experiences within the same social world.[16]

Actual moral ideas, practices, norms, patterns of reasoning, and paradigmatic judgments are in fact always in play in moral philosophy at the outset. The philosopher no more asks after the moral authority of "morality" from outside of it than does anyone reflecting on moral demands when the garden variety questions work their way to the surface out of confusion, temptation, or ennui. The moral philosopher may be more relentless, more systematic, and more logically acute in pursuing normative questions. She may invent in thought startlingly simple or idealized or schematic moral views the social realization of which may or may not be determinate, available, or habitable in reality; this, too, may have its uses. But in all cases of moral reflection, she starts where we all do: we start *from here*, for some "we," and some "here."

In moral theorizing, as at other times, we resort in all cases to what Christine Korsgaard calls "reflective endorsement."[17] If we are able to endorse morality once we understand what about us and our world, especially our actual social world, grounds and enables the morality we have, or if we can endorse a change based on the comparison between what we have and what we might, based on these same understandings, then this justifies the extant or revised morality's authority, its "normativity." Reflection can thus produce or sustain, as it can defeat or chasten, confidence in the claims morality makes on us. But we can only test our moral views by *finding them good or not* upon reflective examination. So the normative question requires the application of some morally normative standards or judgments in the vetting of others.

What results when some of our moral practices, judgments, or concepts pass moral review is that our confidence in aspects of ways we live is confirmed or perhaps enlivened; when they fail it is weakened or destroyed. But it is not as if there are our moral beliefs and our (always in part moral) reasons for them, and then there is our "confidence" in them, the way a cherry sits on a sundae. "Confidence" is not something we might have or not have about those standards we hold as moral ones. When we hold some ways we in fact live as "how to live," i.e., the right or better founded or more enlightened ways, this way of holding certain standards marks them as morally authoritative ones. When confidence wanes or is damaged, we are inclined to wonder whether the standards we have held as moral ones are in fact standards of some other kind (for example, etiquette or mores) or whether we have held the wrong moral standards. So, too, confidence does not replace knowing what is right or good; it is confidence *in* our knowing at least some of, or approximately, what is right or good. Our standards and judgments (or some specially central or important ones of them) being, literally *for all we know,* valid constitutes the *moral authority of morality,* whatever other powers of de facto social authority and inertial social practice hold the standards and supporting practices in place.[18]

Naturalized epistemology of science needs to investigate belief-producing cognitive, social, and institutional processes with an eye to uncovering whether or not they are conducive to the kinds of truth the sciences seek, and in doing so uses with confidence what it seems most reasonable to think we already know.[19] Moral epistemology, whether practiced systematically by philosophers or in the event by any thoughtful agent, needs to investigate belief-producing cognitive, social, and institutional processes with an eye to uncovering whether or not they are conducive to the kinds of worth upon which a moral form of life rests its authority or in terms of which its authority is understood. But "worth" here is a dummy expression for some form of value or necessity that will not be identifiable independently of some standards of moral judgment already in hand. Indeed, we cannot so much as characterize what our or someone else's form of moral life is without importing some understandings of what to identify as the moral parts, and in what sort of evaluative language to identify them. Wherever we invoke some moral concepts, standards, and judgments to test whether some others "really" have the authority they purport, the ones we invoke are invested with our confidence in their representing what we (already) reasonably understand to matter morally. This does not prevent the very commitments in which we have reposed confidence from becoming objects of critical reflection in their turn.

An open-minded and empirically robust naturalism about morality readily discovers that morality is not socially modular: moral understandings are (indeed must be) effected through social arrangements, while social arrangements include moral practices as working parts. Our concepts and principles are given meaning by the practices they in turn make sense of. For this reason there is not nor could there have been a "pure core" of moral knowledge completely extricable from some actual social world or other.[20] That is why moral knowledge requires extensive empirical inquiry and intensive reflexivity about both the moral and non-moral conditions under which we believe we know how to live.

A central mode of examination of our moral understandings is "transparency testing," which involves both moral and epistemic aspects.[21] We need to ask whether we in fact know how it is we *do* live in our moral-social worlds. In fact, in most societies, "we" do not all live the same lives, and "we" often fail to understand or do not try to understand how the places our moral-social worlds provide for us are the conditions for the very different places of others of us. Our intermeshed moral and social understandings may be incomplete, self-serving, distorting, or rigged; they may render the lives of some of us morally invisible, incoherent, or diminished. The moral values we "share" may be ones we do not equally freely endorse or enjoy. We need to discover whether what are represented as morally authoritative understandings are ones whose authority is or is not really earned by their being shown answerable to well-founded fact and critically tested moral standards. We need to explore whether practices that purport to embody values, standards, and judgments "we" share and in which "we" trust are really driven and reproduced by coercion, deception, manipulation, or violence directed at some of us by others. Where transparency testing of our actual lifeways does not sustain confidence that "we" know either how we do live or how to live, the understandings in play lose their *moral* authority. Then we really are left with mere customs, habits, or mores; with ways some people in fact live that are no longer credible as "how to live." But to discover whether authority is warranted and confidence is in point, we must bring to bear a lot of, and the most relevant and reliable, information we have about morality and society. This is especially so in moral theorizing and moral epistemology, where we are promised a high degree of sophisticated scrutiny of the tenability of moral conceptions.[22]

5. WHAT DO "WE" KNOW BEST?

I have argued against a purely scientific naturalism, or a scientifically insupportable "scientism," lest we claim prematurely or irresponsibly for scientific theories or findings a relevance to morality that they do not have, or that we do not know they have. A different danger for naturalists, and perhaps a greater, is that preoccupation with science as our best empirical knowledge can turn our attention away from other kinds of inquiry that bear deeply and directly on our understandings of how we live and how to live. Between the Scylla of scientific naturalism about morality and the Charybdis of a transcendent moral reality accessible to "pure" reflection lies a great deal we can and already do know about our social worlds and moral theories and traditions that is crucial for testing our moral understandings. Above, I mentioned humanistic disciplines, critical studies, and the methodologically less rigorous parts of social and political theory and sciences as important resources for moral reflection, that is, for reflection on actual forms of life that claim moral authority for those who live them (and perhaps beyond). Some contemporary philosophical theorizing itself, empirically attentive and reflexively critical about its empirical burdens and moral commitments, offers moral reflection and moral theory materials it cannot honestly proceed without.

I am going to use here, very briefly, a single example of such empirically enriched but normatively motivated work that sharply focuses a point about the kinds of things moral philosophy needs to examine and who is likely to want to find them out. Charles W. Mills's *The Racial Contract* constructs a deliberately stylized theoretical model to foreground both "the most important political system of recent global history—the system of domination by which white people have historically ruled over and, in certain important ways, continue to rule over nonwhite people"; the invisibility of this system and the issues it raises in mainstream ethics and political philosophy; the obscurity to, or outright denial of, this system by most white people; *and* the intimate relations among these.[23] Specifically, Mills argues that the tradition of social contract theory, still a hugely influential tributary of modern Euro-American moral and political theory, cannot be understood in its normative implications and historical reference without seeing the broad and deep Racial Contract—a set of interlocking political, moral, and epistemological assumptions and their effects—that underwrites it.[24] Mills, in effect, proposes that if contractarian models are honored devices in philosophy for exposing the logic of liberal political legitimacy, we ought to consider their potential for diagnosing the logic of politically legitimated racism in liberal polities. More broadly, Mills asks us to try examining the apparent contradiction of modern European moral philosophy as such: "an antipatriarchalist Enlightenment liberalism, with its proclamations of equal rights, autonomy, and freedom of all men, thus took place simultaneously with the massacre, expropriation, and subjection to hereditary slavery of men at least apparently human" (64).

In what he describes as a "naturalized" ethical account, Mills makes use of the large and expanding body of historical, demographic, anthropological, and critical studies of race, colonialism, modern European history, economic development, and exploitation of non- European lands and peoples. He also pays critical attention to aspects of philosophy's own history and to specific texts that have been passed over silently or left out of sight in perpetuating a particular version of a canonical history of philosophy. Mills's project is not a grand unified explanatory theory but a morally and epistemically strategic intervention, a "rhetorical trope and theoretical method" (6) for reorganizing perceptions of fact and by doing so posing questions about what theories and professional discourses of moral and political philosophy have seemed interested or uninterested in knowing about our world. If one looks where he does determinedly enough, it becomes a good deal harder to believe certain things or not to think about others. It becomes harder to think that Kant and other modern European thinkers created visions of an ideal moral polity and merely failed, due to lamentable but local prejudice, to imagine certain people within it. Mills makes a compelling case by direct textual and inductive historical evidence that it was integral to the construction of that ideal polity that certain people be imagined outside it. One is dignified not only by what one is, but by what, or rather whom, one is not.[25]

An ostensibly "universalist" tradition of ethical thinking about "man," "human nature," and "humanity" in Western philosophy, from ancient to contemporary times, has in fact consistently been understood and intended *not* to apply to the majority of humankind, female and nonwhite. Yet it seems to depend on who moral theorists are, and on to whom they give their accounts and are accountable, whether they will question the significance of this. The ostensible universalism of most contemporary moral philosophy and the bowdlerized universalist presentation of its history conceals the actual history in which the enunciation of "universal" truths has not only coexisted with but has served persisting social practices of dividing, excluding, stratifying, subordinating, degrading, and dehumanizing the larger part of humankind. Most moral philosophers continue to import assumptions about the uniformity of moral intuitions, standard conditions of responsibility, or the universal recognizability of "common humanity," in a way that disguises the ways moral perceptions are characteristically formed in societies in which so-cial *and moral* differentiation is nearly universally the rule.[26] Do we know

whether our systems of moral philosophy even now are free of conceptual features or substantive assumptions that continue the actual tradition
and the understandings it has in fact required? Do we routinely and me-
thodically make sure that we use what we know to find out? Do "we"
really know more about the evolution of social co-operation than about
recent histories and ongoing dynamics of social subordination or imperialism? Or do these questions not seem important enough, or philosophical enough, for "us" to address? It depends on who we are.

In fact, it is overwhelmingly women who have explored the sexism of
ethical theory; people of color, ethnically marginalized people, or indigenous people who have insisted that we know about racism or colonialism;
gay, lesbian, and transsexual theorists who ask us to review the moral intuitions of a hetero-normative cultural universe critically. Not all of "us"
know what others do, and not all of us try to, or care to.

Louise Antony says naturalizing knowledge "requires us to give up the
idea that our own epistemic practice is transparent to us. . . . "[27] So too for
our moral practice, and the epistemic practice, moral philosophy, that seeks
to know it, from within it. In moral epistemology, we cannot but ask ourselves what we know best about science, morality, and social life, and how
we know it. Yet here it is epistemically and morally urgent that we open the
question that Moore would never have asked: who are "we"? And how, in
point of fact, do we know that?[28]

NOTES

1. My view is developed in Margaret Urban Walker, *Moral Understandings: A Feminist Study in Ethics* (New York: Routledge, 1998).
2. W. V. Quine, "Epistemology Naturalized," in *Ontological Relativity and Other Essays* (New York: Columbia University Press, 1969).
3. Richmond Campbell claims that Quine views science as "free of" the effect of value judgments, but acknowledges that Quine in at least one context speaks of empiricism as a theory of evidence that "has both a descriptive and a normative aspect" ("On the Very Idea of a Third Dogma," in *Theories and Things* [Cambridge: Harvard University Press, 1981], 39, and 41 on the "empiricist discipline" that makes for "more or less responsible science"). See Richmond Campbell, *Illusions of Paradox* (Lanham, Md.: Rowman & Littlefield, 1998), chapter 5. A useful discussion that rejects the "no normativity" view but recognizes ambiguity in Quine's position about normativity is Richard Foley, "Quine and Naturalized Epistemology," in *Midwest Studies in Philosophy*, vol. 19, *Philosophical Naturalism*, ed. Peter A. French, Theodore E. Uehling Jr., and Howard K. Wettstein (Notre Dame, Ind.:

University of Notre Dame Press, 1994). Certainly for Quine it is no business of science to judge how the world ought to be, but this is not the same as judging what science ought to do in constructing and revising its picture of the world. And Quine invokes predictive success, conservatism in accommodating recalcitrant experiences, and simplicity of laws, as considerations in revising our web of belief (see, for example, W. V. Quine, "Two Dogmas of Empiricism," *Philosophical Review* 60 [1951]: 20–43). Quine seems to like to label these appeals "tendencies" and "inclinations," but this doesn't disguise the fact that they are normative, i.e., parts of the practice of doing *good* science. See, finally, Quine's later discussion in *Pursuit of Truth* (Cambridge, Mass.: Harvard University Press, rev. ed., 1992), chapters 1, 19–21, which calls naturalized epistemology a "chapter of engineering: the technology of anticipating sensory stimulation" (19) concerned with heuristics, with "the whole strategy of rational conjecture in the framing of scientific hypotheses" (20). Here Quine considers the constraint of predictive power not normative but constitutive of a "language-game" of science. I believe it is Quine's earlier views that have set the tone for dominant conceptions of what "naturalizing" is.

4. W. V. Quine, "Natural Kinds," in *Ontological Relativity and Other Essays* (New York: Columbia University Press, 1969), 138. See also "Five Milestones of Empiricism," in *Theories and Things* (Cambridge, Conn.: Harvard University Press, 1981), 72. Peter Hylton makes a good case that Quine's naturalism can go so far as to reject *empiricism* if science, improbably, validated nonsensory forms of knowledge like telepathy and clairvoyance (the examples are Quine's own). See Peter Hylton, "Quine's Naturalism," in *Midwest Studies in Philosophy*, vol. 19, *Philosophical Naturalism*, ed. Peter A. French, Theodore E. Uehling Jr., and Howard K. Wettstein (Notre Dame, Ind.: University of Notre Dame Press, 1994).

5. Lorraine Code presents a detailed diagnosis and critique of the tendentious and unsupported assumptions about science, scientific psychology, and nature that structure Quinean naturalized epistemology. Although she does not discuss naturalized moral epistemology, her critique powerfully exposes the nonscientific ethos of *scientism* at several levels. See "What Is Natural about Epistemology Naturalized?" *American Philosophical Quarterly* 33 (1996): 1–22. See also, Tom Sorrell, *Scientism: Philosophy and the Infatuation with Science* (London: Routledge, 1991), cited by Code.

6. Quine's own meager views on ethics confirm that science will be judge of ethics, at least: ethics is "methodologically infirm," because "lacking in empirical checkpoints" for those ends that cannot be shown instrumental (Quine says, "causally reduced") to others. Our moral judgments, as also our propensity to extrapolate from some applications of ethical standards to others, can only answer back to our "unsettled" moral standards themselves, so "coherence" only and "no comparable claim to objectivity" is the lot of ethics. See "On the Nature of Moral Values," in *Theories and Things* (Cambridge, Mass.: Harvard University Press, 1981), 63–65. Below I return to the idea that moral standards answer back to moral standards, although also to the experience of the world of those who live in social worlds in which these standards have authority.

7. Hilary Kornblith, "A Conservative Approach to Social Epistemology," in *Socializing Epistemology: The Social Dimensions of Knowledge*, ed. Frederick F. Schmitt (Lanham, Md.: Rowman & Littlefield, 1994), 96.

8. I'm using "warranted belief" here in the fairly open sense that Michael DePaul does as "meeting standards that identify what would be epistemically good, excellent, or best." See Michael DePaul, *Balance and Refinement* (New York: Routledge, 1993), 74.

9. I like to think that this model could be adapted to characterize the justification of certain moral sensibilities, attitudes, or endorsings of norms if moral judgments are explained as expressive rather than descriptive, but I do not attempt to show this here. See Alan Gibbard, *Wise Choices, Apt Feelings: A Theory of Normative Judgment* (Cambridge, Mass.: Harvard University Press, 1990), and Simon Blackburn, *Ruling Passions: A Theory of Practical Reasoning* (Oxford: Oxford University Press, 1998), for expressivist views.

10. I neither affirm nor deny "a" or "the" fact/value distinction, being uncertain what it means but certain that it means different things to different people. I consider ethical propositions *bona fide* propositions; but ethical propositions have distinctive and, I believe, multiple roles to play within practices of responsibility structuring social life. These roles include descriptive, expressive, directive, and perhaps other aspects.

11. The empirical-scientific study of morality is, of course, not a "value-free" enterprise. Few today will deny that scientific knowledge is imbued with epistemic norms, if not other kinds. Feminist epistemology has produced the most sustained contemporary philosophical defense (in varied forms) of the claim that scientific knowledge is also inescapably constrained or driven either by non-epistemic (for example, social, moral, and political) norms. For two good samplers, see *Feminist Epistemologies*, ed. Linda Alcoff and Elizabeth Potter (New York: Routledge, 1993), and *A Mind of One's Own: Feminist Essays on Reason and Objectivity*, ed. Louise Antony and Charlotte Witt (Boulder, Colo.: Westview Press, 1993). Some classics are: Lorraine Code, *What Can She Know?* (Ithaca, N.Y.: Cornell University Press, 1991); Sandra Harding, *The Science Question in Feminism* (Ithaca, N.Y.: Cornell University Press, 1986); Helen E. Longino, *Science as Social Knowledge* (Princeton, N.J.: Princeton University Press, 1990); Lynn Hankinson Nelson, *Who Knows?* (Philadelphia: Temple University Press, 1990); Donna Haraway, *Simian, Cyborgs, and Women* (New York: Routledge, 1991); and Naomi Scheman, *Engenderings* (New York: Routledge, 1993). See also Richmond Campbell, *Illusions of Paradox* (Lanham, Md.: Rowman & Littlefield, 1998) for a recent defense of feminist empiricism.

12. One collection that takes up a variety of issues surrounding the meanings of naturalism and the relevance of empirical studies to moral philosophy is Larry May, Marilyn Friedman, and Andy Clark, eds., *Mind and Morals: Essays on Ethics and Cognitive Science* (Cambridge, Mass.: MIT Press, 1996).

13. The phrase "the normative question" is the centerpiece of Christine Korsgaard's *The Sources of Normativity* (Cambridge: Cambridge University Press, 1996).

14. Wittgenstein's fitful but insightful treatment of the grammar of knowledge is one standard locus for this view in *On Certainty*, ed. G. E. M. Anscombe and G. H. von Wright, trans. Denis Paul and G. E. M. Anscombe (New York: Harper & Row, 1972). See also Michael Williams, *Unnatural Doubts: Epistemological Realism and the Basis of Skepticism* (Cambridge, Mass.: Basil Blackwell, 1991), which rejects a global view of knowledge.

15. See Stephen Darwall, Allan Gibbard, and Peter Railton, "Toward *Fin de siè-cle* Ethics: Some Trends," *Philosophical Review* 101 (1992): 115–89, for an anatomy of some contemporary metaethics organized by the issue of "placing" ethics with respect to "empirical science as the paradigm of synthetic knowledge." (The authors attribute the terminology of placing to Simon Blackburn.) In a footnote, they demur from the view that "objective knowledge" has a definite meaning and deny that it amounts to "knowledge as attained in the empirical sciences," leaving room for alternative conceptions of objectivity, as well as the corrective impact of an alternative conception of ethical objectivity upon understanding of objectivity in mathematics and science (see p. 126, n. 29). But the authors' admonitory remark that "Such 'placement' would enable us to see how much of morality remains in order" shows their own investment in the tribunal of science. In contrast, see John McDowell's "Two Sorts of Naturalism," which chastises "neo-Humean naturalism" in favor of a reality that encompasses our "second," moral natures, in *Virtues and Reasons: Philippa Foot and Moral Theory*, ed. Rosalind Hursthouse, Gavin Lawrence, and Warren Quinn (Oxford: Oxford University Press, 1995). But see also essays on Humean epistemology and naturalism in Annette Baier's *Moral Prejudices: Essays on Ethics* (Cambridge, Mass.: Harvard University Press, 1995). There are varied alternatives to scientific naturalism.

16. See Walker, *Moral Understandings*, esp. chapters 1–3, for a critique of epistemic placelessness and lack of reflexivity in moral theorizing, as well as structural and historical analysis of the emergence of the "theoretical-juridical model" of compact theory. See also chapters 1 and 3 for examination of the feminist critique of gender and other bias in moral theorizing.

17. Korsgaard's initially naturalistic treatment of "reflective endorsement" as the way to answer the normative question unfolds into an argument for the universality and necessity of our valuing our humanity as a condition for acting on reasons, hence bringing back in a bit of the old a priori when it comes to securing morality. This view makes for interesting comparison with the naturalized version of reflective endorsement of actual ways of living. See Korsgaard, *The Sources of Normativity*, lectures 2 and 3.

18. Compare Bernard Williams's somewhat elusive appeals to "confidence" in Bernard Williams, *Ethics and the Limits of Philosophy* (Cambridge, Mass.: Harvard University Press, 1985), 170–73. See also J. E. J. Altham, "Reflection and Confidence," in *World, Mind, and Ethics: Essays on the Ethical Philosophy of Bernard Williams*, ed. J. E. J. Altham and Ross Harrison (New York: Cambridge University Press, 1995) and Williams, "Replies," in the same volume. While Williams seems to consider

confidence an alternative to knowledge, I see our confidence as a kind of trust in what we know.

19. See Kornblith, "A Conservative Approach to Social Epistemology," 102ff.

20. See Walker, *Moral Understandings*, chapters 2, 3, and 9, on the genealogy and implications of the "pure core" idea.

21. The idea of "transparency" as an ideal of moral views or social orders appears in Williams, *Ethics and the Limits of Philosophy*, 101–10, and Korsgaard, *Sources of Normativity*, 17. Although she does not use the phrase, I have profited most from Annette Baier's application of what she calls a "minimal condition of adequacy" that a moral view "not have to condemn the conditions needed for its own thriving," that it not fail to acknowledge or deny acknowledgment to that which is a condition of its working as it does. See Baier, *Moral Prejudices*, 96.

22. The thorough intermeshing of moral and epistemic considerations in the reciprocal relationship between understanding who we are, how we live, and how to live, might be a very rich case of what Richmond Campbell calls "fact-value holism." See Campbell, *Illusions of Paradox*, chapter 7.

23. Charles W. Mills, *The Racial Contract* (Ithaca, N.Y.: Cornell University Press, 1997), 1.

24. Among the facets of the Racial Contract that Mills connects with the massive and grim historical record are: a "partitioned social ontology" and juridical elaboration of persons and racial subpersons (14); a racial polity that is obligated to the privilege of necessarily white citizens at the expense of nonwhites (12); a racialized geography that placed most human beings in a irremediable state of nature (13), their lives uncounted (49–50) and their lands unpeopled (49); an "epistemology of ignorance" that precludes understanding of social and political realities (18), produces "moral cognitive distortions" (95) and disqualifies cognition or cultural production of non-Europeans (44).

25. For a primer of short and disturbing selections that exhibit the modern construction of race within Enlightenment terms by Enlightenment thinkers, see Emmanuel Chukwudi Eze, ed., *Race and the Enlightenment: A Reader* (Cambridge, Mass.: Blackwell, 1997). Two sobering historical studies that document the enormous energy and evasion needed by Europeans to avoid the simplest path of taking Africans or indigenous people as *simply* other human beings who lived differently, even exotically differently, from Europeans are Olive Dickason's study of early North American colonization in the Northeast, *The Myth of the Savage: And the Beginnings of French Colonialism in the Americas* (Edmonton: University of Alberta Press, 1984, 1987), and Winthrop D. Jordan's *White over Black: American Attitudes toward the Negro, 1550–1812* (Chapel Hill: University of North Carolina Press, 1968).

26. The importance for moral philosophy of recognizing, not ignoring or obscuring, the pervasive fact of differentiated social-moral positions in human societies is a main theme of *Moral Understandings*. I have elsewhere examined several philosophers' arguments that presuppose, while purporting to prove, that recognizing the "common humanity" of other human beings is in some sense unavoidable. Sadly, it

has been and continues to be avoided in numerous forms more often than not by human beings. See Margaret Urban Walker, "Ineluctable Feelings and Moral Recognition," in *Midwest Studies in Philosophy*, vol. 22, *The Philosophy of Emotions*, ed. Peter A. French and Howard K. Wettstein (Notre Dame, Ind.: University of Notre Dame Press, 1998), reprinted as chapter 10 in this volume.

27. Louise M. Antony, "Quine as Feminist," in *A Mind of One's Own: Feminist Essays on Reason and Objectivity*, ed. Louise M. Antony and Charlotte Witt (Boulder, Colo.: Westview Press, 1993), 202.

28. I thank John Greco, Richmond Campbell, and Bruce Hunter for their helpful comments on an earlier draft. An opportunity to present a shorter version of this paper in a symposium on naturalized moral epistemology at the Canadian Philosophical Association in Edmonton, May, 2000, helped me to rethink the final form of this essay. I thank the CPA for this invitation.

12

GETTING OUT OF LINE: ALTERNATIVES TO LIFE AS A CAREER

For Mommy, who knew how to be here now.

Autonomy has been a central value in influential moral theories and liberal political conceptions in the twentieth century. Autonomy may be taken as part of a characterization of the nature of moral selves, a feature defining the kind of being that moral beings are. Alternatively, autonomy may be set forth as an aspirational ideal for human beings as moral beings and political actors. It is typical in moral theorizing that the descriptive and prescriptive senses do not stay in separate boxes: moral ideals in theory often take something human beings supposedly are as a key to something it is best for human beings to become. It is also typical for moral theorists to offer characterizations and advance ideals of moral personality and moral relations in general that are in fact abstractions and idealizations of historically specific cultural understandings. These cultural understandings are as "thick" as their philosophical counterparts are "thin": they are embodied in concrete imagery and intertwined with social roles, identities, and functions that are familiar or conspicuous in certain times and places.

In this essay I want to explore a culturally thicker version of autonomous individuality, in order to explore why older people in our society, and older women in particular, may not be able to choose to meet concrete social criteria of autonomy or to emulate culturally familiar exemplars of the autonomous individual. While exclusion from culturally valued identities is a common form of marginalization, I want to reconsider whether we all ought to aspire to be "autonomous men" in this culturally thicker sense. In conclusion, I suggest we think about alternative pictures of well-lived and admirable lives, and ones that may be at odds in the concrete with the kind of individuality and autonomy that a certain kind of society elevates as an ideal.

189

PROBLEMS WITH AUTONOMY

The adequacy and desirability of autonomy in both its descriptive and pre-scriptive senses are open to discussion. Autonomy defines individuals and a kind of individualism that have been repeatedly questioned in recent moral thinking. Feminist critics, for example, have noticed a convergence between features associated with autonomy—independence from external guidance, acting under one's own direction, being able to control and to express one-self, self-assertiveness, choice guided by one's own values and interests rather than social expectations or pressures—and those associated with traditional social norms for masculine, but not feminine, personality. If autonomy rep-resents the nature, perfection, or dignified expression of moral agency, but "autonomous man" really is a *man*, how are we to understand women's moral agency? Communitarian and historicist critics, on the other hand, ac-cuse the autonomous agent of liberal individualism with being no one in reality. That agent's autonomy is seen as a destructive myth or an inappro-priate norm. It conceals, distorts, or devalues the human reality of individ-uals who achieve identity and meaning from the cultures, traditions, com-munities, and roles in which they are embedded.

While some feminists continue to prefer the framework of liberal indi-viduality, other feminists have championed ideals of selves as relationally de-fined, mutually concerned, reciprocally trusting, and complexly interdepend-ent. Ethics of "care," "trust," or "responsibility" see these relational selves as fundamentally and necessarily responsive to each others' worth and need.[1] Communitarians and historicists see moral actors as imbued with historically and culturally formed identities that give substance and meaning to moral re-lations in their specific communities. They argue we do not simply choose the places from which we acquire meaningful self-understanding; these are so-cial communities, not social contracts.[2]

Feminists are understandably uneasy with appeals to "tradition" in communities that have traditions of sex oppression, and those who argue a central role for community and tradition may suspect contemporary femi-nism of embodying too much of the individualist quest for autonomy that they find impoverishing. Yet common to these recent lines of thought is their resistance to autonomy as the dominant ideal of self. They claim that autonomy is at best a restricted or partial expression of human moral agency, and at worst an impoverishing aim for it. Autonomy cannot en-compass the realities of human interdependence and community, nor ex-plain the concrete conditions of responsibility, the commitments, and the at-tachments to others that move us to action. If autonomy is a value, on these views, it must be conditioned by and integrated with other values that express our social natures.

The ill fit between norms of autonomous, self-reliant, and self-interested agency and social reality is evident in the situation of aging persons who are vulnerable and dependent and those who are responsible for their care. The moral position of dependently frail, cognitively impaired, and in some cases severely disabled people is not adequately considered in terms of kinds of independence, self-control, or reflective self-direction that are typically associated with autonomy. Ideals of consensual obligation and contractual responsibility for autonomous actors also fail to address the common situations of caregivers to older people who have come to require others' care. Often demands for care fall—by small increments, or suddenly, by dint of disabling illness or injury—upon those, disproportionately female, who see no reasonable and humane alternative to providing it, even at the cost of severe economic disadvantage and practical and emotional strain.[3] These are areas where ideals of autonomous individuality do not meet concrete realities of aging.

Nor does a disembodied, abstract equality among persons defined by their "freedom to choose" help us understand the social situations and self-perceptions of many people whose humanity is defined differently from that of others on the basis of their physical construction, appearance, or state. Social theorist Iris Young calls this a "scaling of bodies" that is at work historically in gender, race, ability, and age stereotyping.[4] Some people live out their sense of personal agency in bodies socially targeted for the fear, disgust, control, or use of more powerful others. The devalued bodies or low-valued social positions of groups of which many people are members keep those people marginal or vulnerable to neglect, violence, or exploitation even as they remain individually theoretically "free to choose." They are also subject to ridicule, humiliation, and misunderstandings driven by others' malicious, patronizing, or prejudiced view of who they can possibly be, and what their actions can mean. Paul Benson argues that "free agency" may be compromised not only by lack of relevant capacities for self-direction, but also by an incapacity to adequately reveal to others in our actions who we are to ourselves.[5] For people marginalized, devalued, or stigmatized, the assumptions that guide many others' reactions to what they do may make it practically impossible to be seen by those others as they see themselves, and to give their actions the meaning in the others' eyes that the actions have in their own. This does not only mean that people will be thought about, stereotypically and repetitively, in ways they cannot control; it means that they will be treated and responded to in accordance with what others think about them in many contexts of daily life.

I have spoken of theoretical conceptions of autonomy that philosophers advance or debate. But here I want to focus instead on the thick fabric of images and exemplars in everyday life and common cultural understandings that attach to, and concretely represent, those philosophical abstractions. Moral ideals such as autonomy cannot be fully separated from social understandings which give them concrete reference, and some social understandings, I claim, always lie behind philosophers' abstract idealizations.[6] It is important to examine, then, not only the theoretical idea or ideal of autonomy, but the concrete, culturally familiar examples or embodiments of it that inform social understandings. But social understandings often picture as morally ideal a social position or function that is not available to all people. While it is in the nature of ideals to escape fulfillment, moral ideals can be linked to social positions and opportunities in ways that make some people destined to fail at them in fact or in the eyes of others.

Autonomy, for example, has long been defined concretely in ways at odds with social demands for appropriately feminine behavior in women.[7] It has also been elaborated in ways that reflect middle-class expectations of stability and control.[8] On the other hand, Joan Tronto's politically informed ethic of care exposes the way caregiving in our society is assigned to, and its values of interdependence and attentiveness to need are in fact associated with, people of lower status: women, the working or lower classes, and people of color. Independence and executive control are linked to higher social status.[9] Other morally valued ideals such as integrity and dignity may be denied application to people who are poor, dirty, unlearned, sick, enslaved, or dominated by those who are "better" or stronger. We need to ask whether prominent conceptions of valuable lives and admirable character might embody assumptions and invoke examplars that are not hospitable to the lives of older women, among others.

AUTONOMY IN BROADER
CONTEXT: OUR LIVES AS CAREERS

In search of a thicker characterization, I situate the idea of autonomy within a broader cultural theme with a longer history, the idea of *each individual life as a career*. This theme of the shape and proper direction of a whole human life has special relevance for thinking about aging and about women. For it is the more deeply rooted and robust picture of a certain kind of individual and that individual's life that gives concrete meaning to autonomy in our social world.

Historian Thomas Cole has persuasively traced the theme of life as a career to "quintessentially modern ideas and images . . . born in Northern Europe between the late Middle Ages and the seventeenth century."[10] Prior to this time, Western European philosophical and religious traditions viewed human life in terms of general "ages" of human existence, such as childhood, youth, maturity, and old age. What emerged in the early modern period was the individualization of each life's journey as a personal drama. Early Protestantism saw the individual's drama as one of personal salvation, achieved over a lifetime through progressive control over body and will, aided by self-examination, work, and devotion. But this theme of a self-controlled and self-superintended existence became steadily more secular with the growth of modern life and capitalism: the later modern idea of a "life course" suggests a track to stay on and a path to follow to success, or at least stability, in worldly life.

The idea of a proper sequence of roles and responsibilities pegged to age-defined "stages" of life was distilled in the seventeenth century in the symbol of the rising and falling staircase. It was "the standard bourgeois image of a lifetime for the next 350 years."[11] This motif was popular in the eighteenth and nineteenth century, fading only early in the twentieth. It is still reflected in the idea of being "over the hill" or "past peak." The image displays what is expected of individuals at different stages to achieve a well-ordered life. But the image has another central function: to teach *internalized self-control*, the ability to govern oneself, a capacity required by the economic and political institutions of modern life. The image reminds individuals of their responsibility to order their own lives properly in society's view. Predictably, from the seventeenth century there were different versions of the stages of life for men and women.

Women (or, at any rate, ladies, women of advantaged class standing) in this scheme were not in fact intended to seek or achieve full self-governance, but rather to set themselves to master roles within the household under the governance of men. Women's life course is depicted in stages of domestic and child-rearing responsibilities, which diminish in later life. Men, on the other hand, were to conduct themselves appropriately in the workplace and public life, with men most economically and socially advantaged being not only governors of themselves but of other men and women. What is reflected in this ideal, then, even down to the present day, is an emphasis on health and control of the physical body for "productive" life, and an inner discipline of conforming to the demands of one's station throughout life. This ideal has always been meant primarily to guide men of middle-class standing in being economically productive and law-abiding citizens. It requires a supplementary plan to guide their female counterparts into the role of wives, that is, women who provide the necessary and helpful complement to men's desired economic and legal behavior.

While the "rigid code of moral self-government" originated several hundred years ago, the "autonomous individual as the ultimate unit of secular authority" is entrenched in the values of the middle-class today.[12] The image of the fit, energetic, and productive individual who sets himself a course of progressive achievement within the boundaries of society's rules and institutions, and whose orderly life testifies to his self-discipline and individual effort, remains an icon of our culture. This picture of autonomy, rather than abstract ideas of acting out of one's own interests and preferences or acting on principles that one can rationally endorse, is really our central cultural ideal. It is a picture of autonomy as energetic self-superintendence with a consistent track-record over a lifetime to show for it. It is instructive to notice how this more robust picture of physical vitality, reliable performance, and cumulative achievement—*an individual's life as a career*—recurs in the late twentieth century both in studies of aging and in contemporary ethics.

My own work uncovers the idea of a *career self* shaping the views of very influential moral philosophers in the late 20th century.[13] In John Rawls's theory of justice as fairness, a signal achievement of the century, Rawls conceives of a person as a human life lived according to a plan. He sees a person's good as determined by the most rational long-term plan of life for that person.[14] Bernard Williams, a strong objector to Rawls's idea of the planned life, thinks of human lives in terms of "constitutive projects," important commitments and attachments that carry us into the future with a reason for living.[15] Alasdair MacIntyre, harshly critical of many facets of modern thought, describes a human self as the subject of a lifelong narrative that gets meaning from the climax toward which it moves.[16] Charles Taylor, both critic and interpreter of the modern sensibility, endorses MacIntyre's idea of an individual life as a "quest." He judges those whose lives as a whole do not sustain a meaningful narrative severely: he says they have failed as persons.[17]

What is revealing in these otherwise ethically diverse views is the repetition of the idea of an individual's life as a self-consciously controlled career. It binds a whole life or lifetime together in a unified way for which the individual is accountable. The individual's ability to account for this life— to bring forward its plan, project, or narrative plot—testifies to the individual's *self*-control. The imagery in each case recycles the cultural theme of autonomous agency, with its self-conscious individual enterprise. We might expect this from philosophers like Rawls who are within the liberal tradition, but we find it deeply embedded as well in the views of other philosophers who are critics of that tradition. I believe that this view has cultural depth, traced historically in part by Cole. This view runs beneath explicit differences in theoretical moral views, yet its cultural entrenchment exerts a pull on theorizing about personhood and character.

On the side of humanistic aging studies, a parallel theme emerges in discussions of the meaning and value of later life. While philosophers in the latter twentieth century speak of narratives and projects that give a whole life meaning, many gerontologists and humanists emphasize *life review* as an appropriate, perhaps indispensable, activity for the old. Theorized originally by Robert Butler in 1963, aging expert Harry Moody describes it as "an effort by the older person to sum up an entire life history, to sift its meaning, and ultimately to come to terms with that history at the horizon of death."[18] Butler apparently thought of life review as a naturally occurring and universal tendency in the old—as reminiscence surely is—and saw it as an experience of integration and resolution.

Contemporary writers notice that belief in the therapeutic power of life review may be optimistic,[19] and that the drive for coherence within a single linear story may be "distinctive of Western culture from the Renaissance to the present."[20] That is, it is possible that the idea of needing a unified and coherent life-spanning story may fit historically shaped and culturally specific ideas about persons and their lives, rather than spontaneous and universal ones. Harry Moody, for example, believes that successful life review, one that finds one's life to have been intelligible, purposeful, or satisfying, does show the meaningfulness of a life. But he admits that summing up one's life, in fact, is not the only way to find meaning in it. He points to the French essayist Montaigne, whose enduring writings show facets of life "at a particular moment, from a glance, over one's shoulder, so to speak."[21]

In light of this apparent cultural specificity, we might ask some questions about "life review." Why is the privileged view of life the one from its ending? Even if that's the last word, must it be the most accurate one? Why is the review of life a primary task for the old? It would seem that older people's enjoyment of reminiscence is bound to be, like all memory, highly selective; so why does life review have to take in life "whole"? Is life review a fact or a therapeutic recommendation? Is it a universal function of aging or the culmination of a particular style of living in a certain culture?

I propose that whole-life narrative is not a necessary expression of human personhood. Instead, it is a recipe for the sort of selves that fit a specific economic and institutional environment. While this model of relentless self-definition and self-control strongly emphasizes individual responsibility for oneself, it eclipses our dependence on and vulnerability to each other, and it overshadows our life-defining connections to and responsibilities for each other. This view of persons when filled in concretely has negative implications for aging selves, and ambiguous implications for women aging.[22]

The ordered life course of our time is the modernized one, no longer with the ten steps of the rising and falling staircase, but with "three boxes." Youth, adulthood, and old age fit us for the school, the workplace, and retirement, which Moody calls the "bureaucratically ordained means" of enforcing these life stages for purposes of the economy.[23] But "retirement," unlike school and workplace, is not a place. It is not an activity, like education or work, nor a role defined by the development of skills or exercise of competence, like that of student or worker. Retirement is defined instead as the cessation of the adult role of worker.

In a society that views the life course as a kind of "career," retirement, without designated role, activity, or development, signifies the end of the life course, even if there's a lot of life left. And if the ideal of self is the career self, the enterprising self busy at its career, the retired person surrenders not only a job, but eligibility for a centrally valued moral and social identity. The robust ideal of autonomy that pictures life as a career is inherently unkind to those growing older: they must compete in an arena where many are eventually destined to lose out to those younger, or they must retire into a state of "postadulthood."[24] It should not be surprising that in much gerontological writing the way to meaning in later life is either through "productive aging" in which we keep "busy" and "active" as before, or through a final project of life review. We must either continue our life-careers or do the only thing left when they are over: reminisce about and document them: to prove to ourselves and to others that at least we *were* socially acceptable persons before our adulthood expired.

The autonomous individual as the striving career self was never a self-ideal intended for women. But it is one to which more women today aspire or are compelled, especially in the literal form of life-long paid work. Women stand in a persistently ambiguous relation to this ideal of self. In one sense, it is an achievement for women to lay claim to the kind of autonomous individuality to which our society attaches great value. But this kind of individuality in its socially salient forms is defined in terms excluded by some women's traditional domestic roles, where those roles require women to play socially subordinate supporting parts (rather than self-determining or self-determined ones) that both free and require men to assume the role of a career self focused on its linear trajectory. This kind of individuality is also precluded or its ascription is deflected by many women's lives of relentless but repetitive labor, paid and unpaid, of precisely the sort that never "goes anywhere," in terms of social status, occupational importance, or increasing economic power. Housework, personal or domestic service, and caregiving are such "women's" works that do not, in the public arena, add up to a "career"; often, they are not perceived as skilled or intelligent. Some women may wish to be freed precisely from the constraints of gender roles that render them ineligible for a socially valued expression of selfhood. Other women may wonder whether they want to be allowed, and inevitably in turn required, to emulate privileged men's social behavior in order to qualify as selves of an estimable kind. They might also wonder who will then supply the other-directed labors that permit career selves to direct so much attention to themselves and their careers. And they might well ask why these are the choices.

At the same time, the recruitment of women to this paradigm of individuality visits on them a cultural life pattern that renders later life, or life-after-employment, an unmapped space at the end of the life course—a space not literally but by social definition "empty." This space is getting wider all the time. The emptiness of this space may be designated "leisure," but little is recommended to fill it by our society except the consumption of goods and services.[25] In the case of men, this may contribute to the sense of "role-lessness" often mentioned in aging literature. Women's social situation in later life, however, cannot be inferred from or modeled upon men's. For many women, later life is a period filled with unceasing caregiving demands, especially for parents and spouses, and not occasionally for grown children, grandchildren, and other people's children, that society does little to acknowledge, much less relieve.[26] The apparent assimilation of women to the male-identified model of "career" followed by "retirement" may then function ideologically, concealing the reality of continuing work by older women that society compensates neither materially nor socially.

The career self was never an option for many people whose lives did not offer substantial promise of successful self-control of particular, conspicuous, and paradigmatic types. Many of those who are poor, chronically sick, very seriously disabled, or those who are objects of other's domination or control, will encounter practical barriers, sometimes insuperable ones, to performing the role of a career self, or to having their performance recognized as one of the type that counts.[27] And the life of continuous progress and achievement must level off or diminish even for the minority who can approximate it. Yet regardless of its lack of fit with many people's early lives and most people's later ones, the self-directing career self is a social norm that encourages people to try to fit themselves to basic structures of a certain kind of economic and social life. This kind of life demands that one continuously "discipline" oneself over the long haul of life to specific forms of socially acknowledged and rewarded competitive striving as a condition of the "success" that is offered to relatively few and achieved by fewer. But, we can ask, should people try to fit themselves to this mold? Are there alternatives to "life as a career," and to the correlative idea that one's individual life has only the meaning one can give it in retrospect "as a whole"? Are there alternatives that would render later life—and all of life— richer?

IDEALS OF SPIRITUALITY AND CONNECTION

Anthropologist Barbara Myerhoff suggests that "vertical" as well as "horizontal" integration can result in a meaningful life. Horizontal integration is precisely that achievement of continuity in which the individual's unidirectional stream of life is seen as adding up to "a life career."[28] Vertical integration instead stresses "timeless transcendent recognition" that endures and does not pass away, what has been called at different times: epiphany, moments of being, revelation, satori, transcendence.[29] Many cultures, including parts of our own at earlier times, have seen later life as a period for the culmination of a spiritual career, rather than a temporal one, or as a time of life ripe for contemplative, reflective, counseling, guiding, or spiritual work. The theme of the "wise elder," and the roles and practices that give it concrete embodiment, including orator, mediator, teacher, and chaperone, seem to have vanished from our society.[30] Feared and venerated ritual positions open to the old in other societies, such as shaman, witch, medicine man, wise woman, or sorcerer, are regarded as scary cartoons in our own.[31] These roles are not only alien or antique. They suggest forces greater than those of intentional human control, or suggest the need for human beings to entrust themselves at times to a wisdom that is not expert scientific knowledge. These suggestions are not easily integrated with the autonomous individual's mission of rational self-control throughout a lifetime. Even the idea of "practical" or "folk" wisdom, something often attributed to the old as a social resource, can be shamed or disqualified in many contexts in our society by comparison with expert discourse by people with professional credentials of recent stamp. Philosophers themselves, including moral philosophers, often do not treat kindly, and sometimes just ignore, the role of spiritual practice or religious worship in providing meaning and wholeness in people's lives.

However, U.S. Census data show significantly increased membership in churches from the fifth decade of life onward, and although it is a complex and contested topic, there is some research to the effect that women are more inclined to religious participation and to prayer.[32] In my own experience women are more often open-minded or curious about, and more likely to engage in, religious, spiritual, meditative, occult, or holistic (and not conventionally Western medical) health practices. It would be worthwhile to overcome commonplace theoretical neglect of, and generic philosophical disdain for, these sources of meaning, coherence, and connection in life to which so many people, perhaps more often women than men, turn. This might lead to more realistic recognition and objective analysis of the diverse ways people *in fact* continue to find value, interest, and sense in and between their own and others' lives in their later years. Perhaps religious commitment or spiritual discipline is a resource for meaning in women's later lives that already plays a significant role underestimated in both theory and practice. Differences in this respect among and within groups defined multiply by age, gender, ethnicity, class, region, education, political affiliation, and so forth, should be a subject of empirical research as well as an object of philosophical interest. I suspect inquiries like this would make the "wholeness" of well-tended career selves appear more and more a very special preoccupation of a particular (and privileged) segment of society. It is a preoccupation conditioned by specific assumptions about what is rational and valuable; it may also presume access to resources and opportunities of specific kinds.

On a more mundane level, however, I would like to offer another idea of "integration" that might be broad enough to encompass diverse commitments and attachments, worldly and otherwise. It is a conception that supports the idea of individual meaning and responsibility, but finds this in connections that enrich but transcend individuals. I would call it a *lateral integration of life*. This kind of integration supplies not only the pleasures of individual memory but the satisfactions of loyalties and meanings that transcend one's individuality. They can even transcend one's life.

We might see our life's stages (whether linked to our chronological ages or not) as characterized by central lessons, tasks, pleasures, experiences, or bonds. These might endure only for certain times of our lives, but we can revisit them in memory, savoring them for their distinctness or uniqueness in our lives, rather than for their continuity or comprehensiveness. Instead of a review of life in which many smaller bits must all add up to parts of ourselves, the memory of these stages will recall times when we were a smaller part of something else: a relationship, a family, a political movement, a partnership, an enterprise, an institution, a creative process, a ritual event. To remember the meaning of our being a part of these things is to remember being parts of the lives of many others, or being parts of things whose existence preceded or will succeed our own. Our lives on this view are more like journeys than careers: our physical trajectories are continuous, but where we stop to visit and what affects us may not follow a linear path. Some of what affects us may transform us into discontinuity with who or what we were before.

Some of what happens will be fulfilling or exhilarating, but other times will be ones of loss or pain: roads that close, people who are lost to us, dreams that are not realized, pain that we cannot avoid. These losses, for which there is no place on the résumé of the career self, may sometimes also have their value. From some losses we might take positive meaning. Where we cannot, we might at least be reminded of our vulnerability and dependence, a point of connection with all living beings, and of the unavoidability of suffering, which we share with all things that feel. Some episodes of this life will be simply delightful or amusing. They will not need to be anything else either to be enjoyed as we live them, or to be remembered with pleasure, wonder, or mirth.

Unlike "life as a career," there is no reason for us to cease *living* this life, even in very late years, short of grave incapacitation. It embodies no eventually unfulfillable demand for achievement or progress; it requires only normal awareness, capacities for feeling, and opportunities to belong to or with something other than or larger than oneself. The meanings in such a life are many, and we do not wholly control much less create them.

I suspect the valued reminiscences of many people, old or not, are of these sorts that link times in those people's lives to something beyond themselves. Empirical studies of remembrance as a valued experience for older people need not be controlled by the idea of life review. They might explore open-mindedly possibilities other than the narrative of a whole life in review. Philosophical ideals of personal integration might stress the extension of selves beyond themselves and *the integration of selves into other lives and collective experiences*, rather than the self-protecting continuity of a career self.

We need to explore and contrast the life-motifs, guiding images of meaning, and ideals of self of women and men in diverse cultural, religious, and ethnic communities. These might be found in autobiographies and memoirs, stories and sermons, rituals and ceremonies, music, artwork, and craftwork with which people identify their experiences in everyday life. Documentary and community projects could be invaluable in uncovering, recovering, and sharing vital images of life's later times from all of our constituent cultures and communities. There must be more for us there than the impending obsolescence of aging career selves.[33]

NOTES

1. For example, Carol Gilligan, *In a Different Voice* (Cambridge, Mass.: Harvard University Press, 1982); Sara Ruddick, *Maternal Thinking* (New York: Ballantine Books, 1989); Annette Baier, *Moral Prejudices* (Cambridge, Mass.: Harvard University Press, 1995); Virginia Held, *Feminist Morality* (Chicago: University of Chicago, 1993); and Margaret Urban Walker, *Moral Understandings: A Feminist Study in Ethics* (New York: Routledge, 1998).

2. For example, Alasdair MacIntyre, *After Virtue* (Notre Dame, Ind.: University of Notre Dame Press, 1981); Michael Sandel, *Liberalism and the Limits of Justice* (New York: Cambridge University Press, 1982); Michael Walzer, *Thick and Thin* (Notre Dame, Ind.: University of Notre Dame Press, 1994).

3. An indispensable study of this is Elaine Brody, *Women in the Middle: Their Parent-Care Years* (New York: Springer Publishing, 1990). See also Emily K. Abel, *Who Cares for the Elderly? Public Policy and the Experiences of Adult Daughters* (Philadelphia: Temple University Press, 1991).

4. Iris Young, *Justice and the Politics of Difference* (Princeton, N.J.: Princeton University Press, 1990). See also Diana T. Meyers, *Subjection and Subjectivity* (New York: Routledge, 1994).

5. Paul Benson, "Feminist Second Thoughts on Free Agency," *Hypatia* 5 (1990): 47–64.

6. This is a central theme of Walker, *Moral Understandings*.

7. See Diana T. Meyers, *Self, Society, and Personal Choice* (New York: Columbia University Press, 1989).

8. See Kathryn Addelson, *Moral Passages* (New York: Routledge, 1994), chapter 5, and Walker, *Moral Understandings*, chapter 6.

9. Joan Tronto, *Moral Boundaries* (New York: Routledge, 1993).

10. Thomas R. Cole, *The Journey of Life* (New York: Cambridge University Press, 1992), xxix.

11. Cole, *The Journey*, 19.

12. Cole, *The Journey*, 93.

13. Walker, *Moral Understandings*, chapter 6.

14. John Rawls, *A Theory of Justice* (Cambridge, Mass.: Harvard University Press, 1971), 92–93; see also 407ff.

15. Bernard Williams, "Persons, Character, and Morality" and "Moral Luck," in *Moral Luck* (New York: Cambridge University Press, 1981).

16. Alasdair MacIntyre, *After Virtue* (Notre Dame, Ind.: University of Notre Dame Press, 1981), esp. 197–202.

17. Charles Taylor, *Sources of the Self* (Cambridge, Mass.: Harvard University Press, 1989), 47–51.

18. Harry R. Moody, "The Meaning of Life and the Meaning of Old Age," in *What Does It Mean to Grow Old?* ed. Thomas R. Cole and Sally Gadow (Durham, N.C.: Duke University Press, 1986), 24.

19. Kathleen Woodward, "Reminiscence and the Life Review: Prospects and Retrospects," in *What Does It Mean?* ed. Cole and Gadow, 145.

20. Bertram J. Cohler, "Aging, Morale, and Meaning: The Nexus of Narrative," in *Voices and Visions of Aging: Toward a Critical Gerontology,* ed. Thomas R. Cole, W. Andrew Achenbaum, Patricia Jacobi, and Robert Kastenbaum (New York: Springer Publishing, 1993), 110.

21. Moody, "The Meaning of Life," 26.

22. See Sara Ruddick, "Virtues and Age," in *Mother Time: Women, Aging, and Ethics,* ed. Margaret Urban Walker (Lanham, Md.: Rowman & Littlefield, 1999) for a more positive account of the role of life review.

23. Moody, "The Meaning of Life," 36.

24. Sarah H. Matthews, *The Social World of Older Women: Management of Self-Identity* (Beverly Hills, Calif.: Sage Publications, 1979), 42.

25. Harry R. Moody, "Overview: What is Critical Gerontology and Why Is It Important?" in *Voices and Visions,* ed. Cole et al.

26. Along with Brody, *Women in the Middle,* Sara Arber and Jay Ginn, *Gender and Later Life: A Sociological Analysis of Resources and Constraints* (London: Sage Publications, 1991), chapter 8, discusses contributions of elderly persons to the care of others. Bayne-Smith reports a study by W. Stafford (1994) for the Borough President of Manhattan based on the 1990 census that indicated "(a) 36% of black households in New York City with children were headed by persons 45 years or older who were caring for children not their own and (b) almost a quarter of all households with children (21%) were headed by black women 45 years and older without a spouse." See Marcia Bayne-Smith, "Health and Women of Color: A Contextual Overview," in *Race, Gender, and Health,* ed. Marcia Bayne-Smith (Thousand Oaks, Calif.: Sage Publications, 1996), 31–32.

27. Anita Silvers disagrees that autonomy is an inappropriate or unachievable ideal for people with significant physical disabilities; see Silvers, "Aging Fairly: Feminist and Disability Perspectives in Intergenerational Justice," in *Mother Time.*

28. Barbara Myerhoff, "Rites and Signs of Ripening: The Intertwining of Ritual, Time, and Growing Older," in *Age in Anthropological Theory,* ed. David Kertzer and Jennie Keith (Ithaca, N.Y.: Cornell University Press, 1984), 322.

29. Myerhoff, "Rites and Signs," 322.

30. Carol A. B. Warren, "Aging and Identity in Premodern Times," in *Special Issue: Constructing, Maintaining, and Preserving Aging Identities,* ed. Tracy X. Karner, *Research on Aging* 20 (1998): 24.

31. Barbara Myerhoff, with Deena Metzger, Jay Ruby, and Virginia Tufte, *Remembered Lives: The Work of Ritual, Story-Telling, and Growing Older* (Ann Arbor: University of Michigan Press, 1992), 125.

32. For percentage figures on membership in churches, see U.S. Bureau of the

Census, *Statistical Abstract of the United States: 1997,* 117th edition, (Washington, D.C., 1997), 70, No. 86, Religious Preference, Church Membership, and Attendance: 1980 to 1995. Elizabeth Weiss Ozorak, "The Power, but Not the Glory: How Women Empower Themselves Through Religion," *Journal for the Scientific Study of Religion* 35 (1996): 17–29, contains references on women's religious participation and attitudes. For a more cautious view of "women's" religiosity, see Margaret M. Poloma, "From Sex Differences to Gender Role Beliefs: Exploring Effects on Six Dimensions of Religiosity," *Sex Roles* 25 (1991): 181–93. I thank Peggy DesAutels for sharing her recent research on women and religion with me; see DesAutels, "Religious Women, Medical Settings, and Moral Risk," in *Mother Time.*

33. I am grateful for the lively and searching conversation among all contributors to *Mother Time: Women, Aging, and Ethics,* during our working conference in February 1998 at The Ethics Center of the University of South Florida in St. Petersburg. Our thinking together about lives, agency, and aging has deepened my understanding, and increased my sense of the complexity, of all of these.

IV

THE "HUMAN" CONTEXT

13

HUMAN CONDITIONS

> To arm people in this way against propaganda is the function
> of moral philosophy.
>
> R. M. Hare, *Freedom and Reason*

One might think that feminist ethics is about women. This, however, is not true, or at any rate, to think of it this way is to miss a larger truth for a smaller one. Feminist ethics has indeed come primarily *from* women; most of the philosophical (and political and legal) theory that has emerged under this description has been written by women. And feminist ethics is indisputably *for* women. Those who write feminist ethics are moved to write as they do by their commitment to the dignity of women. This idea can be variously defined, but it is always understood by feminists as a moral and social standing yet imperfectly realized or unavailable to women. Yet feminist ethics is not about women but *about ethics*. Its project is to rethink ethics, the theoretical practice of understanding and justifying moral beliefs and the forms of life in which the beliefs are embedded. It also aims to critique and correct the moral beliefs and forms of life themselves, what we might just call 'morality.' Feminist ethics isn't a subject matter, but a way of doing ethics. It involves assumptions about what to look at and what to look for in making and testing ethical theory.

Feminist ethics insists we look at the impact of intersections and distributions of social authority, privilege, and power both on morality as an aspect of social life and on ethics as the reflective and systematic representation of morality. What is crucial to feminist ethics and its importance for ethics is the link between these two dimensions of its inquiry, the impact of power on morality, and its effects on ethics. A premise of feminist ethics is that both in theory and in life unequal distributions of power and privilege

will tend to reproduce themselves, and each will tend to reinforce and legitimate the other. Unequal standings in social life will reappear in theoretical representations as the invisibility or inequality of some kinds of people
or their social functions. Ethical theories often in fact represent the characteristics and positions of particular kinds of people (like relatively advantaged men, or people of a privileged racial group, or fully able-bodied people, or those with a certain educational, professional, class or citizen status)
simply as what is "normal." Inevitably, then, the theories treat the life situations, prerogatives, and responsibilities of people like that also as *normative*, as
how people should be or even what it is to be "really" a proper or fully-
fledged person, as well.

   In the most familiar early exercises of feminist ethics this was the pattern feminists repeatedly identified: the life experiences, required self-
images, and social expectations of some men were unhesitatingly put forward
as paradigms of what is "human," while experiences and social responsibilities characteristic of women either did not appear or appeared as that which
was "other," different, inferior, exceptional, or secondary. In this way, theory
reproduced, in the form of exclusion or demotion, the dominance of some
over others in life. Moral theory in this and other ways can reproduce social
distributions of power and their impact on what we do and think even as it
shields these facts of power from view. In this essay I will look at some philosophical arguments that do this in a somewhat different way. They present a
demanding, historically hard won, and still largely unrealized normative ideal
as if it were instead already a fact about "normal" human relations. The ideal
is that identical moral recognition should be extended to all human beings
simply in virtue of their humanity. The curious effect of treating this moral
ideal as already, if implicitly, realized is to erase a great deal of our history and
our present, in which disregard of, or unequal regard for, the basic humanity
of most human beings is the rule. Or, it makes this endemic human propensity look like a sort of aberration or exception. Then moral philosophy becomes uncritical, if not a distorting mirror. But we should expect moral philosophy to be a lucid representation, as well as an informed and critical
investigation, of the worth of the ways human beings do and might live.
Making it more so is what feminist ethics is about.

   A task for moral philosophy is to open and enlarge critical spaces from
within our always situated views within and about morality. We need critical spaces that allow us to identify the differences between ideal and reality
without distortion, and to identify the operations of power, privilege, and
authority that tend to close certain of those critical spaces at certain times
in thought and in social life. A lesson taught by feminist ethics is that moral

philosophy can itself be one of those operations. I provide some illustrations below of ways that happens. My own concluding argument is for naturalized and non-ideal moral theory that keeps social and moral reality clearly in view.

THE FALLACY OF IMPLICIT INCLUSION

Let's begin with three arguments by contemporary philosophers who hold theoretical positions in ethics that are otherwise quite different. The arguments all claim to show that someone who is mistreating or failing to respect another human being is nonetheless in fact *implicitly*, in what he or she is doing, *acknowledging* that the other has a humanity just like his or her own. The arguments conclude in every case that those who mistreat or demean others are caught out in an inconsistency when they withhold from their victims the moral recognition they would see fit for themselves. I'll summarize the arguments briefly.[1]

Kantian moral philosopher Christine Korsgaard argues in her *Sources of Normativity* that if a stranger you are "tormenting" calls on you to stop, asking how you would like it if someone did that to you, you cannot avoid concluding that you are obligated to stop. Korsgaard argues that unless you take the other's words as mere noise, you are acknowledging that this is a human being speaking. Since you take *yourself* to be an end for others "in so far as you are just human, just *someone*," then you cannot deny that the humanity of another makes him or her an end to you.[2]

Aristotelian Martha Nussbaum argues in a paper "Human Capabilities, Female Human Beings," that a "recalcitrant" husband can be led to the conclusion that women are entitled to development of their intellectual and moral capabilities, by reflecting on the many responsibilities and forms of companionship that he expects from his wife. He relies on "his wife's capability to engage in practical reasoning and ethical distinction making. . . . So, in his daily life he acknowledges her humanity, her possession of the basic (lower-level) capabilities for fully human functioning."[3] To deny her the development of those human capabilities just like his own is to be inconsistent. Generalizing, Nussbaum claims that ". . . to deny humanness to beings with whom one lives in conversation and interaction is a fragile sort of self-deception stratagem, vulnerable to sustained and consistent reflection, and also to experiences that cut through self-deceptive rationalization."[4]

Laurence Thomas, a virtue theorist with an eye to social psychology, argues in several articles that certain kinds of ongoing relations in oppressive systems, like those between masters and slaves in U.S. slavery, occasion certain feelings in both.[5] Masters will find it unavoidable to *trust* the people they enslave, and will find themselves *resentful* of the ingratitude they perceive in slaves' disobedience, hostility, or lack of deference. But these emotions "logically presuppose the humanity of the oppressed."[6] Since the common humanity of masters and slaves is flatly irreconcilable with one's enslavement of the other, the masters' abilities to sustain this contradiction can only be explained by "a corrosive failure of psychological functioning," in effect a psychopathology.[7]

These arguments have a similar structure. The arguments try to show that the tormentor, or the husband, or the slave master, really cannot coherently go on as they are, treating some others in ways they think it unacceptable to treat *human beings like themselves*. For, each of these arguments claim, what they are doing shows that they *in fact already know* that those they torment, subordinate, or enslave are human beings like themselves. They just don't admit it; they are insufficiently reflective, or pretending, or self-deceived, or hypocritical. What is curious is that all the arguments beg the question they are trying to address.

Korsgaard assumes that the tormentor *already* believes that just being "someone," any human being or other, constitutes an entitlement to moral regard, and that the tormentor understands his or her own entitlement in that way. So, by logical extension, the victim, being "just someone" too, is similarly entitled. Nussbaum assumes the husband *already* sees in his wife's wifely performance the expression of capabilities that evince a basic fully human functioning, and so one *like* his own. Thomas assumes the slave master has *already* gone too far in feeling trust or resentment toward slaves, as these feelings concede that those at whom they are directed are "manifestly" human actors, and so just like the masters themselves. Each argument assumes that a fully symmetrical recognition of "humanity"—I'm just like you in being human, and you're just like me in being human—is *already* there but somehow covered over beneath an unstable outward show of different and unequal terms of relationship that must be propped up by inattention, denial, or hypocrisy. So each presupposes that symmetrical recognition is always already there between human beings. But the arguments need to show that this is there in order to show the mistreaters are inconsistent.

Can we assume that the tormentor, the husband, or the slave master *already* believes that the humanity that human beings share is identical, and that their victims or chattel are "just like themselves?" Can we assume that each *already* believes that being a human being implies the same moral status in every case? Some tormentors, husbands, and slave masters might already believe this. But this is a strangely insulated conception of what is likely to be going on here if these things are happening in our world. It is as if the imagined human beings inhabit a world in which it requires an individualized psychological explanation for their failure to admit what it is supposed they *surely* must *already* know is true: others are of course just human beings exactly like themselves. It is as if a bit of clear thinking or logical homework could straighten them out.

Philosophers may be forgiven a bit of wishful thinking about the force of logic in human affairs. But moral philosophers ought not to be excused from a serious interest in how human beings actually think and live. What's missing in these arguments, even as they invoke images of deliberate physical abuse and of systems of female subordination and racial caste, is something in plain view if one will see: the ubiquity, depth, and grip of a human propensity to see in humankind *different human kinds*. Given this, it does not follow logically that if I recognize another being as human, I recognize that other as *just like me*. Nor does it follow that if I accept that another's humanity requires moral consideration that I must conclude the other deserves that same consideration that I would have for myself, and certainly not that every human being deserves the same moral consideration. These implications do not hold in all possible worlds, but let's take a closer look at why they don't follow logically in this one.

HUMAN KINDS

First, the history of some human beings' thinking of other human beings as deeply different kinds is ancient and enduring. It is not occasional, eccentric, or anomalous. It is typically institutionalized elaboratedly and redundantly, in forms of hierarchy, domination, or exclusion. It is probably true that most people who have ever lived have lived on such terms. The study of philosophical, religious, medical, and political thought about sex difference alone through the ages suffices as an example. The history of early European colonialist and modern racialist thinking also counts decisively against presuming that the concept of "humanity" must have a univocal sense.[8] Sustained philosophical and theological discussion of whether there is a single human species of common Biblical or natural descent is a part of the historical record of Euro-American thought only a couple of centuries past.[9] And practices of enslavement, slaughter, oppression, social restriction, and subordination are with us as they have ever been, not by any means confined to particular peoples, cultures, or epochs. Without consideration of these histories and realities, moral philosophers cannot decide in the abstract what it is possible or necessary for human beings to believe in human encounters, nor can they determine by conceptual analysis what it is exactly that people concede in recognizing that another being is human.

Closer to home for philosophers, "Western" philosophy's own history is one that has repeatedly produced theories on which the majority of human beings, even at mature functioning, fail to qualify fully under one or another definition of "humanity" that functioned normatively precisely to sort and scale human kinds. Aristotle is hardly alone in having made embarrassingly explicit arguments in the cases of women and of natural slaves. It is negligent philosophical practice to politely excise or downplay views on sex, race, and ethnicity in the great philosophers that offend a modern sensibility. Instead we should study closely how the conceptual structures that sort human beings into different (and invariably unequal) kinds are constructed, and whether these parts of a philosopher's thought do or do not bear on the other parts to which we prefer to attend.

The logic of human-kinds thinking need not deny common properties of human beings. This logic can be constructed precisely upon attributes that are common to human beings and even ones thought distinctive of them as human beings; it can be these very features that form the basis for rankings of human kinds. Philosopher Elizabeth Spelman reminds us, "what they [humans] have in common can be used either to mark ways in which they are the same, or provide the means by which to mark significant distinctions among them. To take an invidious example, unless it were believed to be the case that all humans have 'racial' characteristics, there would be no way to compare or contrast people 'racially.'"[10] Or, to take a philosophically central case, if "Man is a rational animal," it may yet be decided that some kinds of human beings are more fully or truly so. Even if our humanity is undeniable, the humanity of some may not be denied but may be *affirmed* in one of its *different* and usually hierarchical stratified versions. All human beings may be included in the aptly imaged Family of Man but some may be incorporated within authoritative, and others within subordinate or supporting, roles. Some early modern arguments for the domination of non-European peoples invoked Aristotle's views about the appropriateness of the rule of male over female and adult over child.[11] In the logic of human kinds as soon as somebody is found relevantly different, somebody else can be "like them," rather than "like us" if we are the ones with powers to define. The tropes of immaturity and incompetence are favorite choices in justifying the subordination of normal adult human beings, because young children and the mentally incompetent present the least arguable cases of justifiable control by others.

All this goes to show that it is *not true* that if I recognize you as a human being, I recognize you, in respect of being human, as *just like what I am.* For that to follow, I must not already think in terms of categories or scales that differentiate or grade human beings according to kind, or I must already have rejected such categories or scales. I must not already be well inside any social world in which ideas like this are integral to self- and social understanding. For the point of thinking of human beings as distinctive kinds isn't that they aren't all *human*; the point is that *human beings differ in kind.*

If we are *already* some kind of universalist egalitarian thinkers, then these arguments may for that reason seem compelling to us. Our *moral* commitment to equal worth would compel symmetrical recognition, rather than the other way around. *We* would know we were cheating the victim, subordinate, or captive of what she or he clearly deserves. We would be amenable generally to Golden Rule thinking applied in a particular way; we would ask ourselves whether what we do to them would be justified for them to do to us, given that they are *human beings just like us.* Unfortunately, if one is already well inside a social world in which the standards for considering recognition and desert are not egalitarian, then the Golden Rule format will not by itself "logically" compel a symmetrical interpretation. In a setting of differentiated social and moral statuses, the Golden Rule might with perfect consistency imply: "Do unto others what you would deserve if you were what they are," a point Richard Hare made long ago.[12]

Hare saw that logic, in the form of universalization, did not prevent a Nazi fanatic from holding that "If we were Jews, we should go to the gas chamber." Still, he argued that "there is a form of argument which, without assuming any antecedent moral premises, but given that people are as they are and the world as it is," will lead the great majority away from such "fanatical" attachments to, for example, racism or homophobia.[13] That people and the world "are" (even now) corrigible in this way is a "fortunate contingent fact" that shows for practical purposes, in his view, how effective universalization is likely to be.[14] But it doesn't seem to be so in fact, and a later passage of Hare's reveals why. In *Freedom and Reason*, Hare gives an example in which he imagines himself "becoming black, but retaining my other characteristics," and so being unable to universalize the breaking of families for commercial gain, as in chattel slavery. But on the next page he says:

> "We think that there is a real and relevant difference between men and animals in this respect. We can say 'If I were turned into an animal, I

should stop having any desire for political liberty, and therefore the lack of it would be no hardship to me.' It is possible to say this even of men in certain stages of development. Nobody thinks that children ought to have complete political liberty; and most people recognize that it would be foolish to introduce the more advanced kinds of political liberty all at once in backward countries, where people have not got to the stage of wanting it, and would not know what to do with it if they got it. So this mode of reasoning allows us to make the many distinctions that are necessary in assessing our obligations towards different *kinds* of people, and indeed of sentient beings."[15]

Hare doesn't suggest that I imagine that I am the animal or the child or the allegedly politically immature person but that I nonetheless retain "my other characteristics." In some cases it isn't even clear what this could mean. But it is clear that some of the characteristics relevant to whether I should enjoy political liberty are precisely ones I am pretty sure beings like small children and many animals, at least, do not have, and *nor would I*, if I were what they are.

Logical thought and sympathetic imagination are unlikely to dislodge many beliefs of that kind, and in some cases, such as that of small children, for good reasons. They are also unlikely to dislodge the views of sexists, racists, homophobes, or colonial paternalists that being female, black, gay, or backward is a relevant difference. The logical space of similarity and difference is already shaped by prior assumptions of what it is to *be* a certain kind of human or other animal. Hare thinks that the logical exercise of universalizing has decisive powers for most people without their presuming "antecedent moral premises," but his optimism about it is misplaced. Its results are quite determined by prior assumptions that are in part constituted by *moral* understandings—by a conception of which beings can stand in relations of trust and mutual expectations, or in ones of certain kinds. They may be faulty moral understandings, but they have often been the ones that pattern human beings' judgments and feelings of obligation and responsibility. The unfortunate contingent fact about human beings, openly displayed in history and many present practices, is that human beings are prone to think of humankind as *human kinds*, but only in some cases defensibly so.

I want to consider one more contemporary example that illustrates this point, and how it can be missed if one happens not to look in certain directions.

Jonathan Glover's recent book *Humanity: A Moral History of the 20th Century* is an impressively researched compendium of human cruelty and destructiveness in twentieth-century war, atrocity, and totalitarian violence.

Glover argues that a "humanized" ethic will be "tentative, exploratory, and partly empirical," exploring the moral resources there are in ordinary human psychology, independent of strenuous metaphysical commitments, to resist failure in the "moral emergencies" of mass violence.[16] These moral resources include our "moral identity," our sense of the importance of being a certain kind of person, and so the unacceptability or the necessity in our own eyes of engaging in certain kinds of behavior. Yet moral identity can be overridden or disconnected in contexts of violence. Responses of sympathy and respect for other human beings are also moral resources which, while fragile, are in the end for Glover more fundamental. "Human responses are the core of the humanity which contrasts with inhumanity. They are widely distributed, but to identify them with humanity is only partly an empirical claim. It remains also partly an aspiration."[17]

One problem Glover identifies is "a moral gap" between the respect and sympathy likely to be extended to those who are members of our community, compared to what may be aroused by those "outside."[18] Quoting a famous passage from Thucydides early in the book, Glover reminds us that the Athenians advised the Melians "the standard of justice depends on the equality of power to compel and that in fact the strong do what they have the power to do and the weak accept what they have to accept."[19] His book as a whole offers a grisly parade of twentieth-century instances of mass violence confirming the prevalence of that Athenian point of view. In concluding, Glover says that "luckily, the ethics of preventing atrocities are an extension of the ethics of everyday life," so that we might learn to fortify or protect our everyday moral resources even in "the moral emergencies."[20]

I admire Glover's book and applaud his program for "humanizing" ethics by taking a tentative, empirical approach to understanding what human beings actually are capable of and are apt to do in situations where this matters enormously. He does not help himself to assumptions about how people surely do or must think in those situations he calls "moral emergencies," but asks us to look and see before we reflect on our "humanity," or our failures to express and honor it as an ideal. His book is filled with many actual case studies of patterns of unsuccessful moral thought and justification that had dreadful consequences, and he repeatedly looks at how contexts and conditions precluded certain moral considerations from taking hold or being entered.

Even so, Glover's confidence in some of our moral resources is not well founded. His residual faith in sympathy and respect as the backbone of "everyday ethics" doesn't reckon with how elaborately *within* communities these sentiments are trained to track social distinctions and hierarchies. Respect and sympathy are indeed "widespread and deep-rooted" but they are highly selective in their operations between and among people in very different social places in the same societies. The chilling counsel that the Athenians gave to the Melians—that in unequal power relations the strong will rule and the weak will have no appeal—could have been said by the Athenians to their own wives and slaves. Those bound together in everyday relations of interdependence or intimacy need not learn to acknowledge or expect their positions to be symmetrical, and more often than not they learn otherwise.

The rule in human societies, ever and now, is unequal moral and social standings that are inextricably intertwined, where different moral standings are defined by different responsibilities, entitlements, and relations of accountability that social arrangements embody. Social experience schools moral feeling and perceptions to fit normative expectations the social arrangements require. Our social identities shape and delimit our responses of sympathy and respect not only outside our societies but within them. Significant social identities and the responses they require are often internally related: the reason you may command, for example, is the same as why I must obey, that you possess authority over me in a certain context; or I am respected as a man when I am not treated as a woman, and may be respected as a man only if my treatment of women makes clear that they do not merit the respect or sympathy that men, or men of my own status, do. The moral differentials created by standing social hierarchies expose those despised or subordinated or marginalized to humiliation, misery, and violence. The "everyday ethics" that Glover hopes might support humane responses in moral emergencies is itself, sadly, often not humane.

NATURALIZED NON-IDEAL THEORY

We are returned to the problem of our original arguments. To put it simply, it seems that you *can* very well think in particular ways morally without contradiction or even significant strain *if you live that way.* Indeed it will not be easy to do otherwise. The epistemologies and logics of inequality and domination that are a central study of feminist, race critical, and postcolonial theory are also essential to ethics. For ethics must look at actual languages of morals to grasp how people can in fact think and live. It must look for the conditions for *critically* assessing those actual moral logics within the always limited perspectives available in human epistemic conditions. But what are those conditions? This question goes to the epistemology and methodology of moral theory. I present briefly my own conclusions about this.

Foundationalism is largely discredited in epistemology, whether as a metaphor for the structure of knowledge or a claim about the a priori, self-evident, or incorrigible status of certain items of knowledge. The burden of proof should now fall upon those who would exempt knowledge about how it is best for human beings to live from this result. In my own view moral knowledge can only be holistic and fallible in the way of other experiential knowledge; moral knowledge should be seen as natural knowledge, and moral epistemology as a kind of naturalized epistemology.[21]

A naturalistic understanding sees our claims to moral knowledge as resting on moral understandings of which we are confident, as well as whatever else we have reason to think we know about human beings and our world, at a given time. This does not preclude some of those same supporting beliefs from coming under scrutiny at another time; sometimes they will be rejected in turn under the impact of additional information or shifts in understanding in the bootstrapping, nonfoundational way that knowledge is now generally understood to grow and change. Applied to moral knowledge, this means that moral knowledge is open-ended, fallible, and indefinitely revisable too; we use what we already think we know about how we ought to live in order to discover more, and we may discover at points that what we relied on at some prior time is no longer warranted. This goes for moral theory too; it is an empirically obligated practice that needs to avail itself of many kinds of knowledge human beings have of their lives, through history, literature, sciences, arts, critical and hermeneutic methods, and personal experience.

A naturalized view of moral knowledge provides an explanation of the gender bias—explicit or covert—that feminist critiques have invariably uncovered. Whatever theorists have claimed about the non-empirical provenance of some ingredients of their moral theories, the truth is that their theories about how to live cannot help but be rooted in the lives they *in fact* live. Moral knowledge, like other knowledge, is situated. Moral theories will bear the marks not only of culture and history, but of the ways that the cultural and historical situation presents itself to those who make theory from particular social positions within specific social worlds. The tradition of claiming nonempirical or transempirical status for views about morality has served powerful ideological functions, including the function of hiding the social location of moral philosophy, and its exercise of intellectual authority backed by social and institutional power, even from moral philosophers themselves. Now we need morally and epistemically responsible candor about the bases of moral thought, including philosophical ethics.

Feminist theorists who support naturalistic or experiential views of moral knowledge do not go in for the kind of naturalism that practices scientific reductionism about morality, because feminists are committed to establishing the normative authority of moral judgments, including of course those that condemn oppressive practices and cruel and wasteful social hierarchies that diminish human lives. But what Christine Korsgaard has called "the normative question," the question about morality's authority to command or demand things of us, in a naturalized view cannot be seen as a question about the authority of morality as a whole that can be posed from some reflective standpoint outside morality altogether.[22] For one has to stand on some moral judgments to assess the authority of any other moral judgments. So there is not *one* normative critical question asked about moral norms from outside any of them, but a recurrent kind of question: whether this or that way we or others think people should live is really worthy of human effort and conviction. Such questions are posed and answered from the perspective of those moral and other beliefs in which we repose confidence; we cannot do better. We never get outside normativity, but are never done testing the normative authority of some of our beliefs in light of other, for the while, surer ones. Moral thinking is indeed *reflective* thinking, involving sustained examination of how we actually live. The lesson from feminist ethics is not to lose sight of the situated and contingent character of *the matter on which we reflect* and *the place within a moral and social order from which that matter comes into view.*

If morality is a socially embodied but improvable practice of making people responsible in various ways, the reflective space for normative questions is always there to be opened. It is possible to ask questions about whether moral understandings are truly shared, whether they are what they appear to be, whether we and others can be trusted to be responsive to them, and whether they really represent a worthy way to live compared to whatever we know about or can imagine as a way of human life.

Morality is grasped by its participants not merely as "how we live" but as *how to live*, as a way of going on together that has real authority. The human condition for establishing the authority of moral ideas is close and comparative attention to those actual ways of life in which particular moral ideas are embodied or have no hold. For the embodiment of moral ideas in social practices reveals the real force and meaning of those ideas. Close attention to actual social worlds reveals that moral ideas are often not meant to apply universally, but only selectively or on a sliding scale, and that these ideas mean only what their applications show, and not whatever else we might have hoped they meant.

I believe we should see moral theory as "non-ideal" theory, although only partly in the sense in which John Rawls introduced that phrase. Rawls used "non-ideal theory" to describe the study of how and whether principles that would be ideal if all complied with them could guide us under "less happy conditions" when injustice is common or reigns.[23] In his picture we first work out an ideal theory assuming perfect compliance, and only later turn to problems posed by injustice. If moral theory in fact arises out of our non-ideal social arrangements and situated epistemic conditions, we have good reasons in advance to expect that the understandings enshrined in theory are not in fact ideal. They show the effects of social arrangements that are imperfect not only in people's degree of compliance with standards, but in the nature of the standards with which people learn to comply. Demonstrating this has been a central task of feminist ethics, to show where the supposedly ideal theory tracks all too closely the imperfections and exclusions of the real social world. The task for ethics should be to keep finding out where reality exposes an ideal to criticism, as well as where refined ideals show us that our reality does not yet measure up to something better that we glimpse from where we are. This is a piecemeal and reflexive task that cannot just fix the ideal first and look at the realities later. It is consistent with thinking of moral theory, like morality itself, as an imperfect but improvable practice of collective self-understanding.[24]

NOTES

1. I discuss these arguments in more detail in "Ineluctable Feelings and Moral Recognition," *Midwest Studies in Philosophy, Volume XXII, Philosophy of Emotion*, ed. Peter A. French and Howard K. Wettstein (Notre Dame, Ind.: University of Notre Dame Press), 1998: 62–81, reprinted as chapter 10 of this volume.

2. Christine Korsgaard, *Sources of Normativity* (Cambridge: Cambridge University Press, 1996), 143.

3. Martha Nussbaum, "Human Capabilities, Female Human Beings," in *Women, Culture, and Development,* Martha C. Nussbaum and Jonathan Glover, eds. (New York: Oxford University Press, 1995), 98.

4. Nussbaum, "Human Capabilities," 96.

5. I'm not doing justice to Thomas's valuable analyses of power systems here in attending to this particular aspect of his argument in "Power, Trust, and Evil," in *Overcoming Racism and Sexism*, ed. Linda A. Bell and David Blumenfeld (Lanham, Md.: Rowman & Littlefield, 1995). See also Laurence Thomas, "Evil and the Concept of a Human Person," in *Midwest Studies in Philosophy XX*, ed. Peter A. French,

Theodore E. Uehling, and Howard K. Wettstein (Notre Dame, Ind.: University of Notre Dame Press, 1996). The diagnosis of psychological corrosion is found in the latter piece, but see also *Vessels of Evil: American Slavery and the Holocaust* (Philadelphia: Temple University Press, 1993).

6. Thomas, "Evil and the Concept of a Human Person," 51.

7. Thomas, "Evil and the Concept of a Human Person," 53.

8. Emmanuel Chukwudi Eze's *Race and the Enlightenment: A Reader* (Cambridge, Mass.: Blackwell Publishers, 1997) provides a provocative collection of classical modern philosophical texts that construct race distinctions.

9. Richard H. Popkin provides an interesting account of the intertwining histories of biblical and philosophical thinking about race in "The Philosophical Bases of Modern Racism," in *Philosophy and the Civilizing Arts*, ed. Craig Walton and John P. Austen (Athens: Ohio University Press, 1974). Olive Dickason traces European debate about resident peoples in northeast North America in *The Myth of the Savage: And the Beginnings of French Colonialism in the Americas* (Edmonton: University of Alberta Press, 1987) and Winthrop Jordan about African slaves in *White over Black: American Attitudes toward the Negro, 1550–1812* (Chapel Hill: University of North Carolina Press, 1968).

10. Elizabeth Spelman, *Fruits of Sorrow: Framing Our Attention to Suffering* (Boston: Beacon Press, 1997), 169.

11. For example, see the summary of the contemporary position—taken over from Aristotle—to which Bartolomé de Las Casas responds in his famous *In Defense of the Indians* (DeKalb: Northern Illinois University Press, 1992), 11–12.

12. R. M. Hare, *Freedom and Reason* (New York: Oxford University Press, 1963), chapter 9, "Toleration and Fanaticism," and chapter 11, "A Practical Example."

13. R. M. Hare, *Freedom and Reason*, 185.

14. R. M. Hare, *Freedom and Reason*, 172.

15. R. M. Hare, *Freedom and Reason*, 223.

16. Jonathan Glover, *Humanity: A Moral History of the 20th Century* (New Haven, Conn.: Yale University Press, 2000), 406 and 6. For a fuller exposition and critical discussion, see my review of *Humanity* in *The Journal of Value Inquiry* 36 (2002): 117–21.

17. Glover, *Humanity*, 25.

18. Glover, *Humanity*, 28.

19. Glover, *Humanity*, 29.

20. Glover, *Humanity*, 408.

21. For a fuller characterization of a nonscientistic naturalized moral epistemology, see my "Naturalizing, Normativity, and Using What 'We' Know in Ethics," *Canadian Journal of Philosophy*, ed. Richmond Campbell and Bruce Hunter, Supplementary Volume 26 (2000): 75–101, reprinted as chapter 11 of this volume.

22. The "normative question" is the centerpiece of Korsgaard's *Sources of Normativity*.

23. John Rawls, *A Theory of Justice* (Cambridge, Conn.: Harvard University Press, 1971), 245. Rawls says, remarkably, "We must ascertain how the ideal conception of

justice applies, *if indeed it applies at all*, to cases where rather than having to make adjustments to natural limitations, we are confronted with injustice" (emphasis mine), 351.

24. Special thanks to Hilde L. Nelson and Brian Davies for their good suggestions on improving this paper. This paper was presented as the Inaugural Lecture for the Cardinal Mercier Chair in Philosophy (2001–2002) at the Institute of Philosophy of the Catholic University of Leuven, Belgium, in March 2002.

Index

ABOUT THE AUTHOR

Margaret Urban Walker is Lincoln Professor of Ethics, Justice, and the Public Sphere in the School of Justice Studies at Arizona State University. Her areas of research are moral and political theory, the history of ethics, and feminist and critical race theory. She received a Ph.D. in philosophy from Northwestern University in 1975 and taught previously at Fordham University.

Margaret Walker has held visiting appointments at the University of South Florida, Washington University, and the Catholic University of Leuven, Belgium. She has lectured widely in the United States, Canada, Europe, and Australia on moral theory, moral epistemology and psychology, responsibility, and social difference. In 2000, she joined the teaching faculty of the Graduate Summer School on the Ethics and Politics of Care of the Netherlands School for Research in Practical Philosophy in Soesterberg, The Netherlands, and visited the Research Concentration in Applied Ethics at Queensland University of Technology as guest speaker in Brisbane, Australia, in the summer of 2001. Most recently, she was honored to hold the Cardinal Mercier Chair in Philosophy for 2001–2002 at the Institute of Philosophy of the University of Leuven, Belgium.

Walker is author of *Moral Understandings: A Feminist Study in Ethics* (1998) and editor of *Mother Time: Women, Aging, and Ethics* (1999), as well as a contributor of many book chapters, journal articles, and reviews in professional philosophical journals. Her current work is a book on "moral repair," the ethics and moral psychology of responding to wrongdoing in ways that restore the basis of morality in trust and hope.